ON ME 'EADLINE!

ON ME 'EADLINE!

30,000 years of sport, told by the No1 paper

John Perry   Matthew Knight

Dedications

To
Jack, Tom & Luca

To
Alina

First published in 2007 by Collins
an imprint of HarperCollins Publishers

HarperCollins Publishers
77-85 Fulham Palace Road
London
W6 8JB

www.collins.co.uk

ISBN 13 978-0-00-725943-4

Collins uses papers that are natural,
renewable and recyclable products made
from wood grown in sustainable forests.
The manufacturing processes conform
to the environmental regulations of the
country of origin.

Printed and bound in Great Britain
by Butler & Tanner, Frome, Somerset

Credits

Written by
John Perry and Matthew Knight

Design
Dan Newman, Perfect Bound Ltd
Heike Schuessler

Sun Page Design
Matthew Marsh

Picture Research
Matthew Knight

Additional Picture Research
Kirsty Barclay

Cover Concept
John Perry

FOREWORD

SPORT is the lifeblood of *The Sun*. Yet many of its greatest tales took place before the paper launched in its tabloid form in 1969. Even since then, pressures of space and general news have often denied them the kind of front-page headline they deserved.

This book shows you how *The Sun* might have covered some of these momentous events.

We would like, at this earliest opportunity, to nip in the bud all criticism of our choices! Producing a definitive list of sport's biggest stories is impossible, as we found within seconds of attempting it. It is entirely subjective. And had we selected solely on the basis of exceptional achievement, this book would have amounted to nothing more than a worthy procession of record-breakers and gold-medallists.

We have, of course, included some of those spectacular feats, among a smattering of more unusual tales. Our choice was also skewed by trying to cover as many sports as possible. So if you find your favourite football club or sporting hero under-represented, we apologise but hope you understand why.

As with our previous books in this format, on history and science, we thought it important to set each *Sun* page in context. The accompanying left-hand pages thus provide a potted guide to each subject. We have also included a "world events" timeline so you can place each sporting tale in the context of history.

The *Sun* pages are as realistic as we can make them, even down to the cross-references. Don't let these fool you – they are generally there for added authenticity, rather than pointing you somewhere useful, though a few do advertise a *Sun* spread that follows. The cross-references on the left-hand pages, by contrast, will enable you to trace the evolution of a particular sport from the front of the book to the back if you so wish.

Occasionally we have chosen to tell our *Sun* story as a back page. Well, it would hardly be a tabloid sports book otherwise.

John Perry
Matthew Knight

CONTENTS

HOW TO USE ON ME 'EADLINE

YOU can, if you so choose, read this book from start to finish. And why not? But should you wish to follow the thread of one particular sport, keep an eye out for the handy "NOW JUMP TO…" cross-references on each LEFT-hand page. They will direct you, forward and/or back, to the pages most relevant to the one you're on. You'll also find a fascinating fact in each "Sports Spot" and a timeline which sets the sports story in the wider context of world history.

25000BC ARCHERY – THE ORIGIN OF SPORT

MOST people on Earth have played sport. Most people watch it. But how and when did it start? The answer, given the lack of any evidence, can only be speculation. But it seems reasonable to suggest that mankind invented some form of sport to fill empty hours not taken up by hunting, eating, sleeping and mating.

The first evidence of archery as a sport comes from the "cradle of civilisation", Ancient Egypt. But we know from prehistoric cave paintings that humans were using bows and arrows many millennia before that, so it is possible archery became a leisure activity then too.

In honing his hunting skills, early man may have practised firing his bow – and human nature being what it is, it is likely this led to competition between rivals.

Paintings 20,000 years old depicting men in groups hunting with bows and arrows were first found in caves in the Valltorta Gorge, Spain, in the 1880s. Flint arrowheads found in Tunisia, North Africa, are even older,

Below: Depiction of a squad of hunters in the caves at Valltorta Gorge in the Castellón province, Spain. The caves also reveal scenes of dancing, food-gathering and herding.

some carbon-dated to 40,000 years ago. Clear evidence of sports begins in Ancient Egypt (3400BC to 30BC). Near the great Sphinx of Giza, slabs of stone bearing inscriptions and paintings (called Stele) of Amenophis II and other kings are covered in depictions of leisure activities. Scenes show archery, running, wrestling and fishing.

Proof also lies in numerous similar discoveries in tombs in the village of Beni Hasan on the east bank of the Nile. Murals and artefacts dating to around 1850BC show men, women and children playing sports ranging from rowing and swimming to javelin-throwing and gymnastics.

Around 800BC the Greeks advanced organised sport further. At the time of the early Olympic Games, first held in Zeus's honour in 776BC, they were embarking on an expansion of their empire that continued for 250 years. Sport, practised almost exclusively by men, was an essential part of training for battle. Greek philosophers

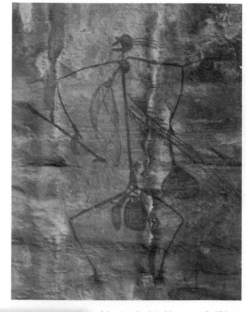

A hunter depicted in a cave in Ubirr, Kakadu National Park, Northern Territory, Australia.

> ### SPORT SPOT
> Archery is arguably as important as the wheel or fire in mankind's development, making him Earth's best hunter. Around 1200, Genghis Khan used bowmen to conquer the known world.

were analysing the meaning of games too. Aristotle (384-322BC) said sport was "the closest human beings come to pure contemplation – the highest of human activities." The great thinker conceded that sport, though it lacked seriousness, contained "a liberty and a joy of its own".

Now, 2,500 years on, sports have changed from being festivals honouring ancient gods to being religions in their own right, with many athletes treated as divine beings.

Sport has successfully stitched itself into the fabric of every nation on earth. The revered cricket commentator John Arlott once said: "Games are as truly part of the history of a nation as its work, wars and art. They are a reflection of the social life of the people, changing with it and conditioned by its changes in economy, religion and politics."

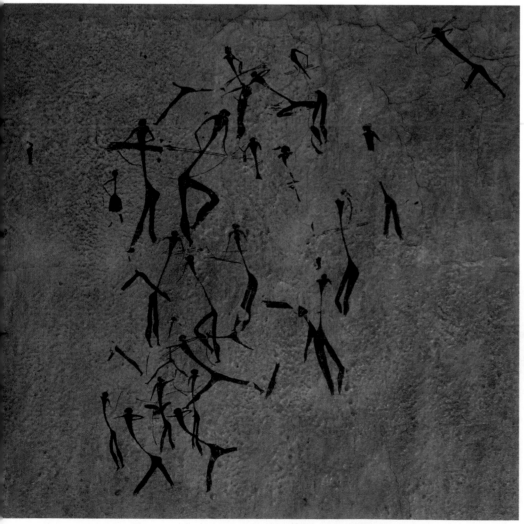

c. 900BC: A carved stone tablet from the ancient Hittite civilisation depicting a deer hunt using a bow and arrow.

> ### FRONT PAGE NEWS
> | | |
> |---|---|
> | 40,000BC | Possible first use of arrows |
> | 10,000BC | End of the last Ice Age |
> | 9000BC | First walled city founded at Jericho |
> | 3150BC | Earliest known hieroglyphic writing |
> | 2560BC | The Great Pyramids are built at Dahshur and Giza |

THE Sun

Friday, April 13, 25066BC   FREE (one copy only per cave)

He SHOOTS ...he SCARS

HUNTING FOR FUN: IS IT OUR FUTURE?

STALK SPORT

A bowman tracking his prey. But could we just shoot at targets for fun?

MANKIND is facing a crisis today — over what on Earth to do with our free time.

Once, our meagre existence was solely about survival, our days entirely filled by hunting, eating and sleeping.

But we are victims of our own success. New technology, such as our superb bows and arrows, has turned us into ruthlessly efficient killing machines.

Often we find ourselves having slept, hunted and

By RICH PICKINGS

feasted by mid-afternoon. Once one has swept out one's cave, there are hours to fill before nightfall.

Today The Sun proposes a radical solution: Using our hunting skills for **FUN.**

We could shoot for the sheer joy of hitting a target. Maiming different animals could earn different numbers of "points".

We could even shoot at inanimate objects (though that doesn't seem much fun).

Turn to Pages 4&5 to find out how to join this crucial debate on all our futures.

There's more to life . . . typical hunt scene Painting: UG GRUNTER

DO SPEARS STILL HAVE A POINT? See Pages 8-9

776BC ANCIENT OLYMPICS AND RISE OF MODERN GAMES

Left: The Statue of Zeus at Olympia was one of the Seven Wonders of the Ancient World. It was carved by the classical sculptor Phidias. The Olympics were in honour of the "King of the Gods".

Above right: Emperor Theodosius I "The Great" (346 – 395AD). **Below:** The stadium at the site of the ancient Olympic Games at Olympia in Greece. Olympia was established around 3000BC.

THE ancient Olympics thrived for more than 1,000 years. They began in the Greek city of Olympia in 776BC – and were the inspiration for the modern Games 2,672 years later.

Olympia is about 95 miles west of Athens on a vast peninsula in the Peloponnesian region. The Olympic Games were centred around a magnificent temple dedicated to Zeus, the supreme Greek god.

Worshippers had flocked to the temple, created by the sculptor Phidias, for decades, but leaders of the new "polis" (city-states) were keen to up the ante and assert their supremacy over rival cities. Grand festivals celebrating both religion and sport, with which the Ancient Greeks were obsessed, served the purpose well. They became common throughout Greece and were also seen as a useful way of getting men fit for military duty.

The first 13 Olympics, which were held every four years, featured just one main event, the stadion race, a sprint up one length of the stadium, probably around 180metres. But the grand finale of the games was a gruelling warriors' race – about 750 metres in helmets and armour.

Chariot racing was introduced in 680BC. Spectators flocked to the Hippodrome to see around 40 chariots, each pulled by four horses, charge chaotically up and down the stadium. Injuries and deaths were common.

The pentathlon soon became a regular event too, testing athletes' skills in wrestling, stadion, long jump, javelin and discus.

More and more events were added, rising to about 12 in total. Boxing, wrestling (Milo of Croton won the event six times) and pankration all became the most an-

ticipated events. Introduced at the 33rd Olympiad in 648BC, pankration (meaning "all strength") combined boxing and wrestling and is best described as an early version of martial arts. Dioxippus – a friend of Alexander the Great – won the event so many times and was so feared that in 336BC he was crowned champion by default because no one would challenge him.

The ancient Olympics were last held in 393AD when the Roman Emperor Theodosius the Great, who had converted to Christianity, banned all pagan festivals. Destruction of all pagan temples, including the statue of Zeus in AD 426, consigned the Olympics to history. It was more than 1,400 years before the site of the Games would be excavated, fuelling interest in a revival of the Olympics.

In June 1894, a French baron named Pierre de Coubertin organised an international congress at the Sorbonne university in Paris to drum up support for a new Games. His ideas led to the establishment of the International Olympic Committee (IOC). Coubertin became its general secretary and saw his dream realised when the first modern Olympics opened on April 6th, 1896, in Athens.

French educationalist and Olympics founder Pierre de Coubertin (sitting, left) poses with members of the first International Olympic Committee (IOC) in Athens in 1896.

SPORT SPOT

Olive wreaths weren't the only prizes for athletes. As the Olympics evolved, winners received fortunes in cash, plus livestock, precious metals and women.

THE Sun

Saturday, August 23, 776BC

They're OFF!

Wreath . . . itchy

Wot, no gongs? Wreath prizes a 'rip-off'

By PENNY PINCHER

FURY erupted at the Olympics last night after it was revealed winners will only be awarded a measly wreath of olive leaves.

Victors are made to don the worthless foliage as they parade around the Games site to the idyllic accompaniment of flute music and lilting songs.

Organisers felt sure athletes would be chuffed to bits with the leaves, because they are plucked from a sacred tree behind Zeus's temple.

But one winner, who refused to be named, stormed last night: "After all the training, all the effort, this is all we get?

"Is some sort of permanent memento really too much to ask? Something in gold, maybe?"

Got To Urn Living — Page 7

D'OH HOMER'S POETRY GETTING VERSE! See Page 8

Hurdling warriors launch 'Olympics'

THE first Olympic Games got under way yesterday with a 750-metre sprint for fully tooled-up warriors.

The gruelling hurdles event was the highlight of the Games, held near the Temple of Zeus in Olympia, Greece.

The winner is unknown. He was too exhausted to utter his name.

The rest of the Games involved more running, albeit without armour, and sporadic wrestling.

Synchronised Stabbing Results — Page 76

From DICK ATHLON in Olympia

490BC THE MARATHON AND THE LEGEND THAT INSPIRED IT

Above: The Battle of Marathon, fought on the Marathon plain of north-eastern Attica. The Athenians repulsed the first Persian invasion of Greece in an afternoon.

Greek shepherd Spiridon Louis (1873–1940), winner of the 40km marathon at the first modern Olympic Games, held in Athens in 1896. He was later chosen to kindle the Olympic flame at the 1936 Berlin Games

THE Battle of Marathon in 490BC is one of history's most famous military engagements and inspired the world's most celebrated long-distance race.

The epic encounter happened during the Persian Wars (499BC – 479BC), which started when the Ionian cities of Asia Minor rebelled against Persian rule. The Greeks sent a fleet to help them but the rebellion was crushed by Persia's emperor Darius I.

Seeking to punish the Greeks for their interference and to expand the Persian kingdom, Darius invaded Greece with 600 ships carrying 20,000 infantry and cavalry. They landed in the Bay of Marathon. Word spread quickly to Athens and 10,000 Greek warriors were mobilised.

In early September 490BC, the two armies met on the plain of Marathon, 25 miles north of Athens. The Athenian army's commander Miltiades ordered his men to charge the Persians in an unbroken line. Soon they had engulfed Darius' army, their sturdy lances more effective than Persian bows at close range. After hours of fighting the invaders retreated to their ships. Miltiades and his army had slaughtered 6,400 Persian infantry, while just 200 Greeks were dead.

Phidippides, an Athenian herald, was ordered to run to Athens and pass on the good

Victorious Greek commander Miltiades (550BC–489BC)

news. Legend has it that he made the distance, exclaimed "We were victorious" - then dropped dead of exhaustion.

His epic, non-stop run inspired the founder of the modern Olympics, Pierre de Coubertin, to create a long-distance race as a tribute to the legend and to Greece, birthplace of the ancient Olympics. The first marathon, at the 1896 Games in Athens, was run over 24.85 miles and won, to the delight of the home crowd, by a Greek water-carrier, Spiridon Louis, who became an overnight hero.

The current official distance, 26 miles 385 yards, was first run at the London Games in 1908. The route was originally 26 miles, from Windsor Castle to White City stadium in West London. But it had to be lengthened by 385 yards so competitors could cross the finishing line in front of the Royal box.

That race ended in controversy. Italian Dorando Pietri entered the stadium in first place ahead of the American Johnny Hayes. Confused and exhausted, Pietri ran in the wrong direction. Officials tried to redirect him but he collapsed. Pietri got up and fell four more times before being helped over the line.

The American team's complaint was upheld and Hayes won gold. Pietri was disquali-

fied, but Queen Alexandra gave him a silver cup for his courage.

The explosion in city marathons and the race's continued success at the Olympics have produced a host of household-name runners. Czech Emil Zatopek will forever be remembered for the 1952 Helsinki Olympics, where he won the marathon, the 5,000m and the 10,000m. In 1960 Ethiopian Abebe Bikila ran barefoot along the streets of Rome, winning the first Olympic gold for Africa and breaking the world record.

The women's race has only been run since 1984. American Joan Benoit Samuelson won the first, and Mizuki Noguchi of Japan won the most recent race at Athens in 2004. It was a race more memorable for Britain's Paula Radcliffe giving up at 36km and weeping at the roadside. But it is only the Olympic title that eludes Radcliffe, undoubtedly the world's greatest-ever female marathon runner and holder of four of the five fastest times ever run.

> ## SPORT SPOT
> **Current men's record holder is Kenya's Paul Tergat (2hrs 4mins 55secs, Berlin, 2003). Fastest woman is Paula Radcliffe (2hrs 15mins 25secs, London, 2003).**

Above, right: Britain's marathon star Paula Radcliffe in 2005
Below: Dorando Pietri, of Italy, on the verge of collapse, is helped across the finish line in the Marathon of the Olympics in London, 24th July 1908.

FRONT PAGE NEWS

THE Sun

Thursday, April 17, 490BC

One coin

What a result . . . Greeks edged Persians in Marathon thriller

Marathon man . . Phidippides collapses after suicidal run

MANIAC KILLED BY 25-MILE RUN

Copycats warned over Marathon suicide dash

A LUNATIC ran non-stop for an astonishing 25 miles yesterday — then dropped dead.

Phidippides, a messenger, legged it to Athens, Greece, from Marathon to announce the invad-

By **DI TRYING**, Classical Affairs Editor

ing Persians had been trounced.

He had just enough time to yell "We were victorious" before he keeled over with exhaustion.

Safety experts warned that **NO ONE** should ape his crazy dash.

BATTLE OF MARATHON MATCH REPORT AND PAINTINGS: PAGE 68

150AD BALL GAMES IN THE EARLY CIVILISATIONS

FRONT PAGE NEWS

c.370BC Philosopher Plato opens school in Athens
44BC Assassination of Julius Caesar
43AD Roman invasion of Britain
79AD Destruction of Pompeii by Vesuvius eruption

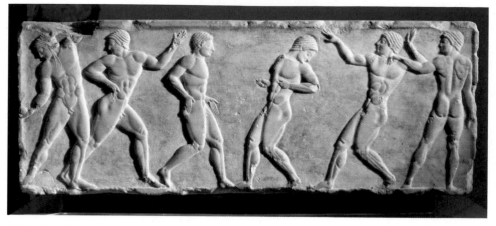

Above: c.510BC: Young men playing a ball game, from a statue base found in the Dipylon Cemetery, Athens.

BALLS have been used in sport for thousands of years. Evidence unearthed from ancient tombs proves that Egyptians played ball games at least as early as 3,000BC – 5,000 years ago.

Between about 3100BC and 332BC, Egypt was the world's most advanced civilisation and sport played a significant role. Ball games may have sprung from a fertility ceremony. As a way to mark the passing of winter and the start of spring, teams engaged in mock combat over a ball representing the "head of Horus" – Horus being the god of law and light. Over time, similar games associated with religious rites spread throughout the Mediterranean and Middle East.

Many balls have been found in excavations in the tombs at Saqqara, nine miles south of Cairo, dating back more than 5,000 years. Often covered in sewn leather or cloth, they were stuffed with palm or papyrus fibres.

More evidence was found in the tombs at Beni Hasan, a small village on the east bank of the Nile, south of el-Minya. Scenes depict groups of girls juggling two or three balls and playing catch while riding piggyback on a partner. Next to these scenes is a drawing depicting what appears to be a forerunner of hockey. Two players can be seen hitting a small ball with long sticks which have been bent and broadened at the ends. These were probably made of palm leaf stalk. This primitive game called Hoksha is still played in Egypt.

Another Egyptian game, "seker hemat", has caused much debate among baseball historians. A recently discovered hieroglyphic dating to around 1475BC shows the Egyptian Pharaoh Thutmose III holding a ball and a bat, suggesting America's favourite national pastime may well date back further

than originally thought. Around 2000BC the Greeks developed a kicking or throwing game, Episkyros (also called Phaininda). The balls were usually made of linen and hair, wrapped in string and stitched together. Later Greek models were made out of a pig's bladder and wrapped in animal skin. These balls were called a "follis", meaning "bag of wind", the word from which our "fool" derives.

It was from Episkyros that the Romans devised Harpastum. It means "small ball game" and was popular for hundreds of years. Harpastum was played on a rectangular field with boundary lines and a line across the centre of the pitch. The object of the game – played by 5 to 12 players – was to keep the ball in your own half, with your opponents trying to steal it. The use of passing and tackling bears a striking resemblance to rugby or early and the mob football which took its inspiration from the Roman settlers.

The ritual function of ball games was equally important to the ancient Mayan civilisation in Mexico and Central America, which played a fiendishly difficult game named Pitz in vast ball courts dating back to about 1500BC. Contested by two teams of between two and six players, its object was to manipulate a solid rubber ball into a suspended stone hoop. Players were not allowed to touch the ball with their hands or feet, only their thighs, hips and upper arms. The price of failure was high: Losers were often sacrificed to the gods.

Above: c.510BC: A hockey-like game depicted on a statue base found in the Dipylon Cemetery, Athens.

SPORT SPOT

The football's basic design, an inflated bladder inside a tough casing, is the same as the ancient Greeks' "follis". Nowadays the bladder is latex and the casing synthetic leather.

Below: View of the north wall of a ball court, Maya-Toltec, c.900AD-c.1200AD

NOW JUMP TO... ➲ FOOTBALL'S ORIGINS page 14 ➲ RUGBY & FOOTBALL page 30

THE Sun

Saturday, February 15, 150AD   One sestertius

ROME 'STOLE KEEPY-UPPY'

OUTRAGED Greeks last night accused Rome of nicking Harpastum from them, then claiming the credit. They say a 1,000-year-old marble relief (left), of a dad showing off his "keepy-uppy" skills to his son, proves it. But Egyptians also put the boot in, claiming THEY used balls first . . . a whopping 2,000 years ago.

SPHERE WE GO, SPHERE WE GO, SPHERE WE GO!

Fine form . . . Roman bikini babe Bella shows off her Harpastum skills, and a good deal besides

Miniature globes set to trigger games explosion

AN ingenious spherical object was last night set to revolutionise our leisure time.

By **MO SAIC**, Classical Sports Editor

The Romans use the tiny globe, or "ball", in an anarchic, violent game called Harpastum.

Players use any means necessary to carry or kick the sphere beyond a line drawn in the sand.

The Romans are almost certain to launch the game in Britain shortly — and top Roman doctor Galen says it is a great way to stay fit: "It exercises every part of the body, takes up little time, and costs nothing."

It is thought the Romans may consider other sphere-based games.

Handsphere, footsphere and net-sphere are just three of the ideas being tossed around.

INSIDE: WIN TEN DENARII IN OUR 'SPOT THE SPHERE' CONTEST

1245 THE UGLY BEGINNINGS OF THE BEAUTIFUL GAME

Left: A ball is pumped up in this football scene from the late 17th Century.
Below, right: Ebenezer Cobb Morley chaired a meeting of 12 teams from London at the Freemasons' Tavern on Great Queen Street in Holborn in 1863. Together they founded the Football Association (FA).

ENGLAND'S claim to being the birthplace of organised football is unquestioned. What is less clear is which nation actually invented the game.

There are numerous theories. In 2004 FIFA President Sepp Blatter officially acknowledged China as football's birthplace. "Tsu chu" – meaning literally "to kick the ball"– was a game played by soldiers during the Han Dynasty between 206BC and 220AD.

The recently-revived Japanese game "kemari" was played around 600AD. Kemari is best described as an ancient form of "keepy uppy" with players standing in a circle kicking the ball to one another without letting it fall.

Probably the most important early advance was made by the Romans. Their game Harpastum (see page 12) can be seen as a crude forerunner of both football and rugby. It was a team game played within a defined area with a small ball being kicked or thrown in an effort to get it past the other team's line.

Tales abound in the centuries after the Romans left Britain of triumphant Anglo-Saxons kicking the heads of conquered Danes around the streets. But it was only in the Middle Ages that primitive modes of the game emerge in written records.

In those days our "beautiful game" was downright ugly. Using a straw-filled, inflated bladder cut from a slaughtered pig, football was a violent, anarchic game between large mobs of young men chasing around the streets of a village or town.

Often neighbouring villages played each other, with the goals being markers at the boundaries of each village, beyond which the ball had to be carried to score. Damage to property was frequent, as were fights and even death. "Mob football", as it became known, became especially popular on Shrove Tuesday. From about the 12th Century, the day before Lent was seen as ideal for men to indulge in a liberal dose of bad behaviour.

Disorder was very much at the heart of the game's appeal. But in 1314 King Edward II imposed the first of many banning orders on football. His son and heir (Edward III) continued to enforce it.

In 1349, 12 years into the Hundred Years' War and with the Black Death ravaging the population, Edward outlawed a range of sports. He ordered healthy young men to practise archery ready for war, rather than indulge in frivolities such as football.

The bans proved impossible to enforce. The outlawed, and lawless, form of the game continued for generations. The first records of more organised football emerge in the 16th Century from an unlikely source – the Headmaster of Merchant Taylor's School in North London. Richard Mulcaster is described by many football historians as "the greatest 16th Century advocate of football".

Mulcaster took the game off the streets, rid it of some of its unruly aspects and promoted it as a way to build school-children's health and strength. He was the first to write about the need to establish teams, positions and referees. Football spread rapidly throughout England's public schools in various forms. Some would play a kicking game, others used hands too.

These different codes would finally separate, into rugby and football, when the Football Association was formed in 1863. The FA outlined 13 rules under which games would be played. It wasn't long before the world followed suit.

SPORT SPOT

Medieval football is alive and well in Ashbourne, Derbyshire. Each Shrove Tuesday and Ash Wednesday unlimited players compete for eight hours a day. The goals (millstones, in fact) are three miles apart.

Right: Mob football took place between rival groups in towns and cities, and also between villages and parishes. Large numbers took part and the goals were sometimes a mile or more apart.

SunSport AT THE BIG MATCH

GORE DRAW
Honours even in 8hr orgy of bloodshed

LOWER WALLOP 1, UPPER WALLOP 1
(SIX DEAD)   (FOUR DEAD)

LOWER Wallop were left to rue what might have been last night after striker Bill Longshanks missed a sitter in the 479th minute.

Longshanks was poised to touch the ball against the mill-

By ED CASE, Chief Football Writer

stone at Upper Wallop for a last-gasp 2-1 when a mob beat him to death with a branch.

Despondent Lower boss Rufus Cavedin said last night: "I was gutted. And so was Bill – quite literally as it turned out." Violence and

death were once again the big winners at the infamous annual derby contested by 254 psychotic yokels drunk as skunks on mead.

Upper took the lead around two hours into the eight-hour mayhem marathon through their 28-stone forward Tommy Tuck.

Lower hit back quickly through musclebound hardman Bill Hook,

nicknamed "The Butcher" because of his job as a butcher.

In all, ten players and bystanders were killed and 41 maimed.

One Lower player was executed for his 423rd bookable offence – quite an achievement in a game with no rules whatsoever.

SUN STAR MAN: Tuck (Upper): Sublime punching.

1536 'REAL' TENNIS ... AND ITS BIGGEST FAN: HENRY VIII

TENNIS as we know it owes much to the participation of England's most notorious Royal divorcee and adulterer King Henry VIII, of whom more later.

As for the game's obscure origins, there is a theory the word tennis derives from the name of an ancient Egyptian city called Tinnis. Indeed, the Egyptians were keen on sport and exercise, but it is unlikely that racket games were played until much later.

More compelling evidence arises in 12th Century France with a game called 'jeu de paume', or 'game of the palm'. This early form of hand-ball seems to have been popular with French monks who played it against monastery walls or over a rope strung across a courtyard. Players would shout "tenez" (meaning 'to take' or 'receive') when they were about to serve. That is most probably where the name tennis comes from.

The game's popularity spread in France during the following two centuries, among kings and paupers alike. By this time players had moved on from hitting the ball – normally made from stitched leather filled with hair – with their bare palms and had begun using protective gloves. These eventually changed into bats and rackets.

By the 16th Century enclosed courts had sprung up all over Paris – some estimates

Above: It is generally thought that the 15th Century Burgundian (French) and Italian courts served as models for the early real tennis courts of Europe.

suggest 1,800 existed by the end of the century. The game had found popularity abroad too. While it retained its 'jeu de paume' name in France, in England it would simply become known as tennis. The prefix "real" or sometimes "royal" was only added in the 19th Century to distinguish it from the modern game that superseded it.

The English game's most famous exponent was King Henry VIII, who built a court at Hampton Court Palace in 1532 and 1533. Despite his ample frame, the King was an extremely athletic and passionate sportsman. He is said to have been enjoying a game of

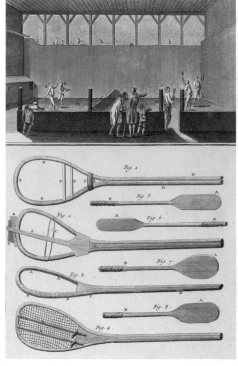

Above: "Real tennis" rackets are smaller than modern rackets. Their asymmetrical head is shaped like a human palm – which relates to how the sport was originally played. The racket was invented in Italy in 1583.

tennis when told his second wife Anne Boleyn had been beheaded on his orders. It is also believed she was watching a game when taken into custody.

The court at Hampton Court is the oldest of its kind in the world and one of a handful in the UK still in use.

The 'game of kings', as it was known, such was its popularity with both the French and British monarchies, became less popular, especially as France edged towards revolution in the late 18th Century.

Outdoor racket games became more and more popular and began taking over from croquet as England's main summer sport.

In 1874, a Welsh army major named Walter Clopton Wingfield designed and patented a game called Sphairistikè (Greek for 'ball game'). His game's obscure title was quickly dropped in favour of 'lawn tennis' and the modern game was born.

> ### SPORT SPOT
>
> In Shakespeare's Henry V, the French King insults King Henry with a "gift" of tennis balls, implying that such frivolous activity is all the English monarch is good for.

Left: Real tennis being played on a Paris court. In France it has retained its original name of 'jeu de paume'. It is 'royal tennis' in Australia, 'court tennis' in USA and 'real tennis' in Britain.

FRONT PAGE NEWS

1337 Hundred Years War begins between France and England

1347 Black Death arrives in Europe and kills 20 million people

1517 Coffee introduced to Europe (Constantinople opens first coffee house in 1554)

1519 Painter, scientist and inventor Leonardo Da Vinci dies at Clos Lucé in France

SEIZED AT TENNIS

BY a grim irony Anne was a big tennis fan and loved to watch her husband play.

In fact she was watching a match at White-hall Palace when was arrested and marched off to the Tower almost three weeks ago.

Anne (left) protested to the guards that they should wait for the end of the game — so she could win a bet she had placed.

Nervous . . . Royal pals let King (left) win yesterday

Henry . . . portrait of a serial killer. Which he will be if he kills further wives

Beautifully executed, your Majesty

(THAT LOB, WE MEAN...NOT THE MISSUS)

By BEA HEDDER, Royal Reporter

KING Henry enjoyed a game of tennis yester-day — as his wife Anne Boleyn was being BEHEADED at the Tower of London.

He was still enthusiastically lobbing, volleying and smashing at Hampton Court when a courtier whispered the news in his ear.

Anne, 29, was executed by a single axe blow after 18 days in custody and on the 1,000th day of her reign as Queen. She was arrested for alleged adultery, incest, treason and witchcraft on May 2.

Henry will waste no time lining up her replacement. He is tipped to get engaged **TODAY** to Anne's lady-in-waiting Jane Seymour, the woman he hopes will give him the son he longs for after Anne's two miscarriages and a daughter.

A Palace spokesman accepted last night that playing tennis during your wife's execution could be seen as insensitive. But he added: "King Henry's a natural athlete — and he really does love the game."

GAME, SET AND MISMATCH: Why Henry can't find love: Pages 12&13

THE ANCIENT ORIGINS OF GOLF, PRIDE OF SCOTLAND

Above: Golf clubs used to have names instead of numbers. A three-wood was known as a "spoon", a five-iron was a "mashie", a nine-iron was a "niblick" and a wedge, whose name remains, was called a "jigger".

Left: St Andrews, 1881: The home of golf is still the most frequent venue for Open Championships and is the largest public golf venue in the world with all six courses open to all golfers.

GOLF'S origins are a source of much speculation among historians and of great pride in Scotland, which lays claim to being the home of golf, if not its birthplace.

Golf's most ancient relation appears to be the Roman game of "paganica", which involved using a bent wooden stick to hit a stuffed leather ball. The game of "kolf" – its name tantalisingly close to the modern one – has been traced back to 1297 by the Dutch historian Steven J. H. van Hengel. Played in the town of Loenen aan de Vecht in The Netherlands, two teams of four used a stick to hit a wooden ball over a 2½-mile course towards a target, usually the door of a public building. Each team tried to hit the target in the lowest number of strokes.

A remarkably similar French game is mentioned in 1353. The object of 'Chole' – played with a wooden-shafted iron club and a wooden ball – was much the same as kolf. Played mainly in winter, it involved striking the ball across fields towards a target, usually a flag attached to a post or tree. Members of a Scottish regiment are thought to have been introduced to "chole" in 1421 when they aided the French against the English at the Battle of Bauge.

The first hard evidence of golf in Scotland comes in 1457. In an attempt to preserve the skills of archery to defend the country from the persistent English threat, King James II banned football and golf ("futbawe and ye gowf") on Sundays. This suggests "gowf", like "futbawe", was already popular with young men. In 1491 golf, along with other pastimes, was banned altogether.

Eleven years later the ban was lifted and golf began to thrive. Catherine of Aragon, Henry VIII's first wife, noted its popularity in a letter to Cardinal Wolsey.

By 1567 even Mary, Queen of Scots, was seen having a round at Musselburgh – the oldest links course in the world. It caused quite a scandal, coming only a few days after the murder of her husband.

The oldest course in England is Blackheath Golf Club in south-east London. It is thought King James I (VI of Scotland) played on Blackheath, behind Greenwich Palace, in the early 17th Century.

During the 18th Century the first golf associations were established. The Honourable Company of Edinburgh Golfers, founded in 1744, produced the first 13 rules of golf for its inaugural competition.

The St Andrews Society of Golfers was set up in 1754 and ten years later reduced the number of holes on its course from 22 to 18, standardising it for all future courses.

Organised golf was booming and equipment improving all the time. More flexible hickory shafts were used by 1826 and the gutta-percha ball – a more durable, water-resistant and rounder replacement for the wooden ball – was introduced in 1848. The first dimpled ball was used in 1880.

St Andrews continued to cement its lofty reputation when in 1834 King William IV became its patron. Building started on the famous old clubhouse in 1854 and in 1873 it hosted its first Open Championship. With Scots dominating its early years, golf had truly found its home in Scotland.

SPORT SPOT

The impact of club on ball lasts a tiny fraction of a second but determines speed, flight and backspin. Backspin changes the airflow round the ball, so it flies higher and further.

FRONT PAGE NEWS

1539 Publication of the Great Bible in England
1546 Georgius Agricola makes first scientific classification of minerals
1549 Book of Common Prayer issued by the Church of England
1564 William Shakespeare is born in Stratford-upon-Avon

Right: The term "golf links" relates to where ancient golf was first played. "Links land" lies between the mainland and the sea. Too barren for cultivation, it became where many golfers, particularly in Scotland, started to play the game.

NOW JUMP TO... ➔ THE OPEN page 28 ➔ TONY JACKLIN page 94

THE Sun

Thursday, February 13, 1567

2 farthings

HAS SHE TEED UP HUSBAND No3 ALREADY?

RUMOURS were sweeping Royal circles last night that the Queen is set to WED randy nobleman the Earl of Bothwell.

Earl .. made the cut

All The Goss — Bizarre, Pages 16 & 17

GOLF WIDOW

Holey inappropriate... Queen's husband was throttled just days ago

Hubby's murdered..but just days later Scottish Queen goes out putting

MARY, the Scottish Queen, caused outrage yesterday by casually playing GOLF just two days after her hubby's murder.

Instead of staying at her Holyrood Palace in mourning, the 24-year-old Monarch enjoyed a few leisurely holes at the Musselburgh course.

Her antics have fuelled speculation that she was involved in

By JUAN OVERPAR, Golf Correspondent

Lord Darnley's strangulation in Edinburgh on Monday.

She is also known to be "close friends" with the Earl of Bothwell, one of several suspects.

Mary and Darnley were going through a rocky patch. It was not helped when he and a gang of noblemen murdered her private secretary before her eyes during a palace meeting last year.

A Royal insider said last night: "That kind of thing can really hurt a shaky relationship."

FROM CLUBHOUSE TO DOGHOUSE: PAGE TWO

1654 CRICKET: KIDS' PASTIME THE PURITANS BANNED

FRONT PAGE NEWS
1577 Francis Drake sets off on his world travels on his ship, the Golden Hind
1587 Mary, Queen of Scots, executed
1640 Stagecoaches introduced into England
1653 Oliver Cromwell appointed Lord Protector in England

Left: The White Conduit Club, forerunner of the MCC, was named after the White Conduit Fields (pictured) where they played many of their matches.

Yorkshireman Thomas Lord (1755-1832) was born in Thirsk and moved to London to seek his fortune. He became a successful wine merchant and involved himself with the White Conduit Club as a bowler and coach.

CRICKET probably started during the Middle Ages, evolving from games such as stoolball (or variations called stow-ball or stump-ball), which was, and still is, played in Sussex by teams of men and women. In stoolball, the ball is pitched under-arm at a stool defended by a batsman armed with frying pan-shaped bat. It is thought cricket and baseball descended from this 14th Century children's game.

The name "cricket" is of uncertain origin. The word "criquet", meaning club, began to be used in Britain after the Norman Conquest in 1066. The Flemish word "krick", meaning stick, also a possible source.

The first definitive reference to the game is found in a 1597 court case concerning a Guildford school's ownership of a plot of land. John Derrick, a 59-year-old coroner, testified that he and his school friends played "kreckett" on the land in Surrey 50 years earlier.

The first reference to adults playing the game came in 1611 when two men in Sidlesham, West Sussex, were fined for playing cricket on a Sunday instead of going to church. A similar

SPORT SPOT

For centuries bowling was solely underarm. Roundarm, or shoulder-height, deliveries were legalised in 1835 and overarm, with a straight arm, from 1864. A 15° elbow bend is now allowed.

instance involving three men is recorded in Eltham, Kent, in 1654, by which time Oliver Cromwell and his Puritans had banned any activities distracting from religious worship. The working class, whose only leisure time was on Sunday, was thus effectively barred from sports, but the wealthier classes kept cricket alive at schools and universities.

After the Restoration of the Monarchy in 1660, sport flourished again.

The first mention of cricket as a commercial enterprise came in 1668 when the landlord of "The Ram" in Smithfield, London, paid rates for a cricket field. By the end of the 17th Century, cricket attracted serious betting. A match in Sussex played in 1697 carried an enormous prize of 50 guineas (£75) for each player on the winning team.

The year 1744 was crucial to the development of English cricket, with the first laws being written by the Noblemen and Gentleman members of the London Cricket Club, which played at the Artillery Ground in East London. A match between Kent and an all-England side on June 18th was the first at which a full scorecard was kept.

The Laws of Cricket were updated in 1774 and included, for the first time, the lbw rule and a standardised width for a bat.

During this time Hambledon Cricket Club was formed in Hampshire. From 1764 until 1792, it was England's foremost club. But

Above: Etching showing cricket being played at Marylebone Fields, late 1700s.

most famous of all – Marylebone Cricket Club – was founded in 1787. Originally called White Conduit Club and based in Islington, it took its name from its second home at Dorset Fields in Marylebone, which had been leased to MCC member Thomas Lord. The MCC moved to the present St John's Wood site – Lord's Cricket Ground, known as the "home of cricket" – in 1814.

In 1788, the MCC became custodian of the Laws of Cricket, standardising the length of the pitch at 22 yards and clarifying the ways in which a batsman could be given out.

The first county sides emerged during the 19th Century and the first international took place in 1844 – not in England, but in New Jersey, between America and Canada.

Twenty years later saw the first-class debut of WG Grace, whose popularity helped spread the game throughout the country.

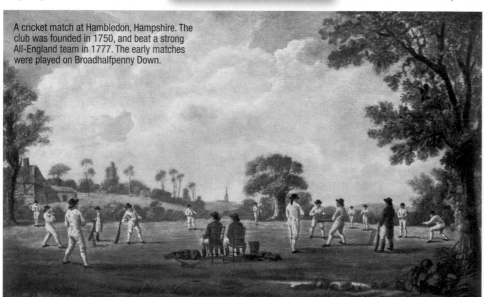

A cricket match at Hambledon, Hampshire. The club was founded in 1750, and beat a strong All-England team in 1777. The early matches were played on Broadhalfpenny Down.

THE Sun

Monday, August 14, 1654   One ha'penny

Sun THE BACKS CROMWELL

THE Sun is proud today to back Oliver Cromwell and his puritan drive against cavalier attitudes. We wish to make clear this has nothing to do with any suggestion he might shut us down.

GOTCHA: We catch cricket yobs dodging church

Howzart . . . undercover Sun oil painter 'snatched' this masterpiece of the Godless wasters in the act

LEG BEFORE WICKED

By HELEN DAMNATION, Puritanical Affairs Editor

IT'S a picture to turn the stomach of every God-fearing Sun reader — a gang of decadent lay-abouts skipping Sunday church to play CRICKET.

The Sun was tipped off to their sick "game" at Eltham, Kent, by a fan of our Lord Protector Oliver Cromwell. Most of the perverts legged it when our reporters approached. But we collared three and handed them over to Cromwell's men. Each was fined a colossal two shillings.

Cromwell's spokesman thanked The Sun last night. He said: "This was evil in its purest form."

Stump Out These Degenerates — Pages 8 & 9

1661 RACING AND ITS ROYAL CHAMPION, CHARLES II

FRONT PAGE NEWS

1655 Saturn's largest moon, Titan, is discovered by Christian Huygens

1658 Oliver Cromwell dies and his son Richard becomes Lord Protector

1660 Daniel Defoe, English writer, is born (died 1731)

1660 MP and naval administrator Samuel Pepys begins writing his diaries

HORSE racing dates back thousands of years but only took off as an organised event in Britain after the restoration of the Monarchy in 1660.

There is evidence of racing's existence as early as 2000BC. The ancient Hittite civilisation wrote about the training of racehorses, and later the Greeks and Romans are known to have raced them to judge their strength and suitability for use in war.

The first races in Britain are thought to have been organised by the Romans around 200AD, although the first recorded meeting was during the reign of King Henry II at Smithfield, London, in 1174.

The sport's modern history can be traced back to 1654 and the ban Oliver Cromwell placed on it and other avenues of pleasure. In 1660, with Cromwell dead and King Charles II on the throne, racing was revived with huge enthusiasm. It became a pastime closely associated with the aristocracy and its patronage by Charles ("the father of the British turf") led to it being dubbed "the sport of kings". The most common form at that time was "match" racing, which pitted two horses against each other. This is regarded as the or-

Above: Eclipse was foaled during a solar eclipse in 1764. He became one of the leading sires of his era. The great-grandson of 'Darley Arabian' won all of his 18 races from 1769-1770. His skeleton is preserved at the Royal Veterinary College.

Star and Garter Tavern in Pall Mall in 1752. It soon relocated to Newmarket and set out a list of rules that remain largely unchanged. Along with sanctioning racing at designated courses, the club introduced a registry of colours for each owner so each horse would be identifiable among a field of runners.

The club accountant James Weatherby was assigned to trace the pedigree of every racehorse in England. His research resulted in 1791 in the "Introduction to the General Stud Book", which detailed the descendants of 387 mares. The "General Stud Book" is still meticulously recorded today and no horse can race unless listed there.

By 1814 the Jockey Club had designated the five "classic" races. Open to three-year-olds, the 2,000 Guineas, the St Leger and the Derby make up the Triple Crown (flat racing's holy grail). The other two classics are the 1,000 Guineas and the Oaks, which are contested by three-year-old fillies.

During the 19th Century steeplechasing developed as a sport. Popular among huntsmen in the winter, it was originally run through the countryside, with horses chasing from one church steeple to the next, negotiating fences and hedges along the way. Stee-

plechasing events began to be run on prepared tracks in the early 1800s and it was first recognised as a sport by the Jockey Club in 1866.

The National Hunt Committee, set up in 1889, amalgamated with the Jockey Club in 1968. Since 1993, horse racing has been controlled by The British Horseracing Board, responsible for planning, training, financing and marketing the sport in the UK.

SPORT SPOT

From 1660, King Charles II moved his Royal Court to the racing mecca of Newmarket, Suffolk, twice a year and regularly rode in races himself.

Below: The St Leger Race, 1836. The St Leger is run over 1 mile 6 furlongs and 132 yards (2,937 metres) at Doncaster. First held in 1776, it is known as "the oldest classic turf race"

Above: A race near Windsor Castle, Berkshire, in the presence of King Charles II (1630-1685), August 14th, 1684.

igin of flat racing. At the turn of the 18th Century racing received its most important and lasting legacy. Three Arab stallions – Darley Arabian, Godolphin Arabian and Byerley Turk – were imported and bred with 35 Arab mares and suitable native mares. Every one of today's thoroughbreds can trace its male ancestry to these three stallions.

In 1711 Queen Anne founded what would become Ascot racecourse and for the first time spectators were able to bet. The popularity of multi-horse races was growing and racecourses sprang up all over the country.

As racing's popularity and profitability grew, so inevitably did corruption, malpractice and cruelty. Racing's first regulatory body, the Jockey Club, was founded at the

THE Sun

Saturday, May 4, 1661 — One halfpenny

LONG MAY YOU REIN!

Joy as King Charles turfs out racing ban

Don't get throne . . . King on horse

By **LES PARDEE**, Entertainment Editor

JOYFUL punters were poised for a betting frenzy last night after King Charles sensationally lifted the ban on horse-racing.

It is one of a host of harmless pleasures, outlawed by Oliver Cromwell's Puritan spoilsports, which the King is poised to reinstate.

Royal-watchers are also optimistic that he will scrap the bans on cock-fighting, drinking dens and brothels, as well as relaxing Cromwell's draconian penalties for blasphemy and drunkenness.

Plays and even **DANCING** may get the nod. And Christmas and May-day festivals will be back on.

One Parliament source told The Sun: "The King is a huge racing fan. He can't see any reason why people shouldn't have a flutter."

Return of the King . . . Charles is back

FREE INSIDE: WEEKEND BEAR-BAITING GUIDE

1789 DEVELOPMENT OF THE NOBLE ART OF BOXING

BOXING is more than 3,500 years old. But it took a young fighter in 18th Century England to invent the "noble art" as we know it today – a battle of brains as well as brawn.

The oldest known depiction of a boxing match is a fresco from the Minoan civilisation, circa 1500BC. The sport was part of the Olympics in 668BC.

The first documented account of a British boxing match appeared in 1681 when a London newspaper, the Protestant Mercury, referred to a bout organised by the Duke of Albemarle between his butler and his butcher at his home in Essex.

James Figg is recognised as the first bare-knuckle boxing champion (1719). A veteran of nearly 300 fights, Figg, backed by the Earl of Peterborough, set up a boxing academy in London where he taught fighters "the noble science of defence".

A pupil of Figg's, Jack Broughton, developed boxing from a bare-knuckle brawl into the beginnings of a sport with rules and regulations. He became English champion in 1738 and is widely recognised as "the father of English boxing".

In 1743, he devised seven "Broughton's Rules" after accidentally killing an opponent. They included giving fighters 30 seconds to recover from a knockdown and the invention of "mufflers" (boxing gloves). These formed the basis of the London Prize Ring Rules, developed by the Pugilistic Society in 1838.

Broughton died and was buried at Westminster Abbey in 1789, the same year another boxer, Daniel Mendoza, published his book "The Art of Boxing". It detailed a list of techniques and emphasised the importance

Above: John Sholto Douglas, the eighth Marquess of Queensbury, supervised the formulation of boxing's rules. In 1895 he was tried and acquitted for libelling Oscar Wilde – an event which led to Wilde's trial and

SPORT SPOT

The concept of paying to watch sport was born at one of three famous bouts between Daniel Mendoza and Richard Humphries around 1789. No record exists of it happening before that.

of brainpower in winning a fight. Just 5ft 7ins and 160 pounds, Mendoza, who was Jewish and from East London, became a folk-hero in England, beating taller and heavier men with his pioneering use of footwork, jabs, counter-punching and defence. He was English champion from 1792-95 and radically altered the stereotype of Jews as weak and inferior, gaining fame and fortune into the bargain.

The London Prize Ring Rules were replaced by the Queensbury Rules in 1867, endorsed by the eighth Marquess of Queensbury. His friend John Graham Chambers drew up 12 guidelines, including three-minute rounds, the ten-count for a knockout and the mandatory use of gloves. They have formed the basis of boxing rules ever since.

Bare-knuckle boxing continued for several years, the last significant fight taking place in 1889, when John L Sullivan triumphed over Jake Kilrain after a marathon 75 rounds in Richburg, Mississippi. Sullivan is widely recognised as the first world heavyweight champion. "Gentleman Jim" Corbett, one of history's greatest boxers and dubbed the "fa-

ther of modern boxing", took the title in 1892. His style was all about skill and technique and less about simple brawling.

The first black heavyweight champion, the "Galveston Giant" Jack Johnson, won the title in 1908 when he beat Tommy Burns. But he was officially recognised as champion only when he beat James Jeffries, a white fighter, in the 15th round in Reno, Nevada, in 1910. He triumphed despite the 22,000-strong crowd chanting racist abuse and a ringside band playing "All coons look alike to me". Decades later, tennis star Arthur Ashe hailed Johnson as the most significant black athlete ever.

Jack Broughton, the father of boxing, was the 2nd heavyweight champion of England after James Figg. Broughton held the title from 1734-1750.

FRONT PAGE NEWS

1675 Sir Christopher Wren begins building St Paul's Cathedral (finished 1710)
1681 First oil street lamps are introduced to London streets
1739 John and Charles Wesley found Methodism at the New Room, Bristol
1768 Captain James Cook begins his first voyage to the Pacific

Jack Johnson (1878-1946), the first black heavyweight boxing champion, held the world title from 1908-1915.

NOW JUMP TO... ⊙ HENRY COOPER page 80 ⊙ MUHAMMAD ALI page 102

THE Sun

Friday, May 1, 1789   Three farthings

'PAY PER VIEW' SHOCKER

BOXING fans will PAY to see Mendoza's big fight with Richard Humphries next week at Stilton, Huntingdonshire. No one has been charged to watch any sport before. The pair will split the takings. The winner also gets a £40 prize.

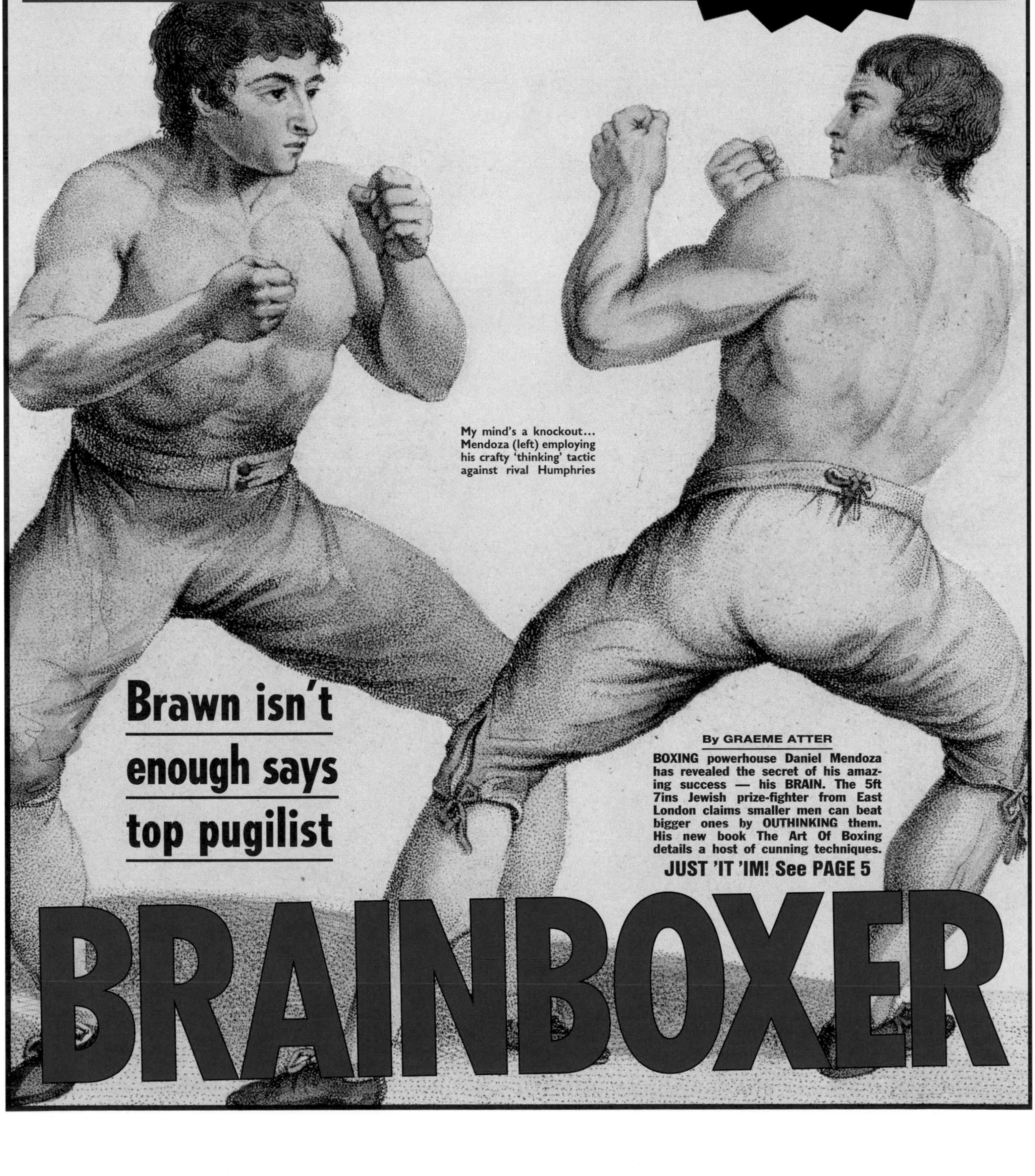

My mind's a knockout... Mendoza (left) employing his crafty 'thinking' tactic against rival Humphries

Brawn isn't enough says top pugilist

By GRAEME ATTER

BOXING powerhouse Daniel Mendoza has revealed the secret of his amazing success — his BRAIN. The 5ft 7ins Jewish prize-fighter from East London claims smaller men can beat bigger ones by OUTHINKING them. His new book The Art Of Boxing details a host of cunning techniques.

JUST 'IT 'IM! See PAGE 5

BRAINBOXER

1850 DOWNHILL SKIING & ITS GREATEST CHAMPIONS

A 17th Century woodcut of a Laplander on skis. The word "ski" is derived from the Old Norse word skið meaning "a piece of split wood".

SKIING was born out of the need to survive harsh winters in the snowbound landscapes of the northern hemisphere thousands of years ago. It did not take off as a leisure activity until the mid-19th Century when a Norwegian farmer's invention paved the way for a high-speed, high risk sport.

Short, broad, carved wooden skis about 4,500 years old have been found in Swedish peat bogs. On the Norwegian coast of Rødøy, near the Svartisen glacier, a rock carving depicting a hunter on skis is also believed to date back more than 4,000 years.

Skiing competitions have been held for nearly 200 years but they were almost entirely conducted on the flat, cross-country, until the appearance of Norwegian Sondre Norheim, widely regarded as "the father of modern skiing".

Born in 1825 in the Telemark region, he was a passionate skier from an early age. As a young man he invented a strong but flexible birch binding which held the ski firmly in place, allowing him to ski downhill and to make turns and jumps without losing his skis. He also created a 'Telemark ski' which was shorter, curved and wider at the tip and tail. It

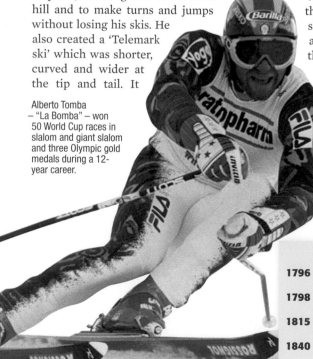

Alberto Tomba – "La Bomba" – won 50 World Cup races in slalom and giant slalom and three Olympic gold medals during a 12-year career.

made turning the skis even easier. Norheim perfected downhill skiing and in 1868, aged 43, won the first Norwegian skiing competition, impressing the crowds in Oslo with his revolutionary new design and his skill.

He is responsible for inventing the Telemark and Christiania turns. It wasn't long before Telemark skis became Norway's most famous export.

Ski clubs sprang up and Norwegian skiers travelled the world spreading the new techniques. Norheim emigrated to America in 1884, settling in North Dakota, where he died in 1897. His gravestone describes him as "the pioneer of modern skiing".

Austrian Mathias Zdarsky (1856-1940) advanced Norheim's invention, developing the first binding suitable for Alpine skiing and demonstrating it in Schneeberg, Austria, in 1905. Zdarsky also wrote the first detailed analysis of skiing technique.

In 1922, the British skier and mountaineer Arnold Lunn invented the modern slalom race and two years later the International Ski Federation was set up, during the first Winter Olympic Games held in Chamonix. Norway won 11 of the 12 titles on offer.

The first alpine skiing races were held in 1948 at the Winter Olympics in St Moritz, with 112 skiers entering the first men's downhill, won easily by Frenchman Henri Oreiller, nicknamed "the Acrobat".

Austrian skiing legend Toni Sailer won the Olympic downhill, slalom and giant slalom titles at Cortina d'Ampezzo in Italy in 1956. Jean-Claude Killy repeated the feat in 1968 at Grenoble, France.

At Innsbruck, Austria, in 1976, home favourite Franz Klammer produced one of the most breathtaking runs in Olympic history. As he took gold by 0.33 seconds, to the delight of 60,000 fans, he admitted: "I thought I was going to crash all the way."

Swede Ingemar Stenmark, who won two golds at the 1980 Olympics in Lake Placid, New York, was

SPORT SPOT

IT took until 1906 before the world's first rudimentary T-bar ski-lift was invented in Schollach, Austria. The first chairlift was built in Sun Valley, Idaho, in 1936.

Celebrated French skier Jean-Claude Killy was the star of the 1968 Winter Olympics, winning the Downhill, Giant Slalom and Slalom titles in front of an adoring home crowd at Grenoble.

the dominant slalom and giant slalom skier of his generation, before the hugely popular Italian Alberto Tomba made the events his own in the late 1980s and 1990s. Norwegian Kjetil André Aamodt amassed the greatest haul of Olympic medals ever for alpine skiing – eight, four of them gold – from 1992 to 2002. During the same period Austrian Herman Maier became the most exciting ski racer of his generation. The double Olympic champion came back from a spectacular crash in the downhill at Nagano, Japan, in 1998 to win the Giant Slalom and Super-Giant Slalom just days later.

Below: Austria's first skiing superstar Toni Sailer, nicknamed "The Blitz from Kitz", was a triple Olympic champion in 1956. He also won four gold medals at world championships before retiring aged 24.

FRONT PAGE NEWS

1796 Edward Jenner discovers the smallpox vaccine

1798 Thomas Malthus publishes his essay on the principles of population

1815 Battle of Waterloo: Napoleon's final defeat

1840 Introduction of penny postage stamps in the UK

THE Sun

Thursday, April 11, 1850   One penny

..BUT HOW WILL THEY GET BACK UP AGAIN?

SCEPTICS claim Norheim has given no thought to the nightmare of climbing back UP the hill one has skied down. One said: "This is a crucial flaw."

Skiers go downhill .. and find it's QUICKER

NOT VERY FAST

Skier's sedate progress on flat

MUCH FASTER

Wheee! He whizzes down hill

SNOW KIDDING!

ASTONISHED skiers have found a way to go downhill safely — and, guess what . . . it's a hell of a lot faster!

Cross-country skiing has gone on for centuries in snowy areas like Norway.

But it has always been too risky to go down slopes because skis would fly off and there was no way to stop. Now Norwegian farmer Sondre Norheim

By CRISPIN EVEN, Ski Correspondent

has developed a wooden binding which firmly fixes skis to a skier's boots. It allows them to make jumps and turns and to stop without crashing. Norheim's new curved-sided skis make turns easier too.

Pundits claim he may have invented an entirely new sport.

One told The Sun: "People will love the idea of racing down slopes, perhaps weaving around obstacles as they go."

It's All Downhill Now — Page 54

Ski's the daddy . . . Norheim

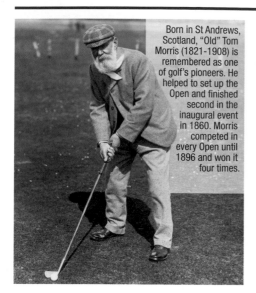

Born in St Andrews, Scotland, "Old" Tom Morris (1821-1908) is remembered as one of golf's pioneers. He helped to set up the Open and finished second in the inaugural event in 1860. Morris competed in every Open until 1896 and won it four times.

THE Open Championship is the world's oldest and most prestigious golf tournament, providing the most varied and testing challenge in the sport.

It was first played at Prestwick Golf Club, Scotland, in 1860, attracting eight contestants who played 36 holes in one day.

Golf pioneer "Old" Tom Morris was expected to win, but Willie Park Senior won with a score of 174 and was presented with "The championship Belt". The Open's famous Claret Jug was not presented to the winning golfer until 1873, when Tom Kidd won the first championship at St Andrews.

Scottish and English golfers dominated the competition until World War One; only Frenchman Arnaud Massy broke the monopoly of home wins, in 1907.

Harry Vardon registered his record sixth win at Prestwick in 1914. Jersey-born Vardon was the top golfer of his day and played a part in spreading the game's popularity in America – albeit by losing the 1913 U.S. Open Championship. Vardon and fellow Englishman

Left: In beating British legends Harry Vardon and Ted Ray in a play-off at the 1913 US Open, Francis Ouimet became America's first golf hero.

Ted Ray were beaten by the little-known American amateur Francis Ouimet in an 18-hole play-off. This stunning victory at the Country Club, Brookline, Massachusetts, prompted a surge of interest in the sport and is recognised as the moment golf in America was born.

Ouimet's victory also began an era of American dominance in all the Major championships. The U.S. Open and USPGA Championship have proved unhappy hunting grounds for overseas players. Since World War One only 12 overseas players have won the U.S. Open and since it was first played in 1916 only ten foreigners have won the USPGA.

Barring the wave of European success at the U.S. Masters in the 1980s and 1990s, the Augusta National Golf Course, designed by the legendary amateur Bobby Jones in 1934, has yielded few victories for non-Americans.

Until recently, American supremacy has also been reflected in Ryder Cup competitions between teams from the U.S. and Europe, with the Americans winning 24 out of 36 since the biennial competition began in 1927.

After World War Two the USPGA Tour produced

The Golf Champion Trophy, now commonly referred to as the Claret Jug, was made by Mackay Cunningham & Company of Edinburgh. The first Open champion to accept it was the 1873 winner Tom Kidd but the first name engraved on it was that of Tom Morris Junior, who won the year before.

SPORT SPOT

The first Open winner received no cash prize at all. Today the overall pot is more than £4million and top prize £750,000.

some of the greatest ever golfers. Jack Nicklaus, Arnold Palmer, Lee Trevino and Tom Watson, to name just four, thrilled audiences and promoted the sport before rapidly growing TV audiences.

Using the American tour as its blueprint, the European Tour was set up in 1971. It quickly blossomed and Seve Ballesteros, Bernhard Langer and Nick Faldo in particular challenged the American supremacy.

Since the Ryder Cup was regained in an historic win at the Belfry in 1985, the game in Europe has gone from strength to strength.

The European tour has produced a constant flow of talented young players and helped the Open Championship retain a more cosmopolitan feel than the other Majors. A truly international field compete in conditions which remain true to golf's ancient origins.

Only 14 courses have hosted the Open Championship but all provide a variety of challenges – bumps, hollows, hillocks and dunes. All have to be negotiated in changeable weather. Almost all the professionals playing today agree that the Claret Jug is golf's most prized possession.

Walter Hagen was the world's first full-time professional tournament golfer and golf's greatest showman. He captivated the public wherever he played.

NOW JUMP TO... ◗ TONY JACKLIN page 94 ◗ NICKLAUS & WOODS page 124

THE Sun

Wednesday, October 17, 1860 — Penny farthing

CHECK 'EM OUT
10 trendy golf outfits: Fashion special inside

Hole-in-one's clothes . . . the Open golfers yesterday. Favourite 'Old' Tom Morris (bearded) is fourth from the left

THE BOGEYMEN

No, not a gang of cut-throats ...they're world's top golfers!

THEY may look like the stuff of kids' nightmares — but this is the world's golfing elite, posing yesterday before the inaugural Open Championship.

The pros will pay 36 holes today at Scotland's Prestwick

By ANDY CAP, Golf Correspondent

Golf Club for the coveted championship belt. Golf legend "Old" Tom Morris is hot favourite.

Fashion pundits have been scathing about the sport's shabby image. One said: "It soooo needs a makeover."

More Frightening Pictures — Page 74

FWORE! SUN'S BIRDIES DRIVE BLOKES BUNKERS: PAGE 3

FRONT PAGE NEWS

1858 First transatlantic telegraph cable laid from Ireland to Newfoundland

1861 Louis Pasteur proposes his germ theory of disease

1863 The London Underground is born. Services begin on 10th January on the Metropolitan Line

1863 President Abraham Lincoln gives his Gettysburg Address during the American Civil War

Above: Parker's Piece, Cambridge. In 1848, Cambridge students H. De Winton and J.C. Thring met 14 representatives from leading public schools and devised a set of standardised regulations known as the "Cambridge Rules". Copies were pinned up around Parker's Piece playing fields.

EGGS AND PLUMS

UNTIL the 1860s footballs and rugby balls were the same shape. They were like plums, that being the shape of the inflated pig's bladder inside their leather cases.

Since 1823 Rugby School had used balls provided by local shoemaker William Gilbert. But in 1862 Richard Lindon, another local bootmaker, started using Indian rubber inner tubes. They were tougher and more pliable, allowing footballs to be spherical. The school, wanting to distinguish its code of football from others, asked Lindon to change the rugby ball from a plum to an egg, which was also easier to carry. Lindon became the principal maker of balls for the "handling game".

By 1892 the RFU endorsed the oval shape. It has since become more streamlined.

THE invention of rugby is popularly attributed to an impulsive Rugby School pupil, William Webb-Ellis. While playing a version of football in 1823 he is said to have caught the ball and charged up the pitch with it, with total disregard for the rules.

The story, first told half a century later, is almost certainly apocryphal and, whether true or not, is most unlikely to have been the birth of rugby. Nonetheless, winners of the Rugby World Cup are awarded the William Webb-Ellis trophy in his honour.

During the early 19th Century, football was popular in English boarding schools. There were few rules, so each school or region developed its own. Some, like Eton, played a kicking game. Others, like Rugby, played a variation where the ball was both kicked and handled. When they competed against each other, half the match would be played by one school's rules and the second half by the other's. This is how half-time evolved.

The differing rules were first drawn together as a single coherent code in 1848 when a group of Cambridge University students who had played variations of football at public school drew up the Cambridge Rules. On October 26th, 1863, several football clubs in London met at the Freemasons Arms pub in Great Queen Street to establish the "Football Association" and propose a single unifying code. It differed from the Cambridge Rules on two crucial points. The ball could not be handled. Nor could a player "hack", or kick in the shins, an opponent to regain possession. These two controversial points were debated at further meetings – and all but two of the public schools represented refused to join the new association. At a fifth meeting, on December 8th, Blackheath football club withdrew its support for the new FA and marked the official split between football and rugby.

In December 1870 the secretary of Richmond Football Club, Edwin Ash, published a letter in the Times stating: "Those who play the rugby-type game should meet to form a code of practice as various clubs play different rules." So on January 26th 1871 representatives from 21 clubs met at a Pall Mall restaurant and founded the Rugby Football Union (RFU).

By June that year the laws had been drawn up by three ex-Rugby School pupils and approved by RFU members. The number of players per team was cut from 20 to 15 in 1877. Initially, points were only awarded for kicking the ball over the posts, but points scored for a "try" were eventually recognised and rose in value to reach three by 1891, staying that way for 81 years. In 1886, Scotland, Ireland and Wales formed the International Rugby Football Board. England initially refused to join, but were members by 1890.

After a complex beginning, full of splits and disagreements, rugby was flourishing. But it wasn't long before it encountered further turmoil, and itself divided in two.

SPORT SPOT

Rugby's major nations are England, Scotland, Ireland, Wales, Australia, New Zealand, South Africa, France, Italy and Argentina, but a host of others have teams, including Uzbekistan, Tahiti and Cambodia.

Left: England and Scotland play the first ever rugby union international at Raeburn Place, Edinburgh, on March 27th 1871. Scotland won 3 goals to 1.

The statue of William Webb Ellis which looks out over the playing fields at Rugby School. Only after Webb Ellis died in 1872 was his story told when a former pupil wrote to the school magazine.

NOW JUMP TO... ⊙ FOOTBALL LEAGUE page 38 ⊙ RUGBY'S SPLIT page 44

THE Sun

Wednesday, December 9, 1863   Penny farthing

It's a fry! Here's one of the egg-shaped balls used for playing rugby. Maybe the breakaway group can start their own Egg Cup!

'Rugby' pals give footie the boot ..so they can chase this barmy ball

EGG-SODUS

By MO MENTUS

A REBEL group of football clubs who play the game's "Rugby" version dramatically voted last night to have their own sport — using a barmy ball shaped like an EGG.

At a tense meeting in London they quit the newly-formed Football Association over its refusal to allow players to handle the ball or "hack" opponents in the shins.

The rebels, led by Blackheath in South-East London, believe both are vital for the sport's success.

Club member Francis Campbell, who was treasurer of the FA, said scrapping the two rules would "do away with all the courage and pluck from the game".

Blackheath and 20 other clubs intend to go it alone. They are expected to use the bizarre oval ball favoured by pupils at Rugby School, Warwicks, where the game began.

The boys say it is easier to carry and is distinctive. Critics argue that it simply doesn't roll properly.

Flown Off The Handle — Pages 4&5

FOOTIE: A GAME

What a carry on . . . our artist's impression of how a 'Rugby' game might look after last night's split at the FA

Ball handler . .
'Rugby' player

THEY'VE OFF THE

By BERTHA SOCKER

THE "Rugby" splitters were accused of petulance last night after walking out on football in the dispute over handling the ball.

One insider at the crunch meeting told The Sun: "We've all been working hard to draw up a set of rules everyone could abide by.

"But they just expected us to adopt the way **THEY** play the game. We don't think handling the ball is right, and put our foot down. They flew off the handle and left. It was ridiculous."

Problems originally began when various schools and clubs started playing organised football earlier this century. Each used different rules, making it tricky to play each other. Rugby School, for example, allowed players to carry the ball, while other schools banned it.

In October several of the clubs got together at the Freemason's Arms at Lincoln's Inn Fields in central London to form

Chaos . . . shambolic game at Rugby School

IN TWO HALVES

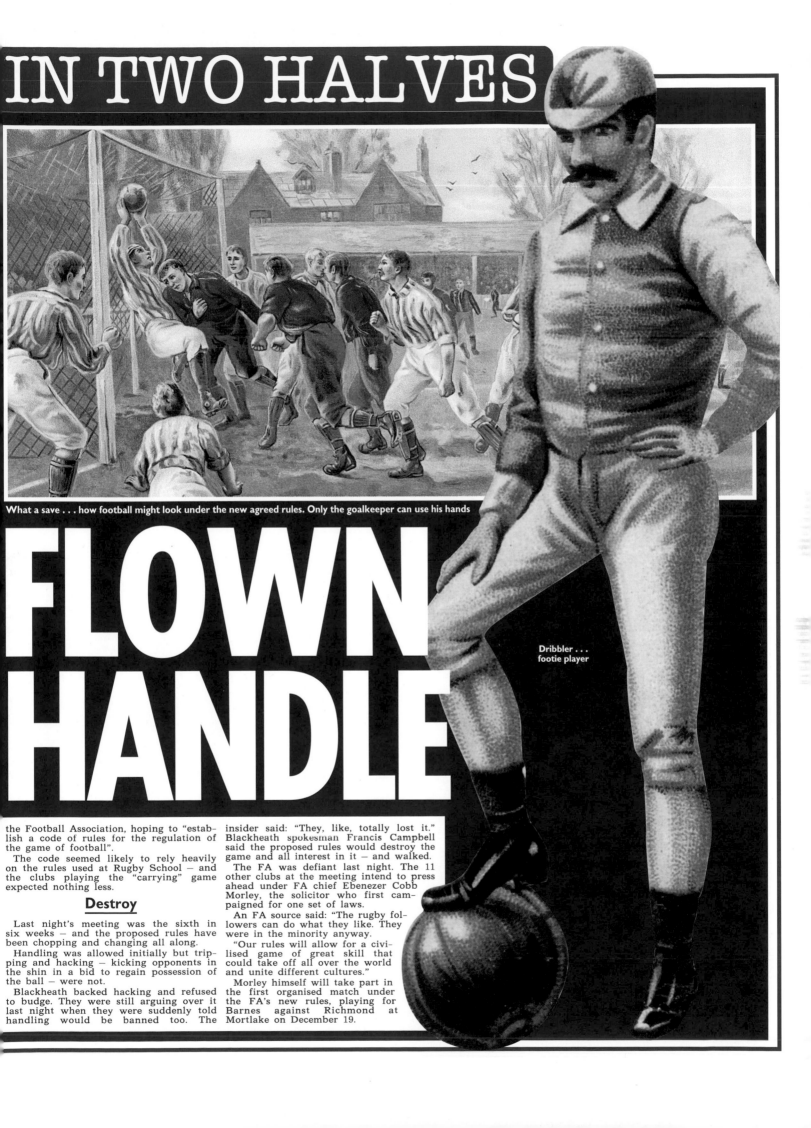

What a save . . . how football might look under the new agreed rules. Only the goalkeeper can use his hands

Dribbler . . .
footie player

FLOWN HANDLE

the Football Association, hoping to "establish a code of rules for the regulation of the game of football".

The code seemed likely to rely heavily on the rules used at Rugby School — and the clubs playing the "carrying" game expected nothing less.

Destroy

Last night's meeting was the sixth in six weeks — and the proposed rules have been chopping and changing all along.

Handling was allowed initially but tripping and hacking — kicking opponents in the shin in a bid to regain possession of the ball — were not.

Blackheath backed hacking and refused to budge. They were still arguing over it last night when they were suddenly told handling would be banned too. The

insider said: "They, like, totally lost it." Blackheath spokesman Francis Campbell said the proposed rules would destroy the game and all interest in it — and walked.

The FA was defiant last night. The 11 other clubs at the meeting intend to press ahead under FA chief Ebenezer Cobb Morley, the solicitor who first campaigned for one set of laws.

An FA source said: "The rugby followers can do what they like. They were in the minority anyway.

"Our rules will allow for a civilised game of great skill that could take off all over the world and unite different cultures."

Morley himself will take part in the first organised match under the FA's new rules, playing for Barnes against Richmond at Mortlake on December 19.

1877 WIMBLEDON & GRAND SLAM TOURNAMENTS

TENNIS as we know it was dreamed up in the 1870s by the inventor Major Walter Wingfield, under the incomprehensible title "Sphairistike", a Greek word meaning 'arena for ball games'. It was quickly renamed "lawn tennis" – and by 1877 had its first, and historically its most important, championship.

It was held at the headquarters of the newly-titled All England Croquet and Lawn Tennis Club, off Worple Road, Wimbledon, South-West London. Around 200 spectators paid one shilling to watch Spencer Gore, an ex-Harrow public school rackets player, take the first and only title then on offer. Gore himself wasn't convinced the new sport would catch on. But it did.

The early championships were dominated by the Renshaw brothers – Ernest and William – who won 13 singles and doubles titles during the 1880s. The period is known as the "Renshaw Rush" and did much to popularise the championships. In 1884, 13 women entered the first ladies' singles tournament, won by Britain's Maud Watson.

The move to new grounds off Church Road in 1922 allowed Wimbledon to forge its iconic status. Many said a 14,000-seat arena would be too big, but centre court was regularly filled to capacity. It took tennis forward as a spectator sport and set the standard for all the world's tennis stadia.

By the 1920s all four "Grand Slam" tournaments were well established. The inaugural U.S. Open men's and women's singles tour-

The courts at the Worple Road site were arranged with the principal court in the middle; hence the title "Centre Court", which was retained when the club moved in 1922 to the present site in Church Road

FRONT PAGE NEWS

1872 Claude Monet's "Impression: Sunrise" gives its name to the art movement Impressionism

1876 George Custer defeated and killed by Sioux at the Battle of Little Big Horn

1876 Alexander Graham Bell invents the telephone

1877 Thomas Edison invents the phonograph (gramophone)

naments were in 1881 and 1887 respectively. The French Open began in 1891, though it was solely a national tournament until 1924. The Australasian Championships, as they were then, started in 1905.

The 1930s was the last golden era for British tennis with Fred Perry winning Wimbledon three years running (1934, 1935 and 1936). Dorothy Round won Wimbledon twice, in 1934 and 1937.

After World War Two the championships were dominated by players from abroad. American women swept the board. Australians and Americans dominated the men's game. The "Open" era, in which professionals competed alongside amateurs, began in 1968 with Rod Laver and Billy Jean King dominant.

Increasing TV coverage gave all the Grand Slam tournaments far greater publicity. For the All England Club it heralded the beginning of a golden era. Classic matches abounded as some of the greatest grass court exponents ever – including Jimmy Connors, Bjorn Borg and John McEnroe – served up extraordinary centre court scripts.

By the end of the 1970s Wimbledon remained the only Grand Slam tournament played on grass. The French had used clay since 1928. The U.S. Open switched to the hard courts at Flushing Meadows in New York in 1978.

Advances in equipment technology during the 1980s tipped the balance towards players

The Renshaw brothers William (Willie) and Ernest, who dominated Wimbledon in the 1880s. William was the more successful, winning the men's singles seven times between 1881-1889. Their success brought the crowds to Wimbledon and helped to establish lawn tennis.

of power rather than skill and threatened the attractive serve-and-volley grass court game. Rallies were shorter and crowd entertainment took a hit. But America's Pete Sampras showed the way, combining power with the traditional delicate grass court touch and winning seven men's singles titles.

With the many improvements to its facilities Wimbledon has managed to embrace change while maintaining its heritage. By 2009 a new retractable roof on centre court will consign rain delays to the history books.

Construction of centre court during 1921. The bigger Church Road site was bought after efforts to buy adjacent land at Worple Road failed.

HAWKEYE TODAY

HAWKEYE is in reality the first new piece of court technology deployed at Wimbledon since 1980 when Cyclops, an infrared laser beam, was introduced to determine whether a ball was out.

Using ten cameras around Centre Court, HawkEye tracks the flight of a ball and provides a virtual replay of the point to settle line calls. It is accurate up to 3mm and has been used in TV's cricket coverage since 2001.

SPORT SPOT

Australian tennis legend Rod Laver is the only man to have won the Grand Slam twice, in 1962 and 1969.

Maud Watson was the winner of the first two ladies' singles championships in 1884/85.

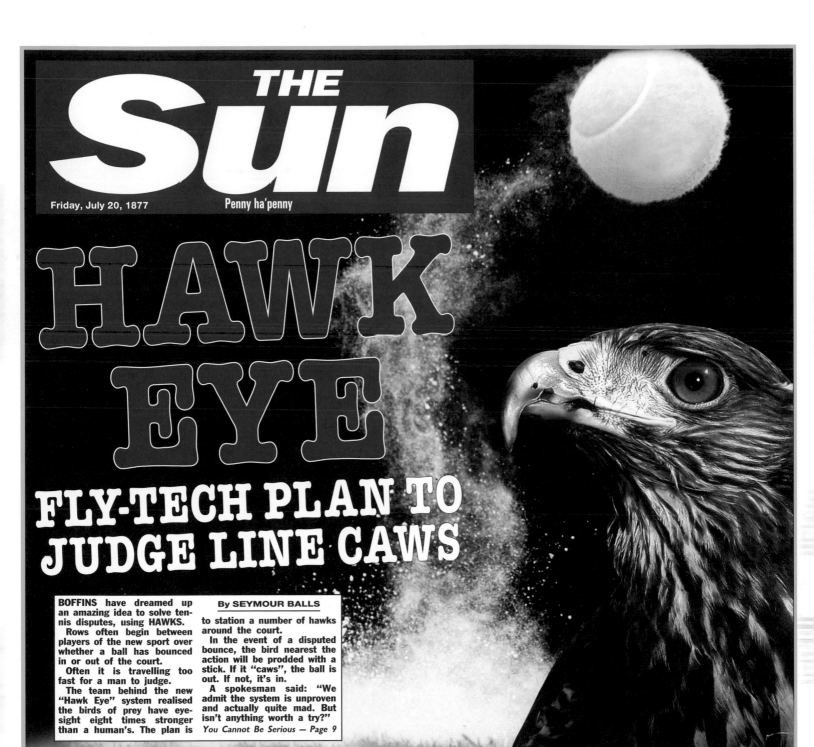

THE Sun

Friday, July 20, 1877 — Penny ha'penny

HAWK EYE

FLY-TECH PLAN TO JUDGE LINE CAWS

By SEYMOUR BALLS

BOFFINS have dreamed up an amazing idea to solve tennis disputes, using HAWKS.

Rows often begin between players of the new sport over whether a ball has bounced in or out of the court.

Often it is travelling too fast for a man to judge.

The team behind the new "Hawk Eye" system realised the birds of prey have eyesight eight times stronger than a human's. The plan is to station a number of hawks around the court.

In the event of a disputed bounce, the bird nearest the action will be prodded with a stick. If it "caws", the ball is out. If not, it's in.

A spokesman said: "We admit the system is unproven and actually quite mad. But isn't anything worth a try?"

You Cannot Be Serious — Page 9

TENNIS IS DULL

Wimbledon ace's astonishing rant

THE winner of the first Wimbledon championships stunned the world last night by sensationally branding tennis "dull".

Spencer Gore, 27, a Surrey county cricketer, is only a part-time player of lawn tennis, invented two years ago.

He beat William Marshall 6-1,

By CON TEMPTUOUS

6-2, 6-4 in a 48-minute final in front of 200 spectators in south-west London yesterday.

Gore *(pictured right)* won 12 guineas and a silver cup.

But in a blistering rant later he said: "Lawn tennis is a bit boring. It'll never catch on." Despite his misgivings, he **DOES** intend to defend his title next year.

Gore Bore — Back Page

1882 THE ASHES: FIERCEST OF ALL CRICKET'S RIVALRIES

FRONT PAGE NEWS

1880   Thomas Edison invents electric light

1880   Russian Peter Tchaikovsky composes the 1812 Overture

1881   Wild West outlaw Billy the Kid shot dead by Sheriff Pat Garrett in New Mexico

1882   Treasure Island by Robert Louis Stevenson is published

THE Ashes urn, the smallest trophy in world sport, is cricket's biggest prize. The coveted award given to the winners of a Test series between England and Australia has inspired some of the sport's finest, and fiercest, matches.

In 1882, on their third tour of the mother country, an Australian team defeated England in the one Test of the summer, at the Oval on August 28th-29th. It was their first Test victory on British soil and a resounding one. England's team, among them the great WG Grace, were bowled out for 77 by paceman Fred Spofforth, who claimed 7-44. The result shook English cricket to its core.

The Sporting Times ran a mock obituary, reading: "In Affectionate Remembrance of ENGLISH CRICKET, which died at the Oval on 29th AUGUST, 1882. Deeply lamented by a large circle of sorrowing friends and acquaintances. R.I.P. N.B. — The body will be cremated and the ashes taken to Australia."

Later that year a team led by Ivo Bligh was dispatched to Australia to "bring back the ashes". England won 2-1, and in commemoration a group of young women are said to have burned a bail, placed its remains in the now famous urn and presented it to Bligh. Some stories suggest the ashes are in fact of an incinerated ball, or even the veil of Bligh's future wife Florence Rose Murphy, who was at the impromptu ceremony.

England dominated the contests for 15 years but by the turn of the century the Ashes had returned to Australia. A

In Affectionate Remembrance
OF
ENGLISH CRICKET,
WHICH DIED AT THE OVAL
ON
29th AUGUST, 1882,
Deeply lamented by a large circle of sorrowing friends and acquaintances.

R. I. P.

N.B.—The body will be cremated and the ashes taken to Australia.

Below: Jack Hobbs (left) was England's premier batsman for almost 30 years and with Herbert Sutcliffe (right) formed probably the best opening partnership ever. Left: Sporting Times 'obit'

memorable series was played in 1902 which Australia won 2-1.

Jack Hobbs – 'The Master' – and Wilfred Rhodes were a formidable opening pair for England before World War One, hitting a record 323-run opening stand at Melbourne in the 1911/12 series which saw England trounce Australia 4-1.

But two years after the war, Australia recorded their first 5-0 whitewash in Ashes history and retained the trophy until 1926 when England won 1-0 at home.

Don Bradman's first Ashes appearances in 1928/29 were unspectacular, as Australia went down 4 matches to 1. But by 1930 he was unstoppable. England's 1932-33 touring side, led by Douglas Jardine, adopted the infamous "Bodyline" tactic purely to stem Bradman's runs. It worked – England won 4-1.

Australia regained the Ashes in 1934 and kept them until 1953 when they were defeated by an England side led by one of the country's finest ever batsman, Len Hutton, who had scored a world Test record of 364 in 1938.

England retained the urn three years later, thanks largely to off-spinner Jim Laker, whose match figures of 19-90 at Old Trafford may never be bettered. Though never really dominant dur-

SPORT SPOT

"Too fragile to travel", the Ashes urn has visited Australia only twice – in 1988 and in 2006 when it flew first-class in a flight-case.

The Oval, 12th September 2005: England celebrate their first Ashes series victory in 18 years. Australia inflicted revenge 15 months later, whitewashing England 5-0.

ing the 1960s, Australia held on to the Ashes until Ray Illingworth's 1970-1971 England touring side, spearheaded by fast bowler John Snow and assisted by a remarkably consistent young batsman, Geoffrey Boycott, won 2-0.

But in 1974-1975 Dennis Lillee and Jeff Thomson – one of the most fearsome fast bowling partnerships in cricket history – proved decisive, Australia winning 4-1.

Ian Botham inspired England to victory in 1981 and after defeat a year later the Ashes were regained again in 1985.

Mike Gatting led England's tour Down Under in 1987. It was to be the last English Ashes victory for 18 years.

Only in 2005 was the talent and brutal efficiency of Australia under successive captains Allan Border, Mark Taylor, Steve Waugh and Ricky Ponting finally vanquished by heroic performances from many England players, chiefly Andrew Flintoff.

The joy was short-lived. England were humiliated by a 5-0 thrashing in Australia during the winter of 2006-2007.

Left: Australian captain Allan Border turned his team's fortunes around in the late 1980s. Australia regained the Ashes in 1989 and dominated for 16 years

England triumph over Australia at the Oval in 1953, their first Ashes series victory in 15 years. As the winning runs were hit, commentator Brian Johnston bellowed "It's the Ashes! It's the Ashes! England have won the Ashes!"

Our destroyer . . . Fred was furious

RIGHT, SAID FRED
How 'Demon' inspired Oz
SEE BACK PAGE

FLAMIN' IDIOTS

Our cricket cretins (77 all out) lose to AUSSIES

R.I.P.

We cremate bails to signify death of English cricket after our pathetic first home defeat against Australia

By **ANDY ZBOLDIM**, Cricket Correspondent

ENGLAND'S cricket bunglers disgraced the nation yesterday by losing to Australia for the first time on home soil.

Set only 85 to win, they collapsed to a measly 77 all out at the Oval in South London.

Paceman Fred "The Demon" Spofforth took 7-44 in an act of furious revenge after WG Grace unsportingly ran out an Aussie batsman who thought the ball was dead.

The Sun yesterday cremated a set of bails in a ceremonial protest at the sorry demise of our national team. We have placed the ashes in a tiny urn.

Now we intend to **AMBUSH** Grace and **TIP** the contents into his beard. A spokesman for The Sun said: "There is no way we should lose to Australia.

"The only crumb of comfort is that it's most unlikely to happen again."

1889 FOOTBALL LEAGUE BRINGS ORDER TO CHAOTIC SPORT

Dixie Dean: the most prolific goal-scorer in English football history. He scored 349 times in 399 appearances for Everton

Spectators crowd around the pitch and scale the roofs of the stand to watch Chelsea at Stamford Bridge in 1946.

WHEN the Football Association sanctioned a switch to professionalism it unleashed pandemonium as far as fixtures were concerned. Teams chased the most lucrative fixtures at the expense of matches they had already agreed to play. New teams sprang up almost every week to satisfy fans' demand. Something had to be done to bring order to the chaos.

Step forward William McGregor, a Birmingham-based Scottish draper. A director at Aston Villa, McGregor wrote to the leading clubs in 1888 proposing they "combine to arrange home and away fixtures each season".

On March 22nd a meeting was convened at Anderton's Hotel in London's Fleet Street and 12 clubs – Preston North End, Bolton Wanderers, Everton, Burnley, Accrington, Blackburn Rovers, Aston Villa, West Bromwich Albion, Wolverhampton Wanderers, Notts County, Derby County and Stoke – formed the first Football League. The first fixtures were played on September 8th.

Preston North End dominated that inaugural season. Not only did Preston's Jack Gordon score the first goal in the new league, the team easily won the first championship. They played 22, won 18 and drew four with no defeats – earning them the nickname "The Invincibles". They scored 74 goals, more than

Born in 1847, William McGregor served his draper's apprenticeship with Richardson and Pearson in George Street, Perth, before moving south to Birmingham in 1870.

three per game, and conceded just 15. Centre forward John Goodall, who was poached by Derby County the next season, scored 20 goals in 21 games. Preston then completed English football's first

SPORT SPOT

Preston won the championship again in 1889-90, but other clubs improved and they never did it again. Their last major trophy was an FA Cup win in 1938.

double by beating Wolves 3-0 in the FA Cup final at the Kennington Oval in front of 22,000 fans.

The new league was hailed a success and the resulting clamour for places made expansion inevitable. In 1892 it was split into two divisions. By 1898 Divisions 1 and 2 consisted of 18 clubs each, rising to 20 in the 1905/06 season.

The league spawned imitators all over the world. Argentina was the first country outside Britain to start a national league and soon McGregor's idea was being replicated throughout Europe.

By 1920 a 3rd Division had arrived in England, as had the first football pools coupon. Wembley opened its gates in 1923 for the "White Horse" Final and by 1930 football was playing its first World Cup, Uruguay beating Argentina 4-2 in the final.

Changes to the rules in 1925 reduced the number of defenders required to place an attacker offside from three to two and led to many more goals. The first season played under the new rules

saw the goal count rise by more than 1,600 to 6,373. In 1927/28 Everton legend Dixie Dean scored a record 60 goals in one season. He finished his career with 473 from 502 games.

During the mid-1920s and early 1930s Sheffield-born Herbert Chapman was establishing himself as one of the greatest football managers of all time, taking Huddersfield to consecutive Division 1 titles, before heading south to win two league titles with Arsenal too.

After World War Two, Matt Busby led his Manchester United team to back-to-back titles before they were torn apart by the Munich air crash in 1958. Busby rebuilt his squad and won the European Cup a decade later.

By this time Liverpool, under the iron rule of Bill Shankly, were laying the foundations for future success. Shankly won three Division 1 championships before handing over to Bob Paisley, who oversaw the most successful period in their history, winning six league championships and three European Cups.

Liverpool dominated domestic football until the end of the 1980s, before the Premiership took the sport into completely new territory.

Below: Bill Shankly, Liverpool manager 1959-74. "Some people believe football is a matter of life and death. I'm very disappointed with that attitude. I can assure you it is much, much more important than that."

FRONT PAGE NEWS

1883	**Volcanic island of Krakatoa explodes, killing 40,000 people**
1884	**First Oxford English Dictionary**
1886	**Karl Benz produces the first car**
1888	**Jack the Ripper begins his murder spree in London's East End**
1888	**George Eastman begins selling the first Kodak cameras**

THE Sun

Monday, April 22, 1889   1½d

PRESTON NORTH END FC

THE INVINCIBLES

Awesome . . . Preston's Invincibles. Back row: Robert Mills-Roberts, John Graham, Bob Holmes, David Russell, Robert Howarth, George Drummond. Front row: Samuel Thompson, Fred Dewhurst, John Goodall, Jimmy Ross, John Gordon

●Preston 'too good'
●'A one-horse race'
●It's ruining footie

By JUAN SIDED, Chief Football Writer

THE first Football League season has ended amid growing fears that it is a one-horse race with little future.

Pundits say Preston North End's mighty "Invincibles" are so dominant that other sides don't have a prayer against them.

Preston's talented local boys and Scottish stars, including 20-goal centre forward John Goodall, won the league and FA Cup with ease. In the league they dropped only four points and were undefeated. One football expert said: "It's crazy. Everyone else is fighting for the runners-up spot."

Goal machine . . . Goodall

RAMS IN FOR ACE GOODO: SEE BACK PAGE

1891-93

TEACHER'S GAME GRIPS WORLD

Head coach of the Boston Celtics, "Red" Auerbach talks with centre Bill Russell in the locker room. The Celtics won eight straight NBA titles – the longest winning run in North American sports.

OF all the major sports in the USA, only basketball can claim to be a truly original American invention.

Seeking a way to keep his YMCA students active through long, cold New England winters, PE teacher James Naismith invented "basket ball" with the aid of a football and a peach basket nailed to the railings above the gymnasium floor.

The first official game was played on January 20th 1892 at the YMCA Training School (now Springfield College) in Springfield, Massachusetts.

Dribbling the ball wasn't allowed but it was soon instated (in 1901) and although there have been numerous adaptations and additions over the years, basketball remains faithful to Naismith's simple rules.

It wasn't long before the popularity of the new game spread through YMCAs and then clubs and colleges across the U.S. In 1904 a demonstration tournament was held at the Olympics in St Louis, Missouri.

Basketball's appeal went around the world and in 1932 eight nations founded the International Basketball Federation. Four years later, at the Berlin Games, the sport officially became an Olympic event. The USA took gold, beating Canada 19-8.

In 1937, 13 teams founded the National Basketball League (NBL). Such was its success that a rival league was established nine years later. The Basketball Association of America (BAA) boasted teams from New York, Boston, Philadelphia, Chicago and Detroit and proved highly successful.

By the end of the 1949 season all the NBL teams had joined the BAA. A three-division league, which soon became two, was set up and renamed the National Basketball Association

Larry Bird's duels with Magic Johnson were legendary. The pair of them turned the NBA from a "minor" pro sport in 1980 into a big-time business.

Above: Minneapolis Lakers in 1949. They were the dominant team of the fledgling NBA.

SPORT SPOT

At 7ft 7in, Romanian Gheorghe Muresan and Sudanese Manute Bol are the tallest players ever in the NBA. Both played in the 1990s.

(NBA). The Minneapolis Lakers, led by centre George Mikan and coached by John Kundla, would dominate the new NBA, winning five championship titles in 1949, 1950, 1952 and 1954.

The Boston Celtics dominated the NBA from 1957 to 1969. The team, coached by "Red" Auerbach, won 11 NBA titles (1957, 1959-1966, 1968 and 1969), including eight consecutively. The Celtics had many stars, with centre Bill Russell arguably their greatest. In his 13-season career, Russell averaged 15.1 points per game and 22.5 rebounds per game. In 1969 the two NBA divisions were renamed the Eastern and Western conferences.

The late 1970s saw organised basketball's appeal begin to wane – even though the Harlem Globetrotters were still pulling in big crowds and TV audiences with their comic exhibition matches. NBA ticket sales were down and TV ratings fell away.

But help was just around the corner as Larry Bird and Magic Johnson transformed the sport in the 1980s.

Bird helped revitalise the Boston Celtics, leading them to three NBA titles in 1981,

At 6ft 9in, Earvin "Magic" Johnson was the tallest point guard ever to play the game.

1984 and 1986. Johnson, along with Kareem Abdul-Jabbar, did the same in Los Angeles, guiding the Lakers to five NBA championships.

In the late 1980s the Detroit Pistons – featuring Isiah Thomas and Dennis Rodman – emerged briefly as a dominant force, taking the title in 1989 and 1990.

The past 20 years have produced a host of stars – Hakeem Olajuwon, Shaquille O'Neal, Kobe Bryant, Jason Kidd – but without question the most important figure in the modern era was Michael Jordan, considered by most commentators to be the greatest player of all time. A born entertainer, Jordan possessed exceptional skills and took the playing and marketing of the game to a new level. He led the Chicago Bulls to six NBA championships (1991-1993, 1996-1998) and led the league in scoring a record ten times.

Below: Michael Jordan won the NBA Most Valuable Player award five times and was included in the All-NBA first team selection ten times.

FRONT PAGE NEWS

1889	Eiffel Tower completed in Paris
1890	Scotland Yard moves to London's Victoria Embankment, becoming New Scotland Yard
1891	Beginning of the Trans-Siberian Railway
1891	The Swiss Army knife is developed
1892	First virus is discovered

THE Sun

Thursday, November 23, 1893   1½d

Basket case . . . PE teacher Naismith invented barmy game

Peach cobblers . . . Naismith's first 'basket ball' court

Sports chiefs mock 'ball in basket' craze

HOOPLESS

By SAM DUNC

A WORRYING new "sport" sweeping America's schools and universities was dismissed as a fleeting craze last night.

Sports experts insisted "basket ball" could never threaten the major sports, almost all invented by ingenious Britons and given generously to the world.

The indoor game was the idea of PE teacher James Naismith to keep his students in Springfield, Massachusetts, active in cold winters.

A player scores a point by lobbing a football into a peach basket nailed on to a wall 10ft above the floor. Each time, the ball must be laboriously fished out with a long pole.

One British pundit said last night: "What a chore! It wouldn't be so bad if they just had a hoop with an open net hanging off it. Mind you, they'll never get anywhere with this whatever they do. It's not exactly cricket, is it?"

Nonetheless, dozens of basket ball clubs have sprung up all over the U.S. in just two years.

Shorties' Fury Over 'Bias' — Pages 78 and 79

COLOSSUS WHO BROUGHT CRICKET TO THE MASSES

CRICKETERS rarely experience widespread fame outside the game, but in his heyday WG Grace was as well-known as Prime Minister William Gladstone. The dramatist and poet Clifford Bax said of him: "There is no more renowned beard in all humanity."

Born on July 18th, 1848, in the Bristol suburb of Downend, William Gilbert Grace was encouraged to take up cricket by his father Dr Henry Mills Grace. It was not long before WG established himself as an all-rounder of great promise.

He began his first-class career at 16, playing, as he always would, for Gloucestershire.

A year later, in 1865, he was picked to play for the Gentlemen (amateurs) against the Players (professionals). The matches drew large crowds and Grace cemented his reputation by turning the Gentlemen from serial losers into regular winners. In 85 matches, his contribution was immense, scoring more than 6,000 runs and taking 271 wickets.

Still only 23, Grace scored a staggering 2,739 runs in the 1871 season. His average of 78 was double that of the next best player. Five years later he would amass 839 runs in three innings inside ten days, with 344 against Kent, 177 against Nottinghamshire and 318 not out against Yorkshire. His lon-

WG Grace was instantly identifiable, even by those who didn't watch cricket.

A young WG Grace poses, ball in hand. He grew his trademark beard in early adulthood

gevity as a top player remains unchallenged in cricket history. In May 1895, aged 47, he was the first player to complete 1,000 runs in May – which included his 100th hundred. Even at 59 he managed the double of 1,000 runs and 100 wickets in a season. By the time he retired in 1908, he had scored 54,896 runs and taken 2,864 wickets.

Yet for all his achievements on and off the pitch – he practised medicine during the winter – stories still abound as to his arrogance on the cricket field.

In one charity match he replaced the bails after being bowled first ball and re-took his guard. "These spectators," Grace told the protesting bowler, "have come to see me bat, not you bowl." He had a point. Such was his celebrity that ticket prices often doubled if he was playing.

On another occasion, against Surrey, a fielder's return throw from the boundary became lodged in his shirt. Grace refused to give the ball back and took an extra three runs. He claimed he did not want to risk being out for handling the ball.

At a momentous Test match at the Oval in 1882, Grace controversially ran out Australian batsman Sammy Jones. Jones had completed a single and wandered out of his crease to repair the pitch, thinking the ball was dead. Grace ambled towards the bowler, before backtracking and throwing the ball at the stumps. Under Grace's strict interpretation of the game's laws, the umpire had to give the hapless Australian out. This act of gamesmanship had lasting consequences. The angry Aussies skittled England for 77 and brought about the famous defeat that gave rise to the Ashes.

There is little doubt that Grace – "The Doctor" – enjoyed and used his celebrity and often used underhand tactics. But for all that, Grace, as is often said, found cricket a country pastime and left it a national institution.

SPORT SPOT

Grace once kidnapped an Australian Test cricketer, about to bat against Middlesex at Lords, and drove him by carriage to the Oval to make good on a promise to play for Gloucestershire.

Above: WG as portrayed by Vanity Fair magazine in 1898.

FRONT PAGE NEWS

1893	**Rudolf Diesel (1858-1913) invents the diesel engine**
1893	**Russian bacteriologist Waldemar Haffkine produces a cholera vaccine**
1893	**New Zealand is first country to give women the vote**
1894	**Guglielmo Marconi invents wireless telegraphy**

NOW JUMP TO... ↻ GREAT BATSMEN page 66 ↻ GREAT BOWLERS page 72 ↻ GREAT ALL-ROUNDERS page 88

SunSport: No1 FOR CRICKET

I'm a celebrity, you won't get me out of here

Grace under pressure
. . . Doctor WG
batting yesterday

Dr. W.G. GRACE.
CRICKET. 1885
Star man . . WG immortalised on cigarette card

'WG' REFUSES TO GO AFTER HE'S BOWLED

By ALBIE DUBBLEYOU

CRICKET giant "WG" Grace stunned fans yesterday by refusing to be given out despite being BOWLED first ball.

In front of a huge crowd, Dr Grace, 47, insisted he was **TOO FAMOUS** to "walk".

He bellowed down the pitch: "They've come to see me bat, not you bowl!"

To the opposition's amazement, play was waved on.

The incident came during a charity match. But Britain's most famous sportsman has been criticised for underhand tactics in his first-class matches for Gloucestershire and England too.

In one innings against Essex he twice bullied umpires into giving him not out, for a catch and an lbw, against cricket's fastest bowler Charles Kortright.

Grace, real name William, only finally trudged off after Kortright knocked two of his stumps out of the ground.

The Essex man sarcastically shouted after him: "What? Are you going, Doctor? But there's still one stump standing!"

Critics say Grace is a bad sport who is forgiven much because his genius has single-handedly made cricket England's No1 game.

DIS-GRACE: PAGES 62-63

1895 RUGBY DIVIDES INTO LEAGUE AND UNION

1935 Challenge Cup final between Castleford and Huddersfield. Castleford won 11-8.

RUGBY'S split into Union and League in 1895 was all about money.

Some Northern teams in the Rugby Football Union (RFU) stood accused of paying players, which was forbidden by RFU rules that insisted on amateur status being maintained. Players at Bradford and Leeds had since 1892 received 'broken time payments' as compensation for taking time off work to play. This was a necessity for the mainly working-class players who could not afford to lose income, and although the Northern clubs lobbied hard for a relaxation of the rules, they were outvoted by 282 votes to 136. Clubs who continued with the payments were suspended.

On August 29th 1895, representatives from 22 Northern rugby union clubs met at the George Hotel in Huddersfield and broke from the RFU, forming the Northern Rugby Football Union, later to become known as Rugby League.

At first they continued using the same rules, but major changes came in 1906. Two forwards were removed to reduce the number of players per side to 13, making the pitch less congested and encouraging more attacking play. Rucks and mauls were abolished. Instead players were allowed to 'play the ball' (heeling it back to a team mate) after being tackled.

SPORT SPOT

Rugby league is the national sport of only one country, Papua New Guinea, where it was introduced by Australian soldiers in the late 1940s.

A year later a team from New Zealand, the All Golds, visited England and played 35 'League' matches. They returned home and spread the new code there. Australia quickly caught on and the first Australian Kangaroos team toured Britain in 1908.

The Northern Union officially changed its name to Rugby League in 1922 and by the end of that decade another significant change had taken place. The Challenge Cup competition, which had started in 1896/97 with Batley beating St Helens in Leeds, had been contested annually at various Northern football grounds. But in 1929 the final took up permanent residency at Wembley. About 41,500 spectators saw Wigan beat Dewsbury 13-2, which started Wigan's love affair with the national stadium. They have secured the cup a further 14 times there, including a record eight consecutive victories from 1988-95. After

Right: Martin Offiah scores another breakaway try for Wigan in their 26-16 defeat of Leeds in the 1994 Challenge Cup final. Offiah scored 501 tries in his 14-year career.

World War Two, crowds of more than 80,000 were common for the final and the trip down the M1 to London became a pilgrimage for League fans.

The League Championship has comprised one or two divisions throughout its history. Hull Kingston Rovers, Huddersfield and Salford dominated before World War Two. Wigan dominated the post-war era, claiming 11 first division titles.

Great Britain was the strongest side internationally until the early 1960s when New Zealand and, more so, Australia began to dominate Test series and the World Cup, which Australia has won nine times since its inauguration in 1954.

The formation of the Super League in 1996 saw the game in the UK switch to being a summer competition a world away from its humble origins.

Gone are the days of playing in a mud bath in December. Team nicknames, cheerleaders, fireworks, music and summer fixtures have transformed rugby league into a 21st Century spectacle.

Above: The first Challenge Cup final in 1897 was contested between Batley (left) and St Helens (right) at Leeds. Some 13,492 spectators watched Batley win 10-3.

VOLLEYBALL'S ROOTS

VOLLEYBALL'S origins can be traced to the same American college which gave birth to basketball.

In 1895 William G Morgan, Director of PE at the Young Men's Christian Association (YMCA) in Holyoke, Massachusetts, wanted a game like basketball but less physical. Taking elements of basketball and handball, and borrowing a tennis net, he invented a game called Mintonette.

The first match was played at Springfield College, Massachusetts, where James Naismith invented basketball four years earlier. It quickly spread to YMCAs worldwide, its name becoming "volley ball".

The current rules were laid down in 1916. The Federation of International Volleyball (FIVB) was set up in 1946 and a year later the first official beach volleyball competitions took place in California.

Volleyball has been an Olympic sport since 1964 and beach volleyball since Atlanta in 1996. Horse Guards Parade in Westminster will host the event in 2012.

FRONT PAGE NEWS

- **1895** Oscar Wilde arrested after losing a libel case against the Marquess of Queensberry and imprisoned
- **1895** Marxist political philosopher Friedrich Engels dies aged 74
- **1895** German physicist Wilhelm Rontgen discovers X-rays
- **1895** French Lumiere brothers invent film projector

THE Sun

Friday, August 30, 1895   1½d

SPORT'S HOTTEST BABES!

THEY'RE the hottest babes in sport . . . the voluptuous vixens of volleyball, the new game taking America by storm. Leaping about in bonnets and hooped skirts, they're a feast for the eyes of any red-blooded bloke. And they're in The Sun today.

MORE TANTALISING ANKLE GLIMPSES: CENTRE PAGES

SCRUM OF THE EARTH

By PHIL YABOOTS

THE warring rugby factions finally tore the sport apart last night.

Northern clubs voted to quit the Rugby Football Union in the bitter dispute over paying players.

They will form their own league, free from the "ridiculous rules and demands" of the RFU in London.

There were even suggestions after their crisis meeting at a Huddersfield hotel that they may change the game's rules.

The row is over working-class Northerners being paid for lost earnings while playing rugby, something rich Southerners do not need.

The RFU's Yorkshire chief James Miller pleaded with the RFU to allow it. It refused, saying players would earn cash without doing "real work". A war of words then erupted between Miller and the Rev Frank Marshall, a referee who insists players must remain strictly amateur.

Let's Give It A Try — Back Page

Unholy row . . . Marshall and Miller are foes

North's rage at South as cash row tears rugby in two

1896 REBIRTH OF OLYMPICS & ITS SPECTACULAR RISE

Pierre de Coubertin (1863-1937) was behind the revival of the Games and was President of the International Olympic Committee until 1925.

The Panathinaiko Stadium in Athens hosted the 1896 Games and was built on the site where more than 2,000 years earlier the ancient Greeks held the Panathenean Games in honour of the goddess Athena.

SOME 1,503 years after they were banned by the Roman Emperor Theodosius I, the Olympics returned. From humble beginnings in 1896 they have blossomed into a vast sporting spectacular, now split into a summer and winter Games.

The first modern Olympics was staged at the home of the ancient Games in Greece, and by today's standards attracted only a small number of athletes. Around 250 competed from 14 nations, compared with more than 11,000 from 201 countries at Athens in 2004. Nonetheless, the eight days of competition in 1896 drew big crowds to the Panathinaiko Stadium.

There were nine different sports – athletics, fencing, gymnastics, shooting, swimming, cycling, tennis, weightlifting and wrestling. Winners were awarded silver medals, not gold, plus an olive branch. James Connolly, a 28-year-old Harvard University student, was the first modern Olympic champion. His 13.71 metres in the "hop, skip and jump" – now the triple jump – won by a metre.

The blue riband event, the 100 metres, was won by American Tom Burke who from a crouched start – unusual at the time – recorded a time of 12 seconds. By also winning the 400 metres in 54.2 seconds he completed a double never since repeated.

Burke's winning time in the 100 metres looks sluggish today. When Justin Gatlin crossed the line at Athens in 2004 in 9.85 seconds, Burke would have been passing the 80 metre mark. Burke's 400 metre time doesn't fare any better. Sally Gunnell, winning gold at Barcelona in 1992, would have beaten him by a second, even though she also cleared ten hurdles.

These extraordinary differences highlight how far athletes have come in the century since the modern Olympics began.

The rise of professionalism is partly responsible. Gone are the days when top athletes had to hold down a day job and train in their spare time. Prize money and sponsorship has enabled them to focus solely on their discipline.

They have the best science and technology at their disposal too. The traditional coach with a stopwatch round his neck has been replaced by a team of specialists, including nutritionists, masseurs, osteopaths, chiropractors and sports scientists. The athletes' bodies are wired up and monitored by computers analysing every detail of their performance and instructing them how to improve it.

Athletes' diets are also immeasurably better than two generations ago.

So too are the conditions under which they compete. In the second half of the 20th Century, quicker all-weather surfaces replaced old cinder tracks. Athletics equipment started to improve. Cotton shorts and vests were replaced by lightweight lycra. Steel-spiked leather shoes gave way to feather-light slippers with titanium pins.

The march of technology goes on, and with it the constant improvements in performance. It is probable that the world-beating times of today's fastest men and women would not qualify them for an Olympic final in 2052.

Pierre de Coubertin, the French founder of the International Olympic Committee, chose his Olympic motto wisely back in 1894: "Citius, altius, fortius" (faster, higher, stronger). Intended as an exhortation to athletes, it proved an accurate prediction too.

SPORT SPOT

The Olympics' explosion in scale since 1896 is breath-taking. The Sydney Games in 2000 was covered by more than 16,000 journalists and watched by almost four billion TV viewers.

On April 6th 1896, American James Connolly won the triple jump to become the first modern Olympic champion. He went on to become a well-known journalist.

Justin Gatlin, the most recent 100m Olympic champion. The joint 100m world record holder – with Asafa Powell – is currently serving an eight-year ban after a positive drugs test in April 2006.

FRONT PAGE NEWS

1896 Charles Dow publishes the first edition of the Dow Jones Industrial Average

1896 The shortest war in history, the Anglo-Zanzibar War, starts at 9am and lasts 45 minutes

1896 Alfred Nobel (b.1833), Swedish inventor of dynamite and Nobel Prize creator, dies

1896 Queen Victoria surpasses King George III as Britain's longest-reigning monarch

THE Sun

Saturday, April 11, 1896 — 1d

Should women compete too?

YOU THE JURY

OUR CRUCIAL OLYMPIC VOTE: PAGE 15

FASTEST MAN ON THE PLANET

Squatever next . . . Burke's 'crouching' start amused spectators, but it worked

Tom wins Olympic 100m in incredible 12 seconds

From MYLES O'HEAD in Athens

SUPERFIT Tom Burke was crowned the fastest human on Earth yesterday as he won Olympic gold in the 100 metres in an astounding time of 12 SECONDS. Burke, 21, a student from Boston, U.S., wowed the crowds in Athens with his wacky "crouching" start. He also won the 400 metres on Tuesday.

Crouching Tiger — Back Page

Hattaboy . . . sprinter Tom

1912 DARK DAY IN THE LONG HISTORY OF BOAT RACE

FRONT PAGE NEWS

1898	Invention of the cornflake
1902	Marie Curie discovers radium
1903	The Wright Brothers become first humans to fly
1905	Albert Einstein's special theory of relativity
1906	San Francisco earthquake kills 700
1912	Royal Flying Corps (forerunner of the Royal Air Force) is established

Left: Oxford and Cambridge are neck and neck at Chiswick on March 24th 1877. The race eventually ended in a controversial "dead heat".

1951: Cambridge University well ahead of Oxford University at Hammersmith Bridge. This was a re-run race following Oxford's sinking in the first. There have been six sinkings in Boat Race history: Oxford and Cambridge have both fallen victim three times each.

THE boat race between Oxford and Cambridge universities is a national institution, attracting enormous crowds on the riverbank and a TV audience of millions. Its popularity cannot have been dreamed of by the two men who thought it up in the 1820s.

The race was the brainchild of former Harrow public school friends Charles Merivale, by then a student at Cambridge, and Charles Wordsworth (nephew of the poet William Wordsworth), who was studying at Oxford.

On March 12th 1829, Oxford accepted a challenge sent to them by Cambridge and on June 10th the two teams convened at Henley on Thames for the first race, which Oxford won. A reported 20,000 spectators attended, sufficient to inspire the launch of the Henley Royal Regatta.

The two teams did not meet again until 1836, by now in their familiar colours – dark blue for Oxford and light blue for Cambridge. This time the race was held in London, from Westminster to Putney. The now famous 4½-mile Putney to Mortlake course was introduced in 1845 and the race became annual in 1856. Perhaps the most famous came in 1877,

when the result was controversially declared a dead heat. Cambridge, the favourites, were ahead for the first half but, buffeted by choppy waters along Chiswick Reach, fell behind Oxford, who maintained a narrow lead right to the finish.

"Honest" John Phelps, a professional waterman who was adjudicating from a boat at the Mortlake finish line, had his view obstructed by other vessels (another version of events claims he nodded off). He announced the result, bafflingly, as a "dead heat to Oxford by 5ft". After an inquiry the umpire recorded the race as a "dead heat".

Thanks to modern boat technology and design, the sight of crews sinking has become far less common. But in 1912 both crews sank in dreadful conditions and had to restart the race the next day. By a grim coincidence, two weeks later on April 15th the same fate befell the "unsinkable" liner Titanic in the Atlantic, claiming 1,523 lives.

One of the most bizarre incidents in boat race history happened in 1984. Before the start Cambridge contrived to row into a static barge moored in the middle of the river and sank. Red-faced and cold, the oarsmen had to paddle back to the riverbank and borrow a boat. The race took place the following day. Oxford won.

Barring 1877's "dead heat", the closest race ever came in 2003. An extraordinary tussle saw the crews side by side right to the finish, where Oxford triumphed by the impossibly narrow margin of one foot.

SPORT SPOT
The annual university boat race has become so ingrained into British culture that it was adopted into Cockney rhyming slang - to mean "face".

Triple Olympic gold medallist Matthew Pinsent rowed three times for Oxford. The Royal photographer Lord Snowdon rowed for Cambridge in 1950 and actor/comedian Hugh Lawrie was part of the losing Cambridge eight in 1980.

The course record was set by Cambridge in 1998 in 16 minutes 9 seconds and, as of 2007, the light blues continue to edge ahead in the overall standing, winning 79 contests to Oxford's 73.

GREYHOUND RACING

GREYHOUND racing evolved out of the controversial pastime of hare coursing and was originally attempted in 1876 when a race was organised along a straight 400-yard track in Hendon, North London. *The Times* dubbed the event "coursing by proxy" and the sport was over before it began.

But when American Owen Patrick Smith invented the mechanical hare in 1912 the traps opened and the sport flourished.

The first track to open in the UK was the Belle Vue stadium in Manchester on July 24th, 1926. London's White City stadium followed in 1927 and soon national attendances were in excess of five million.

Irish-born Mick the Miller took the sport by storm. He won the Derby in 1929 and 1930. He won the Cesarewitch at West Ham the same year, setting a new world record for 600 yards, before claiming the Welsh Derby in another world record time. In six months he won 29 of his 34 races. He retired in 1931 after winning the St Leger.

In the 1960s, attendances began to decline – but "the dogs" continue to excite hundreds of thousands of punters every year.

University boat race 2003: Oxford (left) clinch a thrilling win by just one foot in a time of 18:06. The winning margin was 0.05 of a second.

THE Sun

Monday, April 1, 1912   1½d

OARFUL

Boat race fiasco as BOTH crews sink

By BOB ABOUT, Rowing Editor

THIS was the dramatic moment when the annual university boat race turned to farce — as BOTH crews sank in gale force winds.

The Oxford and Cambridge teams had to call off Saturday's event after being swamped by choppy waves on the Thames.

Cambridge were in the lead when they began to go under. Oxford overtook — but they had the same problem.

The race will be held again today. It is the only time since the event began in 1829 that both boats have sunk.

What A Cox-up — Back Page

TITANIC: ONE SHIP SURE TO STAY UP!

Shipshape . . . the White Star Line's amazing Titanic

JOKERS said the boat race crews should take advice from the builders of the Titanic — the incredible new ship that's dubbed "unsinkable". The huge, state-of-the-art liner is packed with technology to ensure she stays afloat. The Titanic makes her maiden voyage to New York in nine days' time.

1914 HOW FOOTBALL UNITED TWO WARRING NATIONS

"Gassed" (1919) by John Singer Sargent. The scene is the aftermath of a mustard gas attack on the Western Front, as witnessed by the artist. There is a football match going on in the background.

Above: The football used by British troops on the battlefield at Montauban. Hoping to encourage his men to advance, Captain Wilfred Nevill of the 8th East Surreys gave each platoon a football, urging them to see which could be first to dribble it up to the German front line.

FOOTBALL played a crucial role in recruitment for the British war effort in 1914. And it became a unifying force between the two warring armies during the historic truce on the Western front that Christmas.

Throughout the year, Government representatives had travelled the country, urging fit young men to enlist. Public announcements were made and posters put up at football grounds around the country. By November, three months into the war, more than 100,000 had signed up through football organisations alone. It wasn't just fans, it was players too. Around 2,000 of England's 5,000 professional footballers volunteered to fight.

By the end of the year, a million men were positioned along the 500-mile Western Front from the Belgian coast to the Swiss border. On January 1st 1915 The Times published letters from servicemen on the front line that described the extraordinary, poignant truce that still resonates with us today.

"At about 11 o'clock [Christmas Eve night]," wrote one officer, "a very excited Infantry officer came along and told us that all fighting was off, and that men were fraternising in between the trenches."

Another officer wrote: "I found the Bosches' trenches looking like the Thames on Henley Regatta night! They had got little Christmas trees burning all along the para-

pet." On Christmas morning officers from Britain and Germany walked out from the trenches into no man's land, shook hands and exchanged cigarettes and cigars.

News of a truce spread quickly down the line and, but for a few sections, fighting stopped all the way along the Western Front. Impromptu football matches broke out. Some men were lucky enough to have a football. Others used tied-up bundles of straw or empty provision jars and boxes.

Kurt Zehmisch of the 134th Saxons recorded in his diary: "The English brought a soccer ball from the trenches, and pretty soon a lively game ensued. How marvellously wonderful, yet how strange it was. The English officers felt the same way about it. Thus Christmas, the celebration of love, managed to bring mortal enemies together as friends for a time."

An anonymous British soldier wrote on Christmas Day: "This will be the most memorable Christmas I've ever spent. Since

SPORT SPOT

The truce inspired a host of artists and performers, including The Farm, whose 1990 pop hit All Together Now was England's anthem at the Euro 2004 football tournament.

about tea time yesterday I don't think there's been a shot fired. The Germans commenced by placing lights all along the edge of their trenches and coming over to us, wishing us a Happy Christmas.

"We had quite a social party. Several speak English very well. Some of our chaps went over to their lines.

"There must be something in the spirit of Christmas, as today we are all on top of our trenches running about, whereas other days we have to keep our heads well down.

"We've had a few Germans over to see us this morning. After breakfast we had a game of football at the back of our trenches!

"We had a decent chat. They say they won't fire tomorrow if we don't so I suppose we shall get a bit of a holiday – perhaps. We can hardly believe that we've been firing at them for the last week or two. It all seems so strange."

Along some sections of the front, the truce lasted just a few hours. In others it continued into the New Year.

Soon enough, the slaughter resumed. But even in the bloody arena of war, football had for a time transcended the deepest enmity.

British troops go over the top of the trenches at The Somme in 1916.

FRONT PAGE NEWS

1913 Bodies of Captain Robert Scott and two companions found close to the South Pole

1913 Carmaker Henry Ford unveils first moving assembly line at his Michigan factory

1914 George Bernard Shaw's play "Pygmalion", later adapted for film as "My Fair Lady", opens to rapturous reviews

1914 Austrio-Hungarian Archduke Franz Ferdinand is assassinated, triggering World War One

BOXING DAY Sun

Merry Xmas & a Happy New Year to all our brave boys up front

Saturday, December 26, 1914   1d

Whatever you do, don't shout 'shoot' . . . a Brit soldier outwits Germans

They think it's all over...it is for now

WAR OFF AS OUR BOYS PLAY HUN AT FOOTIE

By OLIVE BRANCH

BRITISH and German troops played **FOOTBALL** together yesterday in incredible scenes at the front after calling a Christmas Day truce.

It began after the Hun began singing carols in their trenches at Ypres, Belgium, on Christmas Eve. Our Boys joined in and the guns fell silent. Eventually both sides emerged to swap gifts.

Yesterday they were mixing freely. One amazed Brit said last night: "I never expected to shake hands with Germans on Christmas Day.

"A few came over and we played football at the back of our trenches."

The fighting is set to resume today.

IT'S ALL KICKING OFF AGAIN: PAGES 6 & 7

1919-21 SCANDAL SHAKES U.S. BASEBALL OBSESSION

IT is often called the national pastime, given its tradition and popularity. But America's relationship with baseball could equally be expressed as a long and turbulent love affair, with all its attendant peaks and troughs.

Baseball was probably developed from the English game of rounders, which dates back to the early 17th Century, but its exact origins are much debated.

For many years it was thought baseball was invented in a cow pasture in Cooperstown, New York, in 1839 by a U.S. army general called Abner Doubleday. This theory is now generally considered untrue, not least because of the discovery in 2004 of a document believed to be the earliest written reference to baseball. It is a bylaw, written in 1791, banning the playing of baseball within 80 yards of a meeting house in Pittsfield, Massachusetts.

It is thought that by the 1820s baseball was a common form of recreation in the North-East, around Boston, New York and Philadelphia. In 1845 a set of rules for organised baseball was drawn up by Alexander Cartwright, a fireman. Many are still in use today – and most baseball historians view him as the father of the game.

Baseball spread rapidly and the first professional team – the Cincinnati Red Stockings – began playing in 1869. Seven years later eight teams formed a National League. In 1901 a rival – the American League – was set up and proved successful. Two years later the winners from both leagues played each other in a best-of-nine-match World Series. Today it is best of seven.

Baseball's greatest showcase would provide it with its darkest hour in 1919 when eight members of the Chicago White Sox threw the series against the Cincinnati Reds. It re-

The Father of Modern Baseball – Alexander Cartwright of the New York Knickerbocker Baseball Club.

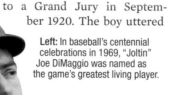

mains the most famous scandal in American sport and rocked a disbelieving nation.

Chicago White Sox owner Charles Comiskey was notoriously tight with money and paid his players a pittance given their status as the world's best team. They were nicknamed the Black Sox either because of the taint of the scandal that followed or because they had to play in unlaundered kit, depending on which theory you believe.

Disaffection about low pay was rife among the team. Bookmaker Joseph "Sport" Sullivan recognised this and offered first baseman Arnold "Chick" Gandil $80,000 to throw the series. Gandil soon had seven team-mates on board and the series was duly thrown. They included star player "Shoeless" Joe Jackson, so-called because he once played a baseball match barefoot. A fix was widely suspected and criminal charges brought in 1920. A law court found the eight men not guilty, but they were issued with life bans from the sport.

The scandal's seismic impact was summed up by a probably fictitious exchange on the steps of a Chicago courthouse between Jackson and a crestfallen young fan after the star's pre-trial "confession" to a Grand Jury in September 1920. The boy uttered

Left: In baseball's centennial celebrations in 1969, "Joltin' Joe DiMaggio was named as the game's greatest living player.

The 4-0 Chicago White Sox victory over the Houston Astros in 2005 was their first World Series win in 88 years and their first appearance in the final since 1959.

plaintively, "Say it ain't so, Joe", to which Jackson replied, "Yes, boy, I'm afraid it is". Given Jackson's stellar performances during the World Series it is unclear whether he was guilty of throwing games, and he protested his innocence to his dying day.

Baseball's reputation slowly recovered and new stars emerged. New York Yankees ace George Herman "Babe" Ruth became one of the greatest home-run hitters of all time in the 1920s and 1930s. Yankees star Joe DiMaggio completed a 56-game "hitting streak" in 1941. It remains one of the greatest feats in the sport's history.

In April 1947, Jackie Robinson of the Brooklyn Dodgers became the first black player to play in the major leagues and so started a new era for the sport.

Another surge in popularity occurred in 1998 when Mark McGwire of the St Louis Cardinals hit 70 home runs in a season, breaking Roger Maris' 37-year record of 61.

In 2005, the Chicago White Sox finally won a World Series and laid to rest the so-called match-fixing jinx that had lasted 86 years.

Left: On August 7, 2007, at the age of 43, Barry Bonds of the San Francisco Giants hit his 756th career home run, setting a new all-time record in the major leagues.

Team of shame . . . White Sox at World Series. Eight now face trial

Chuffed . . . Albert

Double Olympic gold for Bert at 31

By STELLA RUNS

BRITISH track hero Albert Hill was on cloud nine over his amazing Olympic double last night — gold in the 800 metres AND 1500 metres.

The 31-year-old railman from Tooting, South London, also bagged silver in the 3000m in Antwerp.

Albert's triumphs are all the more amazing given that he ran five races in five days — and that selectors almost refused to pick him due to his age.

Flying

The Belgian Olympics are the first since before the war, in which Albert served with the Royal Flying Corps.

In the 800m he set a British record of 1min 53.4secs.

His time in the 1500m was an impressive 4mins 1.8secs.

A spokesman for British athletics said last night: "We're very proud of Albert.

"It'll be a long time before we see any British athlete pull off a middle-distance double like that again."

'BUBBLES' ANTHEM IS MUSIC HALL HIT

BIZARRE: Page 17

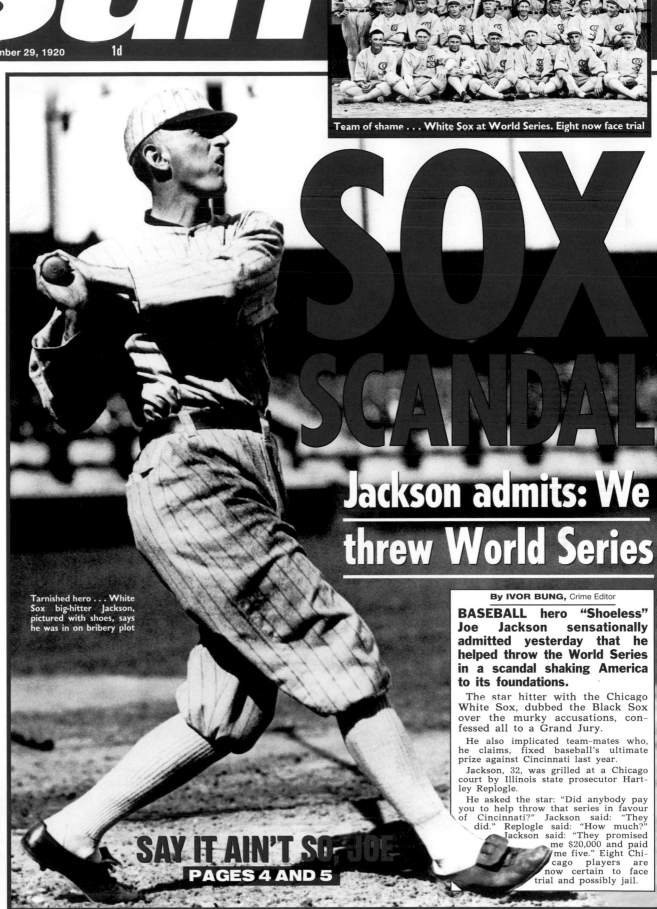

Tarnished hero . . . White Sox big-hitter Jackson, pictured with shoes, says he was in on bribery plot

SOX SCANDAL

Jackson admits: We threw World Series

By IVOR BUNG, Crime Editor

BASEBALL hero "Shoeless" Joe Jackson sensationally admitted yesterday that he helped throw the World Series in a scandal shaking America to its foundations.

The star hitter with the Chicago White Sox, dubbed the Black Sox over the murky accusations, confessed all to a Grand Jury.

He also implicated team-mates who, he claims, fixed baseball's ultimate prize against Cincinnati last year.

Jackson, 32, was grilled at a Chicago court by Illinois state prosecutor Hartley Replogle.

He asked the star: "Did anybody pay you to help throw that series in favour of Cincinnati?" Jackson said: "They did." Replogle said: "How much?" Jackson said: "They promised me $20,000 and paid me five." Eight Chicago players are now certain to face trial and possibly jail.

SAY IT AIN'T SO, JOE

PAGES 4 AND 5

1922 WEISSMULLER AND THE LEGENDS OF SWIMMING

Johnny Weissmuller as Tarzan with co-star Maureen O'Sullivan. He starred in 12 Tarzan movies.

IT is easy to forget that Johnny Weissmuller, the most famous movie Tarzan of all, was also one of history's greatest swimmers – an Olympic champion who set an incredible 28 world records.

Few people have lived the American Dream quite like him. His story, from child immigrant to champion athlete-turned-movie-star, is itself like a Hollywood script.

Weissmuller's Romanian parents emigrated to America shortly after his birth in 1904, settling in Pennsylvania and then Chicago. At 16 Weissmuller joined the Illinois Athletic Club and established himself as a top-class swimmer. He was unorthodox – chest and head jutting out of the water and breathing at every stroke – but unusually powerful. He was nicknamed "the human hydroplane" and the "Chicago whirlwind".

In 1922 Weissmuller swam the 100m freestyle in 58.6 seconds, the first person to break the minute barrier. A year later he won five titles at the national amateur swimming championships.

At the 1924 Paris Olympics, 20-year-old

Weissmuller established himself as an all-time great, winning three golds in the 100m and 400m freestyle and 800m freestyle relay. In 1927 he set a new record for the 100m freestyle that lasted 17 years and won two more Olympic golds in Amsterdam in 1928 before retiring in 1929.

A chance meeting with scriptwriter Cyril Hume at the Hollywood Athletic Club in 1931 led to a screen test for a film based on a Edgar Rice Burroughs' best-selling book "Tarzan of the Apes".

Metro-Goldwyn-Mayer offered him a contract and in 1932 Weissmuller appeared in the first of 12 Tarzan movies. "Tarzan, the Ape Man" was an instant box office hit and Johnny and his echoing yodel passed into film legend. His oft-quoted catchphrase "Me Tarzan, you Jane" was one he never actually uttered.

Weissmuller's swimming feats were acknowledged by the International Swimming Hall of Fame in 1965 and by the International Olympic Committee in 1983, the year before his death at a retirement home in Acapulco, Mexico.

Among those challenging him as history's No1 swimmer is American Mark Spitz who won seven golds at the Munich Olympics in 1972. He won a total of nine during his career and set 33 world records. During the same era, Shane Gould held every women's freestyle world record from 100m to 1500m. American Matt Biondi came close

> **SPORT SPOT**
> Urban legend has it that Tarzan's Yell was a blend of Weissmuller, a hyena, a camel, a dog's growl and a violin. Weissmuller insisted it was him alone.

Shane Gould at the 1972 Munich Olympics where she won three gold medals, all in world record times.

to emulating Spitz when he won five golds – setting four world records in the process – at Seoul in 1988. The 18-year-old Australian Ian Thorpe won five golds at Sydney in 2000. Aided by size 17 feet, he also won 11 world titles and broke 22 world records before retiring in 2006.

British swimmers have had limited Olympic success. At London in 1908 Henry Taylor won two golds, in the 400m and 1500m freestyle. David Wilkie won the 200m breaststroke gold at Montreal in 1976. Duncan Goodhew made himself a household name by winning the 100m breaststroke at Moscow in 1980 and Adrian Moorhouse won the same event in 1988 at Seoul.

Judy Grinham and Anita Lonsborough both won Olympic gold, Grinham in the 100m backstroke at Melbourne in 1956 and Lonsborough in the 200m breaststroke at Rome in 1960.

In the modern era, Sharron Davies – 27 years after she won silver in the 400m individual medley at Moscow – remains Britain's most recognisable woman swimmer.

Below: Ian Thorpe winning the 400m freestyle gold at the 2004 Athens Olympics. Thorpe represented Australia from the age of 14 – the youngest male ever to do so

Mark Spitz at the 1972 Munich Olympics. He won nine Olympic golds in all and set 33 world records before retiring at 22. At 41 he tried in vain to qualify for the 1992 Barcelona Olympics.

FRONT PAGE NEWS

1922 English archaeologist Howard Carter discovers the tomb of Tutankhamun in Egypt

1922 Benito Mussolini assumes power in Italy

1922 BBC begins its first radio broadcasts in the UK

1922 First football pools established

SUZANNE LENGLEN

DURING her heyday in the 1920s French star Suzanne Lenglen was the biggest draw in tennis. She was famed for her "short" skirts (they came up to her knee), her stylish play and unique approach to life – she once revived herself on court by sipping brandy during a match with Helen Mills in Cannes. Lenglen won the Wimbledon singles title six times and the French twice and is one of the greatest female players ever.

NOW JUMP TO... ➔ **FRED PERRY page 62** ➔ **BOB BEAMON page 90** ➔ **NADIA COMANECI page 108**

THE Sun

Monday, July 10, 1922   2d

Ace outfit . . . Suzanne

Glamour queen in Wimbers walkover

By MIKE ROMINI

SUZANNE Lenglen, the biggest star in women's sport, was celebrating last night after winning Wimbledon again, this time with a 26-MINUTE destruction of her deadly rival Molla Mallory.

The 23-year-old French glamour girl took revenge after being jeered off court last year at the US Open by spectators who wrongly believed she faked a coughing fit because she feared American Mallory would beat her.

At Wimbledon's new Church Road site on Saturday, Lenglen hammered Mallory 6-2, 6-0 — and afterwards told her: "I have proved to you today what I could have done to you in New York last year."

Lenglen, who has now won Wimbledon four times, is the darling of the crowd, wearing racy numbers that leave her arms bare and swigging brandy on court.

Floozy Suzie bares arms!

BIZARRE: Page 17

Star quality . . . handsome Weissmuller could be screen hit too

Torpedo . . . Weissmuller sets new record yesterday

SUPER HUMAN

Teenage sensation swims 100m in under minute

By NORMA SMUSSLES, Swimming Editor

A TEENAGER was hailed as "superhuman" last night after becoming the first person to swim 100 metres in less than a minute.

American Johnny Weissmuller, 18, smashed the world record in the 100m freestyle, finishing in 58.6 seconds.

A crowd of 1,000 roared him on at the pool in Alameda, near Oakland, California. The respected San Francisco Chronicle said: "Weissmuller is the greatest swimmer the world has ever known, as near a human speed-fish as the world has seen."

Weissmuller was born in Hungary before his family emigrated to Chicago. He is being tipped for a stack of world records and Olympic titles — and even movie work.

MOVIE CLAMOUR FOR HUNK IN TRUNKS: PAGE 7

1923 WEMBLEY STADIUM AND THE WHITE HORSE FINAL

FRONT PAGE NEWS

1923 New York's Yankee Stadium hosts its first baseball game

1923 Huge earthquake devastates Tokyo and Yokohama, killing 100,000 people

1923 Invention of the Mars Bar

1923 Irish Independence leader Michael Collins is shot dead

WEMBLEY'S status as the home of English football was sealed with its very first match, the 1923 FA Cup final. But had it not been for a horse called Billy, the game might have been remembered for farce and tragedy.

Left: The Cup Final gets under way. Crowds were crammed along the touchline and some daring spectators watched from the stadium's rooftops.

Built on the site of "Watkins' Folly", a bungled attempt in 1891 to build a steel tower to rival the Eiffel Tower, the Empire Stadium, as it was originally named, was the centrepiece of the Empire Exhibition of 1924. It took only ten months to construct, at a cost of £750,000 (around £30million today).

No tickets were issued before the final, between Bolton Wanderers and West Ham – the first and last time this would happen – and a tidal wave of fans poured into the new stadium in North-West London. Bright sunshine and the presence of King George V and a London team swelled the numbers to unmanageable levels. The Times reported that, though Wembley was built to hold 125,000, "at least 300,000 must have turned up".

As fans streamed through the gates, the crowd in the lower stands was forced further and further forward. Soon thousands engulfed the pitch, while scores of police tried in vain to move them back.

Eventually they were pushed back – but only by the arrival of mounted police and in particular PC George Scorey on his horse Billy – a grey who appeared white in the newsreel footage. "Don't you want to see the game?" Scorey asked the crowd as he rode through them, urging that they "join hands and heave" backwards. Billy pushed some fans back by nuzzling them with his nose. The photo of George and Billy, surrounded by an endless mass of spectators, is one of English football's most famous images.

By 3.45pm the pitch had been cleared, but only just. The game went ahead with fans standing on the touchline. Ted Vizard, of Bolton Wanderers, said: "It was an unforgettable sight, with a solid wall of spectators round the touchlines. It felt as though we were going to play in a human box."

Bolton won the Cup 2-0, with a goal in each half. The game was halted twice when the crowd spilled on to the pitch. It was a remarkable debut for Wembley, made all the more so by the fact no one died in the crush. The stadium went on to host innumerable classic sporting encounters, including Rugby League Challenge Cup finals, the 1948 Olympics, European Cup finals and the unforgettable World Cup victory in 1966.

Only in the 1950s did it begin hosting regular England fixtures. Before the visit of Argentina in 1951, the only internationals England played there were against the Scots, with others played at club grounds up and down the country.

In May 2000, the old Wembley hosted its final game, a 1-0 defeat to Germany. Seven years later, a new Wembley opened. The iconic twin towers had been replaced by a 1,750-tonne steel arch towering 133metres above the pitch. The capacity is now 90,000, the facilities state-of-the-art.

Billy lives on in people's memories. In 2005, the new footbridge linking the rebuilt stadium to the local town centre was named the White Horse Bridge after a public vote.

SPORT SPOT

Brazilian star Pele, perhaps football's greatest-ever player, called the old Wembley Stadium "the cathedral of football and the heart of football".

Above: The construction of Wembley's famous twin towers in 1923.

Right: Aerial view of the stadium before kick-off in the White Horse Final.

THE Sun

Monday, April 30, 1923   2d

Partners in climb . . pals help each other over Wembley fence

Old Billy . . . PC George Scorey talks to crowd from his white horse

NAGNIFICENT

Hero horse calms 300,000 at Cup Final

A BRAVE cop on a white horse controls a tidal wave of fans in amazing scenes for which Saturday's Cup Final will long be remembered.

PC George Scorey and his mount

From OMAR GAWD at Wembley

Billy restored order after the new Wembley stadium was engulfed by an estimated 300,000 supporters, far

more than it can handle. Many had climbed railings and walls to get in.

George said last night: "I saw nothing but a sea of heads. I thought, 'We can't do it'. I told them to join

hands and heave and they went back step by step until we reached the line." The match finally went ahead with the vast crowd on the touchline.

All White Now — Pages 4 & 5

1933 BODYLINE & CRICKET'S OTHER GREAT CRISES

September 1932: England's opening bowlers Bill Voce (left) and Harold Larwood, on board ship en route to Australia.

BODYLINE, the ruthless and aggressive bowling tactic England used to beat the Australians on the tour of 1932-33, remains cricket's darkest hour. It soured diplomatic and economic relations between the two countries for most of a decade.

England knew drastic measures were needed after being beaten 2-1 at home in 1930 in a Test series which saw the Australian batting sensation Don Bradman score 974 runs at an average of 139, including 334 in one innings.

It was perceived that if Bradman had a weakness at all, it was against a short-pitched, rising ball.

The MCC appointed Douglas Jardine as captain for the tour Down Under in 1932-3. He was a fan of "leg theory" (later dubbed Bodyline), which involved bowling very fast, short-pitched balls on the batsman's leg side, which would rear up and threaten to hit him. The idea was to pack the leg side with fielders to catch any deflection when the batsman raised his bat to protect himself. Compared with the ferocious bowling of modern Test cricket, it seems small beer. But it represented as assault on the gentlemanly spirit of the game in those days before batting helmets and all-over padding.

Jardine had at his disposal the great fast bowlers Harold Larwood and Bill Voce. The Australians lost the first Test in Sydney, but won the second on a placid Melbourne pitch. The third Test, in Adelaide, has been called "the most unpleasant match ever played". Having hit Australian captain Bill Woodfull over the heart, Larwood was instructed by

Left: Sometimes called "The Iron Duke", Douglas Jardine captained the MCC touring side in 1932-33. In 22 Test matches he scored 1296 runs at an average of 48.

Jardine to continue bowling fast and short. The Australian crowd turned ugly as Jardine packed the leg side with catchers. Woodfull did not last long. Bert Oldfield, Australia's wicketkeeper, was then hit on the temple by another Larwood bouncer and had to retire hurt. Mounted police had to control a riotous crowd.

England won the match by 338 runs, but Australian cricket authorities cabled the MCC in London warning that such "unsportsmanlike" play could damage "friendly relations between Australia and England". The outraged MCC demanded a retraction, threatening to scrap the rest of the tour.

The British and Australian publics began boycotting each other's produce. Finally, Australian PM Joseph Lyons warned his cricket board of the dire consequences should Britain boycott Aussie goods and the board caved in. England won the series 4-1 and returned home heroes. New rules limiting leg-side fielders soon made Bodyline redundant.

Jardine is not the only England captain to court international controversy. In 1987 Mike Gatting clashed with umpire Shakoor Rana in Faisalabad, Pakistan. Rana accused Gatting of cheating by moving fielders after batsmen had taken guard. A very public spat resulted in the third day's play of the 2nd Test being abandoned.

Cricket's greatest scandal after Bodyline involved the match-fixing antics of South African captain Hansie Cronje, a devout Christian and clean-cut leader of men.

Cronje, obsessed by money and in league with shady bookmakers, enticed two younger team-mates to help him fix a one-day international in Nagpur, India. He was banned for life and died in a plane crash two years later.

Right: A dejected Hansie Cronje. The South African captain from 1994-2000 admitted he had taken bribes from bookmakers on the sub-continent and tried to fix matches.

SPORT SPOT
England batsman Eddie Paynter left his hospital bed after hearing his team-mates were struggling in the 4th Test at Brisbane in 1933 . . . and scored 83.

FRONT PAGE NEWS
1926 Scottish engineer John Logie Baird invents the television

1929 Wall Street crash helps trigger depression in the U.S.

1930 Amy Johnson becomes the first woman to fly solo from Britain to Australia

1933 Adolf Hitler becomes Chancellor of Germany

Flashpoint in Faisalabad, 1987. England captain Mike Gatting and Pakistani umpire Shakoor Rana have a shouting match about field movements and placings. Gatting was incensed after hearing Rana call him a "f***ing cheat".

Jeff Thomson (left) and Dennis Lillee were the scourge of England's, and the world's, batsmen in the 1970s.

PACE PARTNERS

LARWOOD and Voce turned the Bodyline series – but there have been many even greater fast-bowling partnerships.

West Indians Wes Hall and Charlie Griffith terrified batsmen during the 1960s. During the tour of England in 1963 they claimed 48 Test wickets, contributing to a 3-1 victory.

West Indies seemed to have a never-ending supply of world-class fast bowlers. In the 1970s and early 1980s Michael Holding's languid approach and delivery concealed ferocious speed which earned him the nickname "whispering death". His team-mate Joel Garner, at 6ft 8in, was sometimes impossible to play. During the 1990s, Curtly Ambrose and Courtney Walsh took more than 900 Test wickets between them.

For Pakistan, Wasim Akram and Waqar Younis snared nearly 800 victims during the 1990s with variety, pace and the modern art of reverse swing.

Perhaps the most famous pairing was that of Australians Dennis Lillee (right, below) and Jeff Thomson (left), whose great pace and guile destroyed batting line-ups – English ones especially – during the mid-to-late 1970s. In the 1974-75 Ashes series they took 57 wickets between them, helping to thrash England 4-0.

THE Sun

Monday, January 16, 1933   2d

Gone . . . Larwood bowls Woodfull in First Test last month

Aussies whinge as Larwood hits their skipper over heart

From REX ISAVRAGE in Adelaide

WHINGEING Aussie cricketers were in uproar last night over England's fantastic "Bodyline" fast bowling.

They went berserk when our pace ace Harold Larwood hit their skipper Bill Woodfull over the heart with one particularly fine delivery in Adelaide.

Home fans nearly rioted as he clutched his chest and our captain Douglas Jardine moved his fielders in for the kill.

The Aussies claim our new tactic, in which their batsmen are peppered with ferocious leg-side bouncers, is **DANGEROUS.** England reckon the mighty Aussies simply fear losing at home.

Full Story — Pages 4 & 5

That's gotta hurt . . Woodfull is hit

BODYWHINE

Gutless wonder from Down Under

Catchers win matches . . . Woodfull ducks another of Larwood's 'Bodyline' bouncers as five fielders wait for leg-side deflection

By FINN EDGE and NICK DWUN

BLEATING Aussie cricket captain Bill Woodfull is so shaken by England's ruthless "Bodyline" bowling he has squealed to our boys' tour manager begging them to stop.

Bad loser Woodfull told England boss Pelham Warner: "There are two teams out there. One is playing cricket. The other is making no attempt to do so."

Woodfull spoke to Warner while lying on a treatment table at the Adelaide Oval after being hit over the heart by a short ball from England's 90mph-plus paceman Harold Larwood.

Warner is known to have reservations about Bodyline.

But skipper Douglas Jardine insists the tactic is entirely legitimate. It involves bowling fast, short-pitched, lifting balls down the leg side which force the batsman to defend himself from injury and risk deflecting it to a pack of waiting catchers.

Woodfull became Larwood's latest victim shortly after Australia were reduced to 1-1, replying to England's 341. Don

SKIPPER'S SQUEAL TO TOUR BOSS

Bradman came in, scored a single and left Woodfull facing Larwood. The next ball, a bouncer, hit Woodfull just over the heart.

The Aussie skipper stumbled away from his stumps rubbing his chest in agony. When he finally returned to the crease, Jardine,

Toothless . . . Aussie whiner Woodfull

HITS ENGLAND ACES

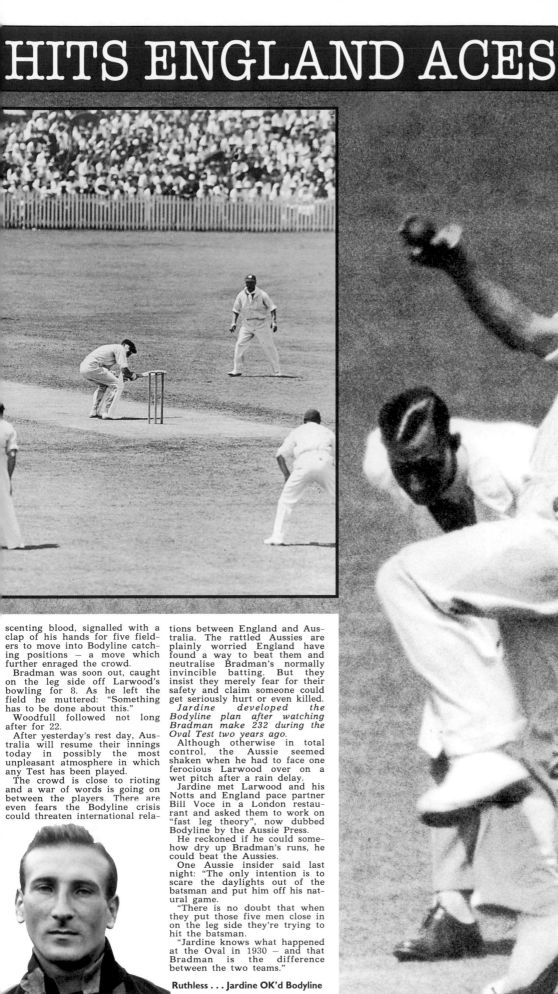

scenting blood, signalled with a clap of his hands for five fielders to move into Bodyline catching positions — a move which further enraged the crowd.

Bradman was soon out, caught on the leg side off Larwood's bowling for 8. As he left the field he muttered: "Something has to be done about this."

Woodfull followed not long after for 22.

After yesterday's rest day, Australia will resume their innings today in possibly the most unpleasant atmosphere in which any Test has been played.

The crowd is close to rioting and a war of words is going on between the players. There are even fears the Bodyline crisis could threaten international rela-tions between England and Australia. The rattled Aussies are plainly worried England have found a way to beat them and neutralise Bradman's normally invincible batting. But they insist they merely fear for their safety and claim someone could get seriously hurt or even killed.

Jardine developed the Bodyline plan after watching Bradman make 232 during the Oval Test two years ago.

Although otherwise in total control, the Aussie seemed shaken when he had to face one ferocious Larwood over on a wet pitch after a rain delay.

Jardine met Larwood and his Notts and England pace partner Bill Voce in a London restaurant and asked them to work on "fast leg theory", now dubbed Bodyline by the Aussie Press.

He reckoned if he could somehow dry up Bradman's runs, he could beat the Aussies.

One Aussie insider said last night: "The only intention is to scare the daylights out of the batsman and put him off his natural game.

"There is no doubt that when they put those five men close in on the leg side they're trying to hit the batsman.

"Jardine knows what happened at the Oval in 1930 — and that Bradman is the difference between the two teams."

Ruthless . . . Jardine OK'd Bodyline

Fearsome . . . superfast and deadly accurate, Larwood is one of the best quick bowlers ever

1936 BRITAIN'S WIMBLEDON HEROES: A BRIEF HISTORY

FRED Perry was one of the most celebrated British athletes of the 20th Century. Throughout his amateur career he won every major title in tennis. His tally of three Wimbledon singles titles stood unchallenged until 1978 when Bjorn Borg won the third of his five.

Born in Stockport, Cheshire, in 1909, Perry only took up tennis when he was 18. His first sport was table tennis, at which he excelled and won the 1929 world championship. He switched to tennis and by 1933 had won the U.S. Open, beating Jack Crawford in the final. He won the title again in 1934 and 1936, by which time he was the dominant figure in the sport.

Perry was famed for his fitness and agility. He could hit a rising ball from both sides of the court and his forehand drive was feared. As a man he was forthright, to say the least, and his self-assurance didn't endear him to committee members at Wimbledon.

Perry's Wimbledon titles came in successive years (1934, 1935 and 1936). He trounced Jack Crawford 6-3, 6-0, 7-5 in his first final and overwhelmed the German Gottfried von Cramm in his second and third.

During this period, Perry also took the French and Australian titles and led the British Davis Cup team to four successive triumphs, beginning with a 3-2 victory over France in 1933 which was the team's first success for 21 years.

He turned professional in 1936, the first man to win all four major titles.

Injury forced Perry to retire from playing in 1942 but he continued to coach and write about tennis and started his sports clothing brand in 1950.

A statue of Perry was unveiled at Wimbledon in 1984 to commemorate 50 years since he won his first singles title. He died in 1995.

His achievements are unparalleled in British tennis. Only Virginia Wade, in 1977, has won a singles final at Wimbledon. She won three Grand Slam titles in all – the U.S. Open in 1968 and the Australian in 1972, but her Wimbledon triumph

In addition to Wimbledon, which she won at her 16th attempt, Virginia Wade won the US Open in 1968 and Australian Open in 1972.

FRONT PAGE NEWS

1933 President Franklin D Roosevelt introduces the New Deal in America, saying: "The only thing we have to fear is fear itself."

1934 Flying Scotsman loco breaks the 100mph barrier

1934 Bonnie and Clyde (robbers Clyde Barrow and Bonnie Parker) shot dead by police in ambush in Louisiana

1934 Cat's Eyes invented by Briton Percy Shaw

remains the most notable. In the Queen's Silver Jubilee year, Wimbledon's centenary year and nine days before her 32nd birthday, she beat Betty Stove 6-2, 4-6, 6-1.

Stove had beaten Sue Barker in the semi-final in 1977, scotching hopes of an all-British final. Barker, ranked as high as world No3, won the French Open in 1976 and reached the semi-finals of the Australian Open in 1975 and 1977.

The British men's game has not produced a major title winner since Perry in 1936. Only John Lloyd – at the Australian Open in 1977 – and Greg Rusedski – at the U.S. Open in 1997 – have reached Grand Slam finals. Rusedski's best showing at Wimbledon came in the same year, reaching the quarter-finals, but he was plagued by injuries and announced his retirement in April 2007.

Tim Henman single-handedly carried hopes of a British victory at

Above: Tim Henman first picked up a tennis racket when he was 2½ years old. By the age of five he had decided that he wanted to be a professional tennis player.
Left: Ranked as high as No3 in the world, Sue Barker won the French Open in 1976 and narrowly missed out on the Wimbledon final a year later, losing to Betty Stove in the semi-final.

Wimbledon for almost a decade, reaching the semi-finals four times. His best chance to reach the final came in 2001 when he faced eventual winner Goran Ivanisevic in the semi. Leading 2-1 in sets, Henman was in control of the match, but a rain delay in the fourth set allowed Ivanisevic time to compose himself and the Croat returned to take the match into a fifth set which he won comfortably. Henman's best year in the Grand Slams came in 2004 when he reached the semis of both the French and U.S. Opens and the quarters at Wimbledon. His best ranking was world No4.

Hopes are high that the young Scot Andrew Murray will finally break Britain's Grand Slam duck. By the summer of 2007 the boy from Dunblane was ranked in the world's top ten thanks to his power, variety and cunning. His best seems yet to come.

Right: Scotland's Andy Murray seems to have all the makings of a future Grand Slam champion.

THE Sun

Saturday, July 4, 1936   2d

ENOUGH'S ENOUGH

BRITAIN invented fair play.

Page One opinion

And in that spirit, we must say to Fred Perry: Enough is enough.

If Fred or any other British players keep winning Wimbledon so easily there's a grave risk of us deterring foreign competition.

Turn pro now, Fred. You've had a good run. **It's time other tennis nations had a chance.**

Perry wins Wimbo for Britain (YET AGAIN)

He was a ping pong ace too

FRED has only played tennis nine years — he was too busy being world champ at TABLE tennis.

Fred was a ping-

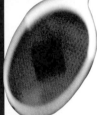

pong prodigy at a youth club in Ealing, West London, after spending hours practising at home by hitting balls against the kitchen wall.

He progressed to the world championships in Budapest, Hungary, in 1929 and won.

When he finally took tennis seriously he found table tennis had given him immense speed and a powerful wrist.

Fred qualified for Wimbledon for the first time the year he won the world table tennis title.

One pundit said: "He is extremely fast, has sharp reflexes and hits a forehand with a snap, slamming it on the rise."

Ping-pong .. he was No1

FRED WHITE AND BLUE

Another smashing win... Fred's on his way in the one-sided final yesterday

FRED Perry won Wimbledon yet again yesterday.

The world No1, from Stockport, Cheshire, trounced Germany's Gottfried von Cramm 6-1, 6-1, 6-0 in just **40 MINUTES.**

Last year he beat him 6-2, 6-4, 6-4. It is the third Wimbledon final in four years that the British ace has won without dropping a set.

Fred, 26, has also won the Australian and French championships and the U.S. championships (twice). Three

By HUGO FETCH, Tennis Reporter

years ago he led Britain to our first Davis Cup triumph in 21 years.

He is now said to be considering turning professional, which would bar him from all tournaments and provide his rivals with much-needed respite.

Fred, a working-class Labour MP's son, has long been at odds with the posh set at Wimbledon.

He said: "I've always been regarded as an upstart, without the right credentials for this noble game."

Genius Perry — Page 7

Brit of all right . . . Fred

1936

JESSE OWENS SCUPPERS HITLER'S OLYMPIC DREAM

FRONT PAGE NEWS

1936 Beginning of the Spanish Civil War which lasts until 1939

1936 King Edward VIII abdicates and marries American divorcee Wallis Simpson

1936 German troops occupy the Rhineland violating the 1919 Treaty of Versailles

1936 The Hoover Dam on the Colorado River is completed

1936 First public TV transmissions in Britain

THE triumphs of James Cleveland "Jesse" Owens – a black athlete – at the 1936 Berlin Olympics made a mockery of Adolf Hitler's claims of Aryan superiority. They turned him into one of the sporting icons of the 20th Century.

Hitler was determined to use the Games for propaganda. With the eyes of the world trained on Germany, it was his chance to showcase his country's collective and individual strength. Winning was everything. The Fuhrer demanded his athletes demonstrate their racial supremacy.

Discrimination, especially against Jews, was widespread throughout Germany. It was part of everyday life for Owens too, in America's largely segregated society. He and his fellow black team-mates travelled to Germany third class on the SS Manhattan. White officials went first class on the higher decks.

The previous season Owens, from Cleveland, Ohio, had shown all the signs of being a future Olympic champion. In just one hour at the 'Big Ten' athletics meeting in Ann Arbor, Michigan, he set three world records, in the long jump, the 220-yards sprint and the 220-yards low hurdles. He equalled a fourth record, running the 100 yards in 9.4 seconds. Owens was the perfect athlete. He had power in his lower body – his legs working like pistons – combined with relaxation in the upper.

His achievements were widely reported in Germany and he found the German people friendly enough. Not so the Nazi-controlled media, who attributed his brilliance to his 'animal qualities'. Some newspapers printed his photo alongside pictures of apes.

On Tuesday August 4th, the second day of competition, Owens claimed the first two of his record haul of medals. He coasted to victory in the 100 metres in 10.3 seconds, which equalled the world record he had set in the heats. Later that day he won gold in the long-jump, producing the first 26ft leap in Olympic history. The next day he won the 200 metres in another world record time of 20.7 seconds. He won his fourth gold as part of the 4x100 metres relay team.

In five days Owens raced ten times and jumped twice. He didn't lose once. To Hitler's fury, Owens became the Games' star, not his Aryan athletes. Indeed, he received a standing ovation every time he entered the stadium.

Hitler had intended to congratulate personally every winning athlete. But he refused to do so after Day Two when he watched aghast as Owens and his black team-mates dominated the competition.

After Berlin, Owens was a household name worldwide, attracting interest from movie producers and commercial sponsors. But the American Olympic Association took a dim view of his professional activities and banned him from amateur events shortly after he returned. Owens was forced to work as an entertainer, tak-

SPORT SPOT

Owens may have been the Games' star, but Germany won easily the most medals – 89, including 33 golds. Next best was the U.S. (56, 24 of them golds).

Above: Owens in the long-jump. In 1950, a US Associated Press poll voted him the greatest track and field star for the first half of the 20th Century.

ing part in money-making stunts involving him racing horses, dogs and trains. He ended up working in menial jobs before his 35-year smoking habit claimed his life through lung cancer aged 66.

Above: The men's long jump medal ceremony. Jesse Owens, centre, salutes the flag after winning gold, with left, Naoto Tajima, Japan (silver) and right, Wilhelm Leichum, Germany, (bronze).

Jesse Owens returns to the Olympic Stadium in Munich in July 1965. "I remember seeing Hitler coming in with his entourage and the storm troopers standing shoulder to shoulder like an iron fence. Then came the roar of 'Heil, Hitler!' from 100,000 throats, and all those arms outstretched. It was eerie and frightening."

SunSport at Berlin Olympics

Champ . . . Owens storms to victory in 100m last week

Heil be damned . . . Hitler with Bulgaria's King Boris

From MARK SETGO, Athletics Correspondent, in Berlin

JESSE Owens won his **FOURTH** Olympic gold in Berlin last night in a hammer blow to Adolf Hitler's propaganda war.

The 22-year-old American sensation bagged a 4x100 relay gong to go with his 100m, 200m and long jump titles. It was a devastating setback for Germany's vile Chancellor, who had hoped his Olympics would prove Aryan superiority.

ADOLF'S NAZI SHOCK: PAGE 68

Who you calling 'inferior'?
The star in action yesterday

This one's 4 you, Herr Hitler

TYRANT FURY AT OWENS' FOURTH GOLD

1948 DON BRADMAN ... AND OTHER BATTING LEGENDS

FRONT PAGE NEWS

1939 Germany invades Poland, ultimately triggering World War Two

1941 Japan attacks U.S. fleet at Pearl Harbour – America enters war

1945 Germany defeated; U.S. drops atom bombs on Japan, forcing surrender

1947 Palestine divided into Jewish and Arab states

1948 Apartheid begins in South Africa

DONALD Bradman – "The Don" – is unquestionably the greatest batsman ever to grace a cricket field. In his final Test match he seemed destined to end a flawless career with an unprecedented average of a century per innings. But fate intervened on a rain-sodden pitch at the Oval.

In a Test career spanning almost 20 years, Bradman strode to the crease 80 times. On 29 occasions he returned to the pavilion with a century. On 12 of those 29 occasions he made a double century. Two of those 12 he converted into a triple. A technique based on technical perfection and unstinting mental application yielded 6996 runs in just 52 matches.

Even when Douglas Jardine's England touring side rattled him by bowling a barrage of short-pitch deliveries in the infamous Bodyline series, he still averaged over 56.

Bradman's farewell series was on the tour to England in 1948, where he captained arguably the strongest ever Australian team. The tourists dominated the series and were 3-0 up when they arrived at the Oval in South London for the fifth Test. On a wet pitch England decided to bat first and collapsed to 52 all out.

In reply, Australia's opening pair of Sidney Barnes and Arthur Morris put on 117 for the first wicket. As the evening shadows lengthened, Bradman emerged from the pavilion to a stand-ing ovation. When he arrived at the crease all the English players doffed their caps and gave him three cheers.

As the crowd settled down the leg-spinner Eric Hollies prepared to bowl to Bradman, who played his first ball defensively. The second, a googly, slipped past the edge of the great man's bat and bowled him. Bradman glanced back at the stumps and then walked off to another standing ovation. He was rumoured to have had tears in his eyes which obstructed his view of the ball – but he always adamantly denied it.

England's poor batting display denied Bradman another chance to bat. His final innings duck left him with an overall Test average of 99.94. A single boundary would have been enough for him to finish with an average of 100.

Decades later, when Bradman was asked to identify the player who most reminded him of himself he invariably mentioned India's Sachin Tendulkar. The 34-year-old blends Bradmanesque application and technical excellence. A Test player by the age of 16, Tendulkar is, as of 2007, the leading century-maker in Test history, with a career average approaching 55.

Two West Indians stand out among a host of great international batsmen. Sir Viv Richards is probably the most stylish and destructive batsman of all time. Capable of seemingly impossible strokes, Richards still holds the record for the fastest century in Test cricket (56 balls) against England at St John's, Antigua, in 1986.

Brian Lara is the only modern Test batsman who has come close to emulating Bradman's feat of 12 double centuries – with nine. Blighted at times by impetuousness, he was unstoppable when his mind was right. He holds the record for the highest – 400 not out – and third highest – 375 – individual Test scores, and the highest score in first-class cricket: 501 not out. Of great English batsmen, Len Hutton probably tops a list including Jack Hobbs, Geoffrey Boycott and David Gower.

He was able to adapt to a variety of pitch conditions and all types of bowling, mixing defence and attack as the match situation dictated. Hutton scored 6,971 Test runs at an average of 55.71, making 19 hundreds in all, with a top score of 364 – the highest ever by an Englishman.

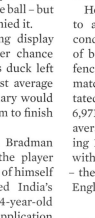

Don Bradman, greatest of all time

> ## SPORT SPOT
>
> In 1994, asked to estimate his batting average against that year's struggling England team, Bradman replied "67", well below his 99.94 career average. "But I am 86," he added.

Sir Len Hutton scored more than 40,000 runs in 513 first-class appearances.

Above: Brian Lara, the gifted West Indies left-hander, made individual scores of 501, 400 and 375, the last two in Tests. **Left:** India's Sachin Tendulkar passed Sunil Gavaskar's record of 34 Test hundreds in 2005. Among modern batsmen, he is Lara's only peer.

Sir Viv Richards, one of five Wisden cricketers of the century, was perhaps the most devastating batsman the game has ever seen.

THE SUPERMUM

DUTCH sprinting legend Fanny Blankers-Koen achieved worldwide fame with her heroic performances at the 1948 London Olympics. A mother of two, her decision to compete was frowned on by some who thought she should be at home looking after her children. Yet the 30-year-old, the oldest athlete at the Games, won 11 races in seven days and claimed four golds in the 100m, 200m, 80m hurdles and 4x100m relay. Her achievements – including six world records – earned her the nickname "The Flying Housewife".

THE Sun

Monday, August 16, 1948   2d

THE DON IS DONE

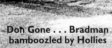

Don Gone . . . Bradman bamboozled by Hollies

'Tearful' star Bradman bowled for a duck in his farewell Test innings

THIS was the amazing moment when Don Bradman, cricket's greatest batsman of all time, was bowled for 0 in his last Test innings.

His duck on Saturday left

By GLADYS ALLOVER

the Aussie genius, who has dominated the game for 20 years, with a Test average of **99.94** runs per innings.

Don, 39, needed to score just four when he went out to bat

against England at the Oval to keep his average over 100, way ahead of any other batsman in history. In emotional scenes, he was applauded on to the pitch by both teams.

And there is speculation that he was bowled by spinner Eric Hollies because he could not see the ball through his tears.

Fearsome sight . . . cricket's master strides to crease

NOW LET'S BASH THE AUSSIES: BACK PAGE

1954 DOCTOR'S HISTORIC RUN IN RAIN-LASHED OXFORD

IN the early evening of May 6, 1954, a junior doctor named Roger Bannister burst through the finishing tape at the Iffley Road athletics track in Oxford to secure a permanent place in sports history. In front of a delirious crowd of 3,000 he had become the first man to run a mile in less than four minutes.

The historic day began in rather more mundane circumstances. Bannister, then 25, finished his morning duties at St Mary's hospital in West London and walked to Paddington, hopping on the 11am train for Oxford.

As it pulled out of the station, he cast his eyes to the grey skies and mulled the possibility of a record attempt not taking place at all in such blustery weather. But he was running out of time if he wanted to achieve the landmark first. In the next few weeks his rival, the Australian John Landy, would make his own assault on the four-minute barrier. Bannister was reluctant to postpone.

With his race scheduled to start shortly after 6pm, things didn't look promising. An hour beforehand, Bannister watched the rain and wind buffeting a flag flying from a church tower near the track.

His friends and pacemakers Chris Chataway and Chris Brasher were keen to know if the attempt was still on. They got their answer shortly before 6pm when the clouds parted, the sun appeared and the wind dropped. After one false start, Brasher led the three men away.

The plan was for Bannister to track Brasher for the first half of the race. Then Chataway would take over as pacemaker until Bannister's long, final sprint to the line.

Brasher took them through the half-mile in 1min 58secs, and on target. Chataway sprinted past Bannister to assume the pacemaker role and carried Bannister to 250 yards out, whereupon he kicked for home alone, running through the intense pain to the finish line.

Arms out, head back and his mouth open, sucking in all the air that his burning lungs would accept, Bannister's chest broke the tape. As he collapsed he was surrounded by officials and well-wishers. For the record to stand three official timekeepers had to verify it.

With the stopwatches all showing exactly the same time, the meet organiser Norris McWhirter took centre stage and began to make the announcement:

"Ladies and Gentlemen, here is the result of Event No9, the one mile. First, R G Bannister of the AAA and formerly of Exeter and Merton Colleges, with a time which is a new meeting and track record and which, subject to ratification, will be a new English native, British national and British all-comers, European, British Empire and world record. The time is three..."

Nothing else was heard as McWhirter was drowned out by cheers.

Bannister's world record time of 3mins 59.4secs lasted only 46 days before, as expected, Landy smashed it with a time of 3mins 57.9secs. But the first sub-four minute mile was Bannister's landmark to keep for eternity.

FRONT PAGE NEWS

1951 Winston Churchill re-elected Prime Minister after defeat at polls in 1945

1952 Queen Elizabeth II crowned

1952 U.S. tests first hydrogen bomb

1953 James Watson and Francis Crick reveal DNA's molecular structure

1953 New Zealander Edmund Hillary and Tenzing Norgay are first to conquer Everest

SPORT SPOT

Half a century after his sub-four minute mile, Bannister said that the greatest achievement of his life was not that record but his 40-year career as a neurologist.

Australian John Landy, the second man to run a sub-four minute mile, leads Roger Bannister in the mile race at the Empire Games in 1954. Bannister won it as both men went under four minutes again.

Pacemaker Chris Brasher (right) led Bannister through the first half-mile in 1min 58secs, before peeling off to let Chris Chataway assume the pacemaker role.

Below: Bannister poses at the finish line at the Iffley Road running track in Oxford on May 6th 2004, the 50th anniversary of his epic run.

SEE, AUSSIE? IT CAN BE DONE!
PAGES 6 & 7

Golden mile . . . cheering fans and Press see finish

Vest of friends . . . with Chris Brasher (left) and Chris Chataway

WHAT A MILESTONE

Brit track star Bannister smashes 4-minute barrier

By ANNA CHEEVEMENT

HERO athlete Roger Bannister made history last night as the first man to run a mile in less than four minutes.

The 25-year-old doctor broke the world record in front of 3,000 fans at the Iffley Road track in Oxford.

He admitted the gruelling run, in 3mins 59.4secs, left him feeling "like an exploded flashlight with no will to live."

1956 BERT: LEGENDARY TALE OF SPORTING HEROISM

BERT Trautmann, the former Manchester City goalkeeper, is the definitive example of sporting heroism. He broke his neck during the 1956 FA Cup final but played on, making spectacular saves, to the final whistle.

A German soldier, Trautmann was captured during World War Two and sent to a PoW camp in Ashton, near Manchester.

After the war he joined St Helen's Town football club, signing for Manchester City in 1949. Hostile fans called him "Nazi" and threatened to boycott games, but his performances won

SPORT SPOT
Cricket star Colin Cowdrey came out to bat with a broken arm to save England from defeat against the West Indies at Lords in 1963.

them over. Between 1949 and 1964 he made 545 league appearances.

In 1956, City were 2-1 up against Birmingham in the second half of the cup final. Birmingham were chasing an equaliser and when a cross came into City's penalty area, Trautmann, with typical bravery, went to claim it.

Birmingham striker Peter Murphy caught his neck with his knee, knocking him out. He came round, had a quick sponge down and carried on, in agony and cradling his neck with his hand.

"I wasn't seeing any colour," he later recalled. "It was like walking around in fog." In between three further collapses, Trautmann made important saves which secured City the Cup.

As he collected his winner's medal, he was asked by a typically blunt Prince Philip: "Why is your head crooked?" Trautmann stoically replied: "Bit of a stiff neck, sir."

The next day a London hospital told him he had simply cricked his neck. But an X-ray three days later confirmed the fracture. "You should be dead!" said the doctor.

Trautmann was named player of the year for 1956 – the title's first foreign recipient.

In 2006 he was inducted into the Hall of Fame at England's National Football Museum in Preston.

Left: Captain Roy Paul lifts the FA Cup after Manchester City's 3-1 win.
Below: Bert Trautmann continues to play on, in varying degrees of agony, after his collision with Birmingham striker Peter Murphy.

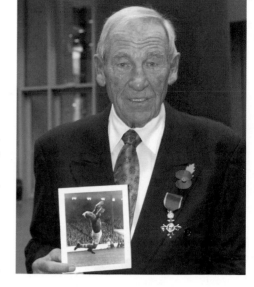

Bert Trautmann is awarded an OBE for his work fostering relations between Germany and the UK, at a ceremony in Berlin attended by the Queen on November 1st 2004.

FRONT PAGE NEWS

1954 First commercial nuclear power station goes online at Obninsk, Russia
1954 JRR Tolkien publishes Lord of the Rings
1955 Ruth Ellis is last woman hanged in Britain
1955 Warsaw Pact formed by Communist states in Eastern Europe and USSR.

DORA RATJEN

THE case of "Dora" Ratjen is one of sport's most bizarre tales.

Adolf Hitler's followers were prepared to go to any lengths to ensure German athletes won golds at the 1936 Berlin Olympics – even entering a man in the women's high jump.

The Hitler Youth ordered young Herman Ratjen to strap up his genitals and pose as Dora. It didn't work, however – he came fourth.

Tracked down two decades later to the Bremen café where he was by then a waiter, Herman admitted the Nazis made him do it "for the honour and glory of Germany".

Similarly nationalistic motives led communist East Germany to pump its women athletes full of male hormones and steroids to dominate their competitions.

"State Plan 14.25" employed hundreds of scientists to create illegal performance-enhancing drugs and masking agents. It brought about countless triumphs.

The state-sponsored cheating was exposed after the Berlin Wall fell in 1989. As many as 10,000 athletes had been affected, among them Kristin Otto, winner of six swimming golds at the Seoul Olympics in 1988.

Drugs had transformed East Germany's sporting fortunes, and its athletes. The dire effects of the steroids forced Heidi Krieger, European shot-putt champion in 1986, to have a sex change. She is now Andreas.

THE Sun

Wednesday, May 9, 1956   3d

GERMAN VILLAIN
EXCLUSIVE by WILLIE HEIDING

A WOMAN high-jumper at Hitler's 1936 Berlin Olympics is today unmasked as a BLOKE dubbed Herman the German. Beefy "Dora" Ratjen was made to pose as a girl to bring glory to Nazi Germany. But he came fourth, and is now a waiter.

Dora . . . 'she' hid privates

Hunmasked — Page Nine

HIGH-JUMP GIRL IS BLOKE

Rub it better . . . Bert after final

GERMAN HERO
By TERRY BULL-PAYNE

GOALIE Bert Trautmann won the FA Cup with a BROKEN NECK, tests revealed yesterday.

And a doctor has told him: "You should be dead."

Man City's German hero, 32, assumed he had a "stiff neck" after his horror clash in Saturday's 3-1 win. He was recovering last night.

Trautstanding — Back Page

BROKEN NECK? I'M PLAYING ON

Cup Final hero Bert was close to death, says doc

1956 JIM LAKER AND CRICKET'S GREATEST BOWLING FEATS

FRONT PAGE NEWS

1956 Elvis Presley enters U.S. charts for the first time with Heartbreak Hotel

1956 Chancellor Harold Macmillan introduces £1 premium bonds

1956 Contraceptive pill is introduced in Britain

1956 Suez Crisis ruins reputation of PM Anthony Eden who resigns the next year

1956 English engineer Christopher Cockerell builds first practical hovercraft

NOT even the great Shane Warne ever came close to emulating Jim Laker's unique achievement of taking 19 wickets in a Test match. His haul in 1956 remains a landmark unlikely to be bettered.

Laker, a 34-year-old Yorkshireman, had already bagged 11 wickets with his off-breaks in the previous Test at Headingley and 20 in total that series. When the fourth Test started across the Pennines at Old Trafford, the notoriously fickle Manchester weather provided the perfect conditions for spin bowling.

England amassed 459 quickly in their first innings and on the second afternoon Australia went out to bat. They made a solid start, with the opening pair of Jim Burke and Colin McDonald sharing a 48-run partnership. But as soon as Laker and his spin partner Tony Lock came on to bowl, wickets started to tumble. McDonald fell first, followed by Neil Harvey, who received an unplayable delivery that pitched on middle and clipped off-stump. Laker had bowled what he regarded as the pivotal ball of the match. It sent shockwaves through the Australian camp and soon they had collapsed from 48-0 to 84 all out, with Laker taking 9-37.

England captain Peter May enforced the follow-on and before the end of play Laker had taken his tenth wicket of the match when Neil Harvey, who had come in for an injured McDonald, completed a "pair" after prodding a full toss to Colin Cowdrey at midwicket for his second duck of the day. Australia closed Day Two on 53-1.

All but 45 minutes' play was lost to rain on the Saturday but it was enough time for Lak-

Above: Jim Laker (left) is presented with the two balls with which he took 9 and 10 wickets during the Test match at Old Trafford.

> ### SPORT SPOT
> Jim Laker also took all ten wickets in an innings for Surrey against the same Australians earlier in the 1956 season.

er to have Burke caught at leg slip. When the players returned on Monday morning, Australia started solidly and looked set to salvage an unlikely draw. But brighter conditions soon dried the pitch, allowing Laker to extract prodigious turn. When Ian Craig was trapped lbw, Australia fell apart. Ken Mackay, Keith Miller and Ron Archer all posted no score, and when McDonald's lone resistance ended when he had scored 89, the match was all but lost. Laker duly completed the job he had started, taking the wickets of Richie Benaud, Ray Lindwall and finally Len Maddocks to finish with figures of 51.2-23-10-53 for the innings and 68-27-90-19 for the match. Tony Lock took the only other Australian wicket. In the five-match series, Laker took 46 wickets, averaging just 9.60 runs each.

Laker's 19 wickets surpassed the figures of England's Sydney Barnes – 17-159 – against South Africa in 1913. Barnes was England's dominant bowler in the early 20th Century. He only played 27 Tests but took a remarkable 189 wickets, averaging a miserly 16.43 and taking five wickets in an innings a staggering 24 times.

Only a handful of bowlers have come close to matching Laker's figures in Tests. India's Anil Kumble alone has equalled Laker's ten-wicket haul in a

Above: Averaging nearly six wickets per Test, Muttiah Muralitharan is one of the most successful bowlers in history and the greatest Sri Lankan player ever.

Test innings, taking 10-74 against Pakistan in Delhi in 1999.

Australian paceman Bob Massie was a one-hit wonder. He played just six Tests but took 16-137 on debut at Lords in 1972 before fading into obscurity.

Sri Lankan off-spinner Muttiah Muralitharan took 16-220 against England at the Oval in 1998 and looks set to overhaul Shane Warne's record tally of 708 Test wickets. Muralitharan's career has been plagued by controversy about the legitimacy of his bowling action but statistically he is the greatest bowler of all time, having claimed more than 1,000 wickets in Tests and One-Day Internationals.

The most efficient and deadly of modern pacemen was New Zealander Richard Hadlee. Apart from being a notable all-rounder, Hadlee stands seventh on the all-time list of Test wicket-takers with 431 victims. He achieved this in remarkably few Test matches, 86, averaging five wickets per Test. Of the bowlers above him, only Muralitharan averages more wickets per game.

Sydney Barnes took 16 for 93 in one day against Northumberland. All his contemporaries considered him the greatest bowler of his era.

Left: In March 2006 Anil Kumble became the first Indian to take 500 Test wickets.

THE Sun

Wednesday, August 1, 1956   2d

Australia 1st innings

CC McDonald	c Lock	b Laker	32
JW Burke	c Cowdrey	b Lock	22
RN Harvey		b Laker	0
ID Craig	lbw	b Laker	8
KR Miller	c Oakman	b Laker	6
KD Mackay	c Oakman	b Laker	0
RG Archer	st Evans	b Laker	6
R Benaud	c Statham	b Laker	0
RR Lindwall	not out		6
LV Maddocks		b Laker	4
IWG Johnson		b Laker	0
Extras			0
Total (all out, 40.4 overs)			84

Laker 9–37

Oops, one got away . . . Jim's first effort

Australia 2nd innings (following on)

CC McDonald	c Oakman	b Laker	89
JW Burke	c Lock	b Laker	33
RN Harvey	c Cowdrey	b Laker	0
ID Craig	lbw	b Laker	38
KD Mackay	c Oakman	b Laker	0
KR Miller		b Laker	0
RG Archer	c Oakman	b Laker	0
R Benaud		b Laker	18
RR Lindwall	c Lock	b Laker	8
IWG Johnson	not out		1
LV Maddocks	lbw	b Laker	2
Extras			16
Total (all out, 150.2 overs)			205

Laker 10–53

I got the lot . . . Jim bags his 'ten-fer'

What did you do today Jim, love?

I BOWLED OUT 19 AUSSIES, TEST HERO TELLS MISSUS

Deadly . . . England spin ace Jim demolishes the Aussies again yesterday

ENGLAND spin king Jim Laker turned in the greatest bowling performance of all time yesterday — then had to explain it to his clueless missus.

Jim, 34, bowled out **ALL TEN** Aussies in their second innings at Old Trafford.

Having taken nine wickets in

By LILIAN THOMSON

the first innings, the Yorkshireman finished with match figures of 19–90, easily the best ever. England won by an innings.

When off-spinner Jim got home, his baffled Austrian wife Lilly said she had taken dozens of congratulatory phone calls but didn't understand them. She had to ask her hubby: "Jim, did you do something good today?"

He'll Never Be Beaten — Back Page

1958 THE GIFTED YOUNG TEAM WIPED OUT ON RUNWAY

Busby's Babes 1958. Back row L-R: Duncan Edwards, Bill Foulkes, Mark Jones, Ray Wood, Eddie Colman and David Pegg. (Front row L-R): John Berry, Bill Whelan, Roger Byrne, Tommy Taylor and Dennis Viollet. Bobby Charlton, Harry Gregg and Geoff Bent are not pictured.

Above: Duncan Edwards was only 21 when he was killed in Munich. Team-mate Bobby Charlton once said of him: "If I had to play for my life and could take one man with me, it would be Duncan Edwards."

THE Busby Babes – the prodigiously gifted young Manchester United team built up by manager Matt Busby – were on the threshold of greatness when tragedy struck on a snow-swept runway in Munich.

In 1956 the team, average age 22, won the English league title by 11 points. The following year they successfully defended it and reached the semi-finals of the European Cup, losing to eventual winners Real Madrid.

In 1958, they had a historic treble in their sights. They were third in the league, through to the fifth round of the FA Cup and into the semis in Europe. Disaster struck on the return trip from the second leg of their quarter-final against Yugoslavia's Red Star Belgrade, which they had won 5-4 on aggregate.

The team began their journey home the morning after the match. The snow that had begun falling during the game had worsened overnight and when they stopped off in Munich to refuel conditions were little better.

Less than an hour after touchdown the passengers were called back on to the plane to fly home to England. Shortly after 2.30pm the first take-off was aborted due to a fault with the engines. Minutes later, a second take-off was aborted for the same reason and the plane taxied back to the airport buildings for examination.

The subdued players and accompanying sports reporters disembarked, hoping another take-off would not be attempted. Star player Duncan Edwards was so sure they wouldn't be flying that he telegrammed his landlady in Stretford saying: "All flights cancelled. Flying tomorrow. Duncan."

A short time later, with the fault seemingly fixed, they were called back on board. As the plane sped down the runway, it became clear they weren't going to abort this time, but they were running out of tarmac.

The pilot Captain James Thain described the moments before the crash. "When it *(the air speed indicator)* reached 117 knots I called out 'V1' – Velocity One is the point on the runway after which it isn't safe to abandon take-off. Suddenly the needle dropped to about 112 and then 105...I looked up from the instruments to see a lot of snow and a house and a tree right in the path of the aircraft."

Flight BE609 careered through a fence and the port wing was torn off as it struck the house, causing it to ignite. The cockpit hit a tree and the fuselage hit a hut containing a truck laden with fuel, which exploded.

Seven of the team – Roger Byrne, Geoff Bent, Mark Jones, David Pegg, Liam Whelan, Eddie Colman and Tommy Taylor – were killed instantly. Duncan Edwards, already an England international and tipped to become an all-time great in the game, died from his injuries two weeks later aged just 21.

Matt Busby was seriously injured but eventually made a full recovery. He rebuilt the team and won the European Cup ten years later.

In total 23 out of 43 passengers were killed, including eight of the nine journalists who had flown with the team.

The cause of the crash has been a source of heated debate. Pilot Thain was sacked and handed a life ban from commercial flying. He had not swept the plane's wings for ice before take-off and was deemed culpable. But the crash was almost certainly caused by a build-up of slush on the runway which made the plane decelerate before take-off.

Manchester United manager Matt Busby unveils a memorial plaque at Old Trafford to the Munich air crash victims.

SPORT SPOT

Former Manchester United manager Tommy Docherty once said: "You can keep all your Bests, Peles and Maradonas. Duncan Edwards was the greatest of them all."

FRONT PAGE NEWS

1957 **Treaty of Rome forms the European Economic Community**

1957 **Launch of Sputnik 1, the first space satellite**

1958 **BBC launches Grandstand and Blue Peter**

1958 **Parking meters introduced in London's Mayfair**

7 BUSBY BABES DEAD

- ## Matt 'critical' after air crash
- ## 14 other passengers killed
- ## Can Manchester Utd survive?

By SUN FOREIGN DESK

SEVEN of Manchester United's "Busby Babes" were among 21 people killed yesterday in an air disaster in Munich.

The victims are captain Roger Byrne, David Pegg, Geoff Bent, Eddie Colman, Mark Jones, Tommy Taylor and Liam Whelan.

Manager Matt Busby and England star Duncan Edwards are fighting for life.

Eight sports reporters and several Man Utd officials are also dead.

The team's plane had stopped in Munich to refuel on the way back from the European Cup victory against Red Star Belgrade in Yugoslavia.

It crashed into a house and caught fire on its third attempt to take off in heavy snow.

Last night the Queen was "deeply shocked".

Pilot yelled 'Run'... but Harry went back for tot

On brink of death . . . stricken Matt in oxygen tent last night. Below left, as he normally looks

STAR IS PLANE BLAZE HERO

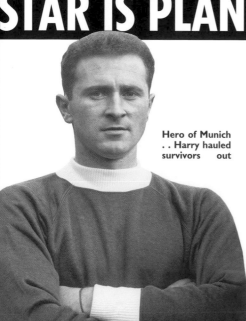

Hero of Munich . . Harry hauled survivors out

MANCHESTER United hero Harry Gregg defied warnings that the team's plane was set to explode — and clambered into the burning wreckage to save a baby.

The goalkeeper, bleeding from the head, also dragged the tot's mother to safety.

Then Harry, 25, hauled teammates Bobby Charlton and Dennis Viollet 20 yards through the thick snow and away from the flames leaping 50ft into the air.

Last night he told how he came to in the dark after the British European Airways charter plane carrying the Man Utd team home crashed in flames, killing 21 of its 44 passengers, as it tried to take off at Munich airport.

Harry said: "I could feel blood running down my face. I thought, 'Christ, I'm not dead'.

"Above me I could see flames and some daylight. I started to

By SUN FOREIGN DESK

crawl towards the light. I looked out of this hole and saw our coach Bert Whalley lying dead in the snow. I thought I was the only one alive . . . then I heard a child's cry from the plane.

"I climbed back into the burning wreckage even though Jim Thain, the captain, shouted, 'Run, you stupid b*****d, it's going to explode!'

"I pulled Bobby and Dennis out and also managed to help a mother and baby out too."

Northern Ireland international Jackie Blanchflower was lying in the snow with his bloodied arm snapped at the elbow and the body of skipper Roger Byrne sprawled across him.

Harry knelt down and used his own tie as a tourniquet for Blanchflower. Lying near the plane was manager Matt Busby, covered in blood, rubbing his chest and moaning, 'My legs, my legs'.

Last night the Scotsman — who built up his young "Busby Babes"

side into English champions — was in an oxygen tent, close to death. He has massive chest injuries and a punctured lung. A priest has read him the last rites.

He is the only club official to survive. Secretary Walter Crickmer, first team trainer Tom Curry and coach Whalley are dead.

England star Duncan Edwards, 21 — one of football's most skillful players — is "critical" with crushed kidneys and multiple fractures.

Ablaze

Nine other Man Utd players survived, including Harry.

They are Bill Foulkes, Ken Morgans, Bobby Charlton, who has a gashed head, Albert Scanlon (fractured skull), Jackie Blanchflower (broken arm), Dennis Viollet (head and face injuries), Ray Wood (cuts and concussion) and John Berry, who is also "critical".

The eight sports reporters who died were named as Alf Clarke, Don Davies, George Follows, Tom

DISASTER IN MUNICH

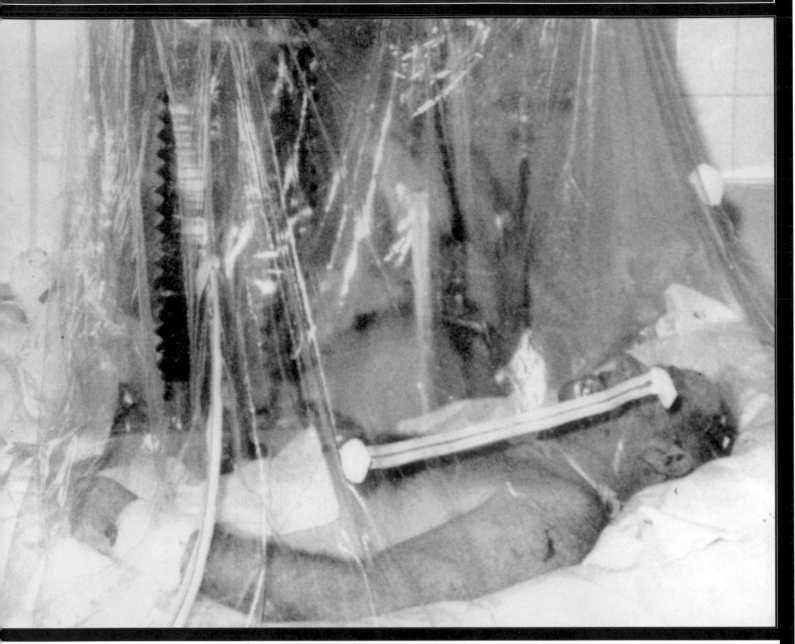

Jackson, Archie Ledbrooke, Henry Rose, Eric Thompson and Frank Swift. Two passengers and one of the crew were killed. Co-pilot Ken Rayment is fighting for life.

The plane was making its third attempt to take off in heavy snow at 3.03pm yesterday after a spate of technical problems.

Slush was preventing the airliner, named the Lord Burghley, from gaining enough speed to get airborne. The engines were at full throttle but it was **LOSING** speed and running out of runway.

Cpt Rayment was heard to shout: "Christ! We won't make it!"

Within moments the plane hit the perimeter fence, bumped across a field and then a road and ploughed into an empty house, setting it ablaze.

It also hit a hut containing a fuel-laden truck, which exploded.

A doctor treating the victims said last night: "It's like looking at a war."

Could Manchester United fold? — See Pages 4 & 5

Horror in the snow . . . Munich police view crash scene last night

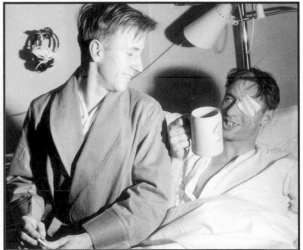

Brave face . . . survivors Bobby Charlton and Ray Wood in hospital

1963 33 YEARS AT THE TOP: SIR STAN'S AMAZING CAREER

FRONT PAGE NEWS

1960   ITV's Coronation Street launched

1961   Russian Yuri Gagarin becomes the first man in space

1961   Construction begins on the Berlin Wall

1961   President John F Kennedy delivers his inaugural address: "Ask not what your country can do for you. Ask what you can do for your country."

1962   Cuban Missile Crisis brings U.S. and Soviets to brink of war

Stanley Matthews dribbles past Bolton midfielder Malcolm Barrass during the FA Cup final on May 3rd 1953 at Wembley.

DURING a 33-year career "The Wizard of Dribble", as he was affectionately nicknamed, was the greatest British player of his generation and the first recipient of the European footballer of the year award . . . aged 42. He only quit the top flight after turning 50.

Born in Hanley, Stoke-on-Trent, in 1915, Stanley Matthews was encouraged to keep fit by his father Jack, a notable featherweight boxer. Hard physical training would be the cornerstone of Matthews' long career.

His talent for football was quickly realised – he once scored a dozen goals in a schoolboy fixture – and by 1932 he was playing for Stoke City, helping them to the Second Division championship a year later.

At 19, Matthews was awarded his first England cap. After an indifferent start to his inter-national career, he quickly became England's chief tormentor of defences. Against Czechoslovakia in 1937, he galvanised an injury-reduced ten-man team with three goals that transformed the match and helped England to win 5-4, thus maintaining their unbeaten home record against foreign teams.

Two years later Matthews turned in one of his finest performances for his country, running rings around the German defence and contributing to a 6-3 mauling. After the war, Matthews formed an irresistible partnership with another legendary winger, Preston North End's Tom Finney.

Although a small and sickly child, Finney was offered a contract by Preston at 14 and stayed loyal to them throughout his career, making 433 appearances and scoring 187 goals from 1946 to 1960.

In 1947 they played together for England for the first time, Matthews on the right and the two-footed Finney on the left, helping England to a 10-0 victory against Portugal. When the two teams met again in 1950 Finney scored four times in a 5-3 victory.

Matthews' quick feet and genuine pace intimidated a generation of left-backs. His great trick was to run directly towards a defender, shape as if to go inside, then flick the ball outside, giving him space in which to deliver a cross. In 1947 Matthews joined Blackpool for £11,500, helping them reach the FA Cup final in 1948, 1951 and 1953. Yet Matthews collected a winner's medal only at the third attempt. The 1953 final against Bolton was considered the 38-year-old's last chance, but with 20 minutes to go Blackpool looked beaten, trailing Bolton 3-1. Matthews came alive, weaving his magic down the wing and delivering a cross which Stan Mortensen met and hit home. After Mortensen had levelled the scores with a free-kick, Matthews embarked on another mazy run and delivered a perfect cross to Bill Perry on the far post who fired home to win the match 4-3.

Finney looked set to emulate Matthews' fairytale when Preston met West Bromwich Albion in the final the next season. It was not to be. Preston lost 3-2 and Finney retired six years later without a major winner's medal. Matthews rejoined Stoke in 1961 and two years later helped them to the Division Two title and was named Footballer of the Year for the second time.

Five days after his 50th birthday, the newly-knighted Sir Stanley Matthews ended his remarkable career. After 710 games for Stoke and Blackpool and 54 England caps, his last game was a league match against Fulham on 6th February 1965. Matthews set up Stoke's only goal in a 1-1 draw. He later said he had retired too soon.

Above: Preston stalwart Tim Finney stayed loyal to the club throughout his career. He also won 76 England caps and scored 30 goals.

SPORT SPOT

A Daily Mail writer in 1934 said Matthews was "slow and hesitant" and "lacked big-match temperament". A spectacular double misjudgment.

Above: Matthews in action for Stoke City

DANNY BLANCHFLOWER

BELFAST-born Danny Blanchflower masterminded Tottenham Hotspur's double success of 1960-61. Spurs dropped only one point in the opening 16 games of the season. At the half-way stage they were 11 points clear and went on to claim the title by eight points. The double was clinched by beating Leicester City 2-0 in the FA Cup final. Spurs became the first club in the 20th Century to complete the domestic double and almost did it again the next season. Blanchflower was one of the few celebrities to turn down This Is Your Life, walking off the show on live TV.

SPURS ACE DANNY: WHY I SNUBBED THIS IS YOUR LIFE

SPURS ace Danny Blanchflower has told why he walked off his own This Is Your Life tribute on live TV. The double-winning skipper said: "It's an invasion of privacy."

Full Story — Pages 12 and 13

I'M STILL

The double . . . Stan's gong in 1948

Matthews is Footballer of Year..at 48!

By IAN DURANCE

SOCCER veteran Stanley Matthews was sensationally named Footballer of the Year last night — aged 48!

The superfit wing wizard was given the top gong for the second time in his long career for inspiring Stoke City to the Second Division championship.

Football writers first gave the ex-England superstar, a legend with Stoke and Blackpool, their prize back in 1948.

Can He Make It To 50? See Back Page

Play on . . . Stan, a teetotal vegetarian, is still amazingly fit

OUTSTANDING

1963 COURAGE OF OUR 'ENRY & BRITAIN'S TOP BOXERS

ON June 18th, 1963, at a packed Wembley Stadium, Henry Cooper – "our 'Enry" – floored Cassius Clay with a stinging left hook. With that one punch he secured his place in British boxing folklore and almost derailed the most celebrated career in all sport.

Undefeated in 18 bouts, 21-year-old Cassius Clay (later Muhammad Ali) was the clear favourite and eyeing a showdown with world heavyweight champion Sonny Liston. For Cooper, the British and Commonwealth champion, it was the 37th bout of a distinguished career.

Clay entered the ring wearing a cardboard crown and a robe bearing the words "the greatest". Boos turned to cheers as Cooper, a modest, down-to-earth Cockney whom Clay had labelled a bum, was greeted by 40,000 fans chanting his name.

Cooper made a strong start, taking the fight to Clay, all the while trying to tee him up for his famous left hook (known as "Enry's 'ammer"). But Clay fought back in rounds two and three, nicking Cooper's right eye and then, with a swinging right hand, opening up a deep cut above his left.

Cooper was struggling to land a punch and Clay's corner urged him to finish the fight quickly. Clay didn't listen. Moments before the end of the fourth round, Cooper threw the most famous punch in British boxing history. Clay fell, stunned, but the bell saved him.

Cooper has always maintained that Clay's trainer Angelo Dundee sneakily bought his man a few extra minutes to recover by cutting his glove and requesting time to fetch a new one. But TV footage shows the delay was a few seconds, not minutes.

Clay targeted Cooper's left eye during round five and, with blood streaming down the Londoner's face, the referee stopped the fight and declared a relieved Clay the winner. Years later, Clay said Cooper hit him "so hard that my ancestors in Africa felt it".

Britain's love affair with home-grown heavyweights continued with the emergence in the 1980s of Frank Bruno, who fought five times for the world title.

Bruno was a fearsome puncher but lacked stamina over 12 rounds. His first attempt in 1986 failed when Tim Witherspoon knocked him out in the 11th round. He fought Mike Tyson twice, in 1989 and 1996, being knocked out both times. Lennox Lewis inflicted a round seven knockout in 1993. But Bruno finally won the World Boxing Council (WBC) title in 1995, defeating Oliver McCall by unanimous decision.

Two years earlier, Lewis had become the first British heavyweight in a century to win a world title fight, beating America's Tony Tucker on points. He would win a further 13 world title fights. His only career losses were

Above: Lennox Lewis defeats Evander Holyfield on November 13th 1999 to become the undisputed world heavyweight champion.

SPORT SPOT

Henry Cooper became the face of Brut in the 1970s, urging men to "Splash it all over" in TV adverts for the after-shave.

to McCall in 1994 and Hasim Rahman in 2001, but they were both avenged with knockouts in the rematch. Lewis dominated heavyweight boxing for eight years and never ducked a fight. He is regarded as one of the greatest heavyweights of all time. Other UK boxing heroes include Northern Ireland's Barry McGuigan, who won the world featherweight crown in 1985 and defended his title twice.

Lloyd Honeyghan, from Bermondsey, London, produced one of the biggest upsets in boxing history when he beat Don Curry in 1986 to become world welterweight champion. "The Ragamuffin Man" went on to win the title four more times.

Nigel Benn, from Ilford, Essex, became world middleweight champion in 1990 before dominating the super-middleweight division from 1992-96.

In 1997, Welshman Joe Calzaghe beat Londoner Chris Eubank to claim the vacant WBO super-middleweight title and as of mid-2007 has made 20 successful defences.

Cassius Clay on the canvas at Wembley, still reeling from Cooper's punch.

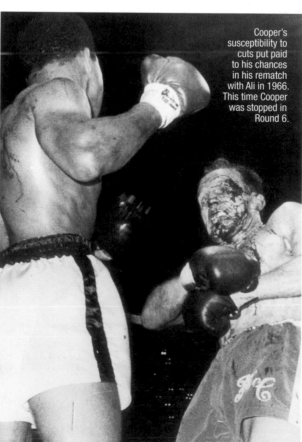

Cooper's susceptibility to cuts put paid to his chances in his rematch with Ali in 1966. This time Cooper was stopped in Round 6.

FRONT PAGE NEWS

1963 Assassination of John F Kennedy in Dallas, Texas

1963 Conservative Government rocked by Profumo sex/spy scandal

1963 More than £2.5m stolen in the Great Train Robbery at Ledburn, Buckinghamshire

1963 Beatlemania grips Britain as "She Loves You" passes one million sales

Above: "Get in there, Frank," commentator Harry Carpenter implored, but Bruno (left) lost to Mike Tyson in five rounds in their first world title fight in 1989.

THE Sun

Wednesday, June 19, 1963   3d

Bloody hero . . . Henry, after fight, with Clay, felled by punch in fourth

'Cheat' fury at Cassius trainer

By HUGH CROOK

CASSIUS Clay's trainer was accused of cheating last night — by slashing the boxer's glove to buy him time to recover from 'Enry's 'Ammer.

After the fourth round knockdown Angelo Dundee told the ref that Clay's glove was split and showed him horsehair sticking out of it.

Dundee was told to fetch another pair from the dressing room, which gave Clay precious extra minutes to recover

What a crock . . Dundee

from 'Enry's assault. Dundee insists the split had been there most of the fight and he merely stuck his finger in it to show the ref the damage.

Clay's camp say the delay it caused was tiny and that the normal minute between rounds overran by only a few seconds.

But there are claims that the American used a razor blade to worsen the split.

Enry's camp reckon the delay lasted several minutes.

Slash it all over
BACK PAGE

Our 'Enry decks Clay ...so what if he lost?

BOXING hero Henry Cooper was the toast of Britain last night after decking the American motormouth Cassius Clay in a night of incredible drama.

The popular Cockney landed his devastating left hook, dubbed 'Enry's 'Ammer, on Clay's chin in the fourth round of

By STAN DINGCOUNT

their heavyweight clash at Wembley Stadium.

The 35,000 crowd went berserk as Clay fell, dazed, into the ropes. He was saved by the bell from a further flurry from 29-year-old Cooper that would have finished him off.

But undefeated Clay, 21, who had dubbed Cooper "a bum" and arrived in the ring sporting a **CROWN**, cut the Brit so badly in the fifth round the fight was stopped.

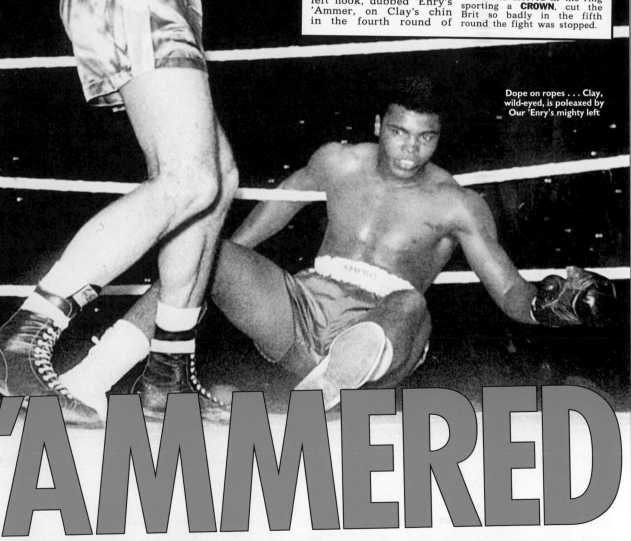

Dope on ropes . . . Clay, wild-eyed, is poleaxed by Our 'Enry's mighty left

'AMMERED

1966 4-2 AT WEMBLEY: A DAY WE WILL NEVER FORGET

FRONT PAGE NEWS
1965 U.S. enters Vietnam War in earnest
1965 UK abolishes capital punishment
1966 Ian Brady and Myra Hindley jailed for life for the Moors Murders
1966 Aberfan coal tip disaster kills 116 children and 28 adults in Wales

ENGLISH football's greatest achievement engulfed the nation in a tide of unrestrained joy. But the team's triumph set the standard for their successors – and the spectre of '66 has placed an unenviable burden on every England manager and player since. More than four decades on, we are still waiting for a repeat performance.

On that gloriously sunny July day in 1966, captain Bobby Moore and his England teammates, plus manager Alf Ramsey, paraded the Jules Rimet trophy around Wembley to delirious fans and reflected on a match fit to grace football's biggest stage.

With close to 100,000 in the stadium and a further 32 million viewers huddled round their TVs at home, England took on the old enemy West Germany. England made a nervous start, conceding a goal in the 12th minute, but Geoff Hurst equalised seven minutes later.

The scores were level until the 77th minute when Martin Peters volleyed home from close range. England looked destined to win in 90 minutes, but with seconds left a West German free-kick ricocheted around the penalty area before being bundled in.

The most talked-about goal in English football history came ten minutes into extra-time. A cross from Alan Ball found Hurst who turned and hit his shot, which rebounded down off the crossbar and over the line. Or was it?

Then, in the dying seconds, Hurst collected the ball just inside the West German half, ran up the pitch and blasted it high into the net to complete his hat-trick. England were world champions.

Expectations of a similar result in Mexico four years later were high. England started as one of the favourites, but West Germany inflicted the first of many painful revenges

German referee Rudolf Kreitlein sending off the Argentine captain Antonio Rattin (left) during the World Cup match against England at Wembley, 23rd July 1966. Rattin refused to leave the pitch. The confusion led to the use of red and yellow cards.

SPORT SPOT
Four months before the tournament, the Jules Rimet trophy was stolen. A dog called Pickles found it under a bush in a South London garden.

in the quarter-finals, winning 3-2 in extra-time. It wasn't the first time England had been knocked out at that stage – losing to Uruguay 4-2 in 1954 and eventual champions Brazil in 1962. Nor would it be the last.

England failed to qualify for the next two World Cups in West Germany and Argentina and their return to the finals in Spain in 1982 was notable only for a Bryan Robson goal scored after 27 seconds of their opening game against France. England's challenge would peter out in the second round.

Maradona single-handedly – in both senses of the phrase – saw off England in the quarter-finals in Mexico in 1986.

Four years later, in Italy, it was again West Germany who twisted the knife, though it was England's most valiant attempt to win the World Cup since 1966. Inspired by the genius of Paul Gascoigne, England were one step away from a final against a poor Argentinian side, but could not match the Germans' precision in a penalty shoot-out. A nation wept, as did Gazza.

Qualification for the 1994 World Cup ended in farce, with England having to win by 11 clear goals against San Marino in their final group match. They conceded a goal within ten seconds, leav-

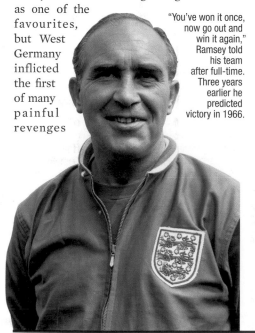

"You've won it once, now go out and win it again," Ramsey told his team after full-time. Three years earlier he predicted victory in 1966.

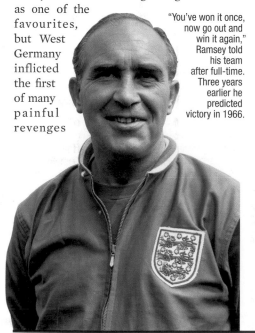

Above: Paul Gascoigne weeps during 1990 penalty shootout in Italy. He would have missed the Final through suspension.

ing them staring into the abyss. It was Argentina's turn to boot England out on penalties in 1998 in France, a game memorable for 18-year-old Michael Owen's wonder goal and for David Beckham petulantly kick-starting his notoriety.

Before the old Wembley was demolished, England hosted Germany one final time. On a rain-swept day, England lost the World Cup qualifier 1-0. Manager Kevin Keegan's resignation immediately after the match cleared the way for Sven Goran-Eriksson to take charge and inflict England's heaviest ever defeat of a German side, thrashing them 5-1 at the Ol-

The thrilling 5-1 victory over arch-rivals Germany in September 2001 remained the pinnacle of Sven Goran Eriksson's controversial reign as England manager.

ympic Stadium in Munich in September 2001. England played with unusual flair, apparently scoring at will – especially Owen, who bagged a hat-trick. The victory convinced fans and the media that World Cup glory was a real possibility.

But Eriksson's tenure ultimately promised more than it delivered. England were knocked out of the 2002 and 2006 World Cups in the quarter-finals.

The long wait for another gold star to be embroidered on the England shirt goes on.

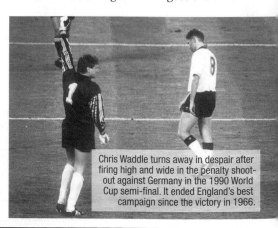

Chris Waddle turns away in despair after firing high and wide in the penalty shoot-out against Germany in the 1990 World Cup semi-final. It ended England's best campaign since the victory in 1966.

Moore the merrier . . . Bobby and Jules Rimet trophy are carried aloft

DON'T MENTION THE SCORE

Bobby's world champs are toast of nation after drubbing Germans 4-2

BOBBY Moore's band of heroes were officially England's greatest team ever last night after being crowned champions of the world.

Captain marvel Bobby and the rest of the lads were yesterday still celebrating Saturday's historic triumph over old foes West Germany.

They were looking forward to splitting a bumper £22,000 bonus and each receiving a luxurious new raincoat.

Meanwhile the entire nation was having its biggest knees-up since VE Day. Every household in England was

By SAUL OVER at Wembley

talking of little but hat-trick hero Geoff Hurst, goal-scorer Martin Peters, battlers Bobby Charlton and Alan Ball and the extra-time nail-biter at Wembley.

Today The Sun demands a knighthood for manager Alf Ramsey and MBEs for our boys.

0-1 Jack Charlton looks on aghast as a desperate dive from Banks fails to stop Helmut Haller's shot after 12 minutes of the final

1-1 Hurst leaps in the air and heads the ball into the net from Moore's pinpoint cross to level the scores on 19 minutes

2-1

DID THAT WHO

3-2 Hurst's shot hits bar and bounces down. There is an outside chance it may not have been quite over the line

CHAMPS AT LAST

Peters volleys in a deflection to put England in lead after 77mins

2-2 Oh no! A chaotic goalmouth scramble ends with Weber lunging past the diving Banks. It's extra time

4-2 No quibbling with that! Hurst's rocket heads for top corner of the German net to seal win

GO IN? CARES?

DEBATE was still raging last night over England's third goal on Saturday — but only among Germans!

They insist Geoff Hurst's strike failed to cross the line — and they intend to bring the tedious matter up for decades.

But The Sun has a blunt message for them today: **WHO CARES?**

It was good enough for the linesman and ref. And besides, Hurst clinched the World Cup with a fourth anyway.

Saturday's thriller was, as the BBC's Kenneth Wolstenholme said on TV, "the day we've all been waiting for".

The game had a scrappy start, with both sides nervous amid the deafening roar from a 97,000 Wembley crowd which included the Queen, the Duke of Edinburgh and PM Harold Wilson.

German fans were outnumbered ten to one. But their men drew first blood.

After 12 minutes the ball fell perfectly for Helmut Haller, who scored despite the efforts of goalie Gordon Banks and defender Jack Charlton, who raised an arm in protest.

Seven minutes later England were back level. Wolfgang Overath conceded a free kick, which skipper Bobby Moore floated beautifully into the German area. Hurst ran in and headed the first of his hat-trick.

The crowd went potty and he jumped for joy on the spot with his knees tucked under him. A drum sounded: "Bang-bang, bang-bang-bang, bang-bang-bang-bang" and our fans, as one, bellowed "ENG-LAND" in reply.

Volleyed

A rousing chorus of When The Saints Go Marching In also struck up.

The evenly-matched teams went in for half-time at 1-1. And so it stayed until the 77th minute when a Hurst shot from outside the penalty area was deflected into the path of Martin Peters who unhesitatingly volleyed it home for 2-1 with 12 minutes left.

Peters ran back to the half-way line screaming with delight. Goalie Banks ran all the way out to hug him and Bobby Charlton said: "We've won."

He spoke too soon. In the last minute his elder brother Jack gave away a free-kick. It was taken by Lothar Emmerich, hit Karl-Heinz Schnellinger on the arm and fell for Wolfgang Weber, who lunged forward with his right leg and tucked it under the diving Banks.

It was 2-2 after 90 minutes and the crowd was in agony. Before extra-time

From SAUL OVER at Wembley

kicked off, Alf Ramsey told our dispirited boys: "You've won it once. You'll have to go out there and win it again."

The crowd screamed "ENG-LAND! ENG-LAND!", desperate for our weary team, their red shirts stained dark with sweat, to fulfil their destiny.

The dream came true after ten minutes. Hurst, in space, received a cross from Ball, swivelled and shot. The ball hit the underside of the bar and bounced down around the goal line.

Was it over? Roger Hunt was convinced — and raised his arm. The Germans were just as sure it wasn't.

Confused

TV's Wolstenholme was confused: "Yes, yes, yes — no! The linesman says no! The linesman says no . . . It's a goal! It's a goal!" The furious Germans protested to Swiss ref Gottfried Dienst but the Soviet linesman said it was OK and the goal stood.

And then, a minute from the end, with the crowd singing Rule Britannia, came the coup de grace. Moore picked out Hurst with a 40-yard pass and the striker charged for goal as the crowd began to encroach on the playing area.

Wolstenholme said: "Some people are on the pitch, they think it's all over." With that, Hurst blasted the ball into the top corner of the net — and Wolstenholme added: "It is now. It's four!"

The commentator was on fine form again as Bobby collected the trophy from the Queen. He said: "It's only 12 inches high, solid gold, and it means England are the world champions."

HOW THEY RATED (OUT OF TEN)
Gordon Banks (goalkeeper, Leicester City, aged 28): **10**. George Cohen (right-back, Fulham, 26): **10**. Jack Charlton (central defender, Leeds, 31): **10**. Bobby Moore (central defender, West Ham, 25): **11**. Ray Wilson (left-back, Everton, 31): **10**. Alan Ball (midfield, Blackpool, 21): **11**. Nobby Stiles (midfield, Man Utd, 26): **10**. Roger Hunt (striker, Liverpool, 28): **10**. Martin Peters (midfield, West Ham, 22): **10**. Bobby Charlton (midfield, Man Utd, 28): **10**. **SUN STAR MAN:** Geoff Hurst (striker, West Ham, 24): **12**.

One's won . . . Queen, Bobby and trophy

1968 DON FOX, POOR LAD, AND OTHER CHOKERS

IN sport, no one remembers who finishes second. If only that were true for sport's greatest chokers.

Prop Don Fox was Man of the Match at Rugby League's Challenge Cup Final at Wembley in 1968. But no one remembers that, because the game between Wakefield Trinity and Leeds will forever be famous for his gaffe that cost his team victory.

Trailing Leeds 11-10, Fox had the opportunity to win the match with the final kick. It was a simple conversion in front of the posts, but he sliced it wide. The final whistle sounded immediately and Fox collapsed in a heap on the sodden turf. "He's a poor lad," said commentator Eddie Waring. His tale of woe is by no means alone in rugby's annals. The shocking penalty miss by Scotland's Gavin Hastings against England in the 1991 World Cup semi-final at Murrayfield proved equally costly. They lost 9-6.

Golf has had its fair share of chokers. American Doug Sanders missed a tap-in to win the 1970 Open at St Andrews. He lost the resulting play-off to Jack Nicklaus. Similarly, Scott Hoch was labelled "Hoch the Choke" after he missed a 2ft putt which would have clinched the 1989 Masters.

When Greg Norman wasn't being robbed of Major tournaments – Bob Tway holing out from a bunker on the 18th green at the 1986 USPGA Championship and Larry Mize holing an impossible chip during the play-off for the 1987 Masters – he did an excellent job of letting winning positions slip. At the 1986 Masters – the year Jack Nicklaus claimed his 6th Masters title – Norman, needing a par 4 to tie, blasted his second shot at the 18th high and wide of the green and eventu-

SPORT SPOT

For all his talent, charisma and success, snooker legend Jimmy White has reached the World Championship final six times – and lost them all.

ally took five. Ten years later, going into the final round at the same event, Norman led by six strokes but slumped to a six-over-par 78. His playing partner Nick Faldo shot a 67 and won the tournament.

And then there was Frenchman Jean Van de Velde. His catastrophic 72nd hole at the Open at Carnoustie in 1999 was a model example of how to lose a championship. Needing only a six to win on the par 4 18th hole, Van de Velde carded a seven. A poor drive was followed by an abysmal 2-iron, which ricocheted off a grandstand and landed short of the moat protecting the green. Playing from thick rough, he then hit the ball into the water. The Frenchman took off his shoes and socks, paddled into the water and contemplated playing the submerged ball. He saw sense and took a drop, only to see his 5th shot land in a bunker. He managed to get up and down for a triple-bogey seven and squeezed into the play-off, but he lost out to Scot Paul Lawrie.

Penalty shoot-outs have accounted for England's exit from five of the last seven major football tournaments. It's a familiar rollercoaster for English fans: Hope, despair, hope and then misery.

Sven Goran Eriksson's biggest regret of the 2006 World Cup was not taking a sports psychologist to Germany. After 17 years of choking over those free shots from ten yards, it's probably time we did.

Gavin Hastings completed a distinguished career for Scotland and the British Lions in 1995. The missed penalty kick against England in the semi-final of the 1991 World Cup was the only blemish.

Golf's most famous miss. Doug Sanders watches his 2ft putt for victory slide by the hole on the 18th green at St Andrews in the 1970 Open Championship. He lost the playoff to Jack Nicklaus.

Above: The greatest and most bizarre blow-up in golf ever. Jean Van de Velde contemplates playing his ball from the Barry Burn. Thankfully he chose not to, but still managed to snatch defeat from the jaws of victory.

Below: David Beckham consoles a weeping John Terry after England's exit from the 2006 World Cup in yet another penalty shootout.

FRONT PAGE NEWS

1967 Direct dialling is introduced between Britain and the United States

1967 Dr Christiaan Barnard carries out first successful heart transplant

1967 Beatles release Sgt Pepper's Lonely Hearts Club Band

1967 Six-day war between Israel and Arabs

FRED TITMUS

DURING the 1968 tour of the Caribbean, England off-spinner and vice-captain Fred Titmus had four toes on his right foot severed by an outboard motor while swimming in Barbados just before the third Test. Astonishingly, Titmus was back playing within weeks and took 111 wickets in the 1968 season. He even made four more Test appearances in 1974-75. Titmus received £98 compensation for his toes.

THE Sun

Monday, May 13, 1968   4d

TOE HORROR TITMUS BACK

ENGLAND cricket ace Fred Titmus is back bowling for Middlesex — only three months after losing four toes. A boat propeller maimed Fred during a swim on England's Caribbean tour.

Full Story — Back Page

Slice of bad luck . . . Don hoofs wide in last kick of game

Torment . . . Don falls as Leeds players leap for joy

DESPERATE DON

By ED INHANS

THIS was the moment when distraught Don Fox collapsed after bungling a simple conversion that gifted opponents Leeds rugby league's biggest prize.

The Wakefield prop needed only to kick over in front of the posts in the dying seconds of Saturday's Challenge Cup Final at Wembley. But in front of 87,100 fans he sliced it wide. Don's agony was unbearable to watch. TV's Eddie Waring said only: "He's a poor lad." Ironically, Don was Man of the Match. But he said: "No one will remember that." Leeds won 11-10.

Rugby ace's agony as kick bungle blows Cup

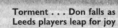

IT'LL HAUNT HIM FOREVER: BACK PAGE

1968 GENIUS OF SOBERS AND CRICKET'S ALL-ROUNDERS

Garry Sobers excelled at all aspects of the game. An elegant and powerful batsman, he was able to bowl quick and turn his hand to spin.

NEITHER the match – Nottinghamshire v Glamorgan – nor the location, Swansea, were the most glamorous, but the achievement was. Garry Sobers became the first cricketer to hit six sixes off one over on August 31st 1968. It was a stunning exhibition of precision hitting by probably the greatest all-rounder the world has ever seen.

With his Nottinghamshire team in need of quick runs, Sobers seized his opportunity. But far from just slogging the ball, Sobers' assault was, as the Glamorgan captain Tony Lewis would later comment, "scientific hitting with every movement working in harmony".

The hapless bowler was Malcolm Nash. Sobers smashed the first two balls over midwicket and into the stands in front of the Cricketer's Inn. The third ball was crashed high over mid-off's head and into the pavilion. Unsure of what to do next Nash dropped his fourth delivery short. Sobers swivelled and deposited the ball over the scoreboard behind square-leg.

The fifth six was a streaky one. Sobers sliced the ball high in the air towards the mid-on boundary. Fielder Roger Davis had an age to think about it, but in making the catch, he fell over the boundary rope. Six more. The sixth ball was promptly smashed over square leg, out of the ground and down St Helen's Avenue. It was only recovered the next day and in November 2006 sold at Christie's auctioneers for £26,400.

Sobers graced the Test arena for 20 years, amassing 8,032 runs at an average of 57.78 (the highest of any Test all-rounder) including a top score of 365 not out. His left-arm bowling, whilst not as destructive as his batting, still earned him 235 wickets.

The title of greatest all-rounder is a hotly debated topic. Sobers is generally regarded to take the honour, but he does have some notable rivals.

Ian Botham was the first player to score 5,000 runs and take 300 wickets in Tests and remains England's leading Test bowler with 383 victims. But Botham's game wasn't about statistics, it was about entertainment. Few cricketers have drawn crowds as he did and his swashbuckling performances with both bat and ball encouraged thousands of youngsters to take up the game.

He almost single-handedly took on and beat the touring Australians in the 1981 Ashes series with performances of skill and character. He played his cricket with a rare vigour and was, at his best, one of the world's most exciting cricketers.

The 1980s produced an abundance of all-round talent. Pakistan's Imran Khan was, at his peak, one of the world's quickest bowlers. His slinging action brought him 362 Test

Above left: Kapil Dev was voted India's cricketer of the century and was for a period the world's leading Test wicket taker, with 434.
Above: The great Pakistan all-rounder Imran Khan, a world-class performer during the 1980s and early 1990s.

wickets and he scored 3,807 runs. He is, by common consent, the finest cricketer his country has produced. His career got better as he got older, averaging 50 with the bat and just 19 with the ball in his last 50 Tests.

Kapil Dev was India's greatest all-rounder, taking 434 wickets in 131 Tests and scoring more than 5,000 runs. Perhaps his greatest achievement was leading India to glory in the 1983 World Cup Final against the then mighty West Indies. It was a tournament where he also smashed 175 not out against Zimbabwe in a group match.

> ## SPORT SPOT
> When Brian Lara overhauled Garry Sobers' world record Test score of 365 not out at Antigua in 1994, Sobers walked out to the middle to congratulate him.

Above: Keith Miller (1919-2004) was probably Australia's greatest all-rounder. An immensely popular fast bowler and classical batsman, he took 170 Test wickets and scored 2,958 Test runs.

Left: Sir Richard Hadlee was New Zealand's greatest all-rounder, the first player to 400 Test wickets (his exceptional fast bowling eventually claiming 431), and a powerful batsman who scored two Test hundreds.

FRONT PAGE NEWS

1968	**Senator Robert Kennedy shot dead at the Ambassador Hotel in Los Angeles**
1968	**Civil rights leader Martin Luther King assassinated in Memphis, Tennessee**
1968	**The last steam passenger train service runs in Britain**
1968	**Richard Nixon is elected President**
1968	**Soviet invasion of Czechoslovakia**

NOW JUMP TO... ➡ BOTHAM'S ASHES page 116 ➡ SHANE WARNE page 128

SunSport: BRITAIN'S BIG-HITTER

Another dull day's cricket at Swansea ..

Ball One . . . Six! Nash said: "It was like a VC10 taking off. I thought, 'Blimey! That's not bad for the first ball after tea'."

Ball Two . . . Six! Hammered into a restaurant beyond square leg. Bowler Nash said: "I thought, 'Oh, dear me!' "

Ball Three . . . Six! Driven into the members' balcony over mid-off. "At least I'm getting it straighter," thought Nash

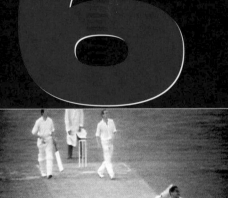

Ball Four . . . Six! The great West Indian wallops it behind square leg. It leaves the ground and bounces in the street

Ball Five . . . Six! Sobers finally mishits one. But fielder (left) falls over boundary catching it

Ball Six . . . Six! The keeper had offered to bet Sobers he couldn't do it. Sobers just grinned and hit it into the street

THESE were the amazing scenes as batting legend Garry Sobers smashed an unprecedented six sixes off one over at the weekend.

The great West Indian all-

By HUGH SLOGGER, Cricket Correspondent

rounder lashed hapless medium pacer Malcolm Nash over the boundary again and again.

His last six went out of the ground and bounced down the street. A small boy found it, kept it overnight and returned it yesterday. Sobers, 32, was skippering Nottinghamshire against Glamorgan at Swansea when Nash came on to bowl the first over after tea.

One ball went into the pitchside restaurant, another into the members' balcony. The fifth ball was caught, but the fielder fell over the boundary. Six more! Sobers already holds the record for the highest Test score, 365. Now he has another.

Nash was good-natured about the nightmare over which is bound to haunt him for the rest of his days.

He joked to Sobers: "We've gone into the record books — and you couldn't have done it without me."

666666 . . . THE NUMBER OF THE BEST: Pages 68-69

1968 BEAMON'S FREAK LEAP 'RUINS' THE LONG-JUMP

FRONT PAGE NEWS

1968   Racing driver Jim Clark is killed in a Formula 2 race at Hockenheim

1968   MP Enoch Powell makes his controversial "rivers of blood" speech

1968   Comedy legend Tony Hancock commits suicide in a Sydney hotel room

1968   France explodes its first hydrogen bomb, becoming world's fifth nuclear power

Left: Beamon breaks down in shock after making his historic jump.

Right: Mike Powell leaps into the record books during his epic duel with Olympic legend Carl Lewis at the World Championships in Tokyo, 1991. Powell still holds the world record.

BOB Beamon's gravity-defying leap in Mexico City is one of the enduring moments of any Olympic Games. In one jump – in an event where records are more often improved by fractions of an inch – he added 21¾ inches (0.5m) to the world record.

Looking for an escape from a turbulent childhood punctuated by domestic violence and brushes with the law, Beamon, then 16, entered a Junior Olympics held in New York and won the long jump with a leap of 24ft 1in (7.33m).

It was the turning point in his life and the first step towards the Mexico Olympics.

Having lost only once all sea-

SPORT SPOT

A Spartan, Chionis, is said to have jumped 7.5m at the 656BC Olympics, enough to have won gold at the first modern Games in 1896.

son, Beamon arrived in Mexico in October 1968 as the favourite. But he was an erratic jumper and almost failed to get through to the final. In the qualifying round he overstepped the take-off board twice and only secured his final place with his third jump.

At 3.40pm on October 18th the final got under way. When his turn came, Beamon composed himself for 20 seconds and then took the first of 19 strides.

He hit the board perfectly and at the apex of his leap reached a height of 6ft. Beamon's initial reaction when he landed in the pit was that he had bungled the jump by landing on his haunches. Such was its length that the optical measuring device – introduced at those Games – fell off its rail.

A steel measuring tape was sent for and after 20 minutes the distance of 8.90m was flashed up on the revolving screen. Unfamiliar with metric measurements, a confused Beamon ran across to his compatriot and rival Ralph Boston, who told him he had jumped

Below: Colin Jackson still holds the indoor 60m hurdles record, set at Sindelfingen, Germany, in 1994.

over 29ft. In fact the distance was 29ft 2½in.

No one had jumped beyond 28ft before, let alone 29ft. Beamon collapsed in tears and his rivals all knew they were jumping for the silver medal.

Igor Ter-Ovanesyan, a Soviet athlete who had until then jointly held the world record of 27ft 4¾in (8.34m), said: "Compared to this jump, we are as children". Britain's Lynn Davies, who had won the title four years earlier in Tokyo, looked on in astonishment. "You have destroyed this event," he told 22-year-old Beamon.

To put Beamon's achievement in perspective, no one, including him, would jump more than 28ft for another 12 years. His record was only surpassed 23 years later when America's Mike Powell jumped 8.95m (29ft 4in) at the 1991 World Championships.

In the modern era, few athletes hold on to their record-breaking times or distances for long, but there are some exceptions. In 1981 Sebastian Coe set world records for the 800m (1min 41.73secs) and the 1000m (2mins 12.18secs) which lasted 16 and 18 years respectively.

Briton Colin Jackson's world record of 12.91secs for the 110m hurdles lasted 13 years before Xiang Liu of China shaved 3/100ths off it in 2006.

The American 400m hurdler Ed Moses went undefeated for an amazing nine years, nine months and nine days. He was only beaten six times throughout his career and broke his own world record four times, holding on to it for 16 years. His best time of 47.02secs, set at Koblenz in 1983, lasted until 1992.

Michael Johnson's world record of 19.32secs for the 200m looks as unassailable now as it did when he achieved it in 1996 at the Atlanta Olympics. In the same year the Czech javelin-thrower Jan Zelezny threw a colossal 98.48m (108 yards). It remains the distance to beat.

Left: Michael Johnson's 200m record at Atlanta, 1996. He still holds the 400m world record of 43.18secs, set in 1999.

Ed Moses beat his own world record four times and won Olympic gold in 1976 and 1984.

THE Sun

Saturday, October 19, 1968   4d

Giant leap for mankind

I can fly . . . Beamon's monster jump yesterday

MIRACLE JUMP 'RUINS SPORT'

AN American athlete stunned the Olympics last night with a freak long-jump certain to remain the world record for decades.

By SANDY PITT, Long Jump Reporter

Bob Beamon won gold in Mexico City with an incredible 29ft 2½in leap.

That's almost **TWO FEET** more than the record it smashed. The 22-year-old star was immediately told by the defending champ, Welshman Lynn Davies: "You've destroyed this event."

Beamon, from the Bronx in New York, collapsed and wept with joy and disbelief.

Beamon Smile — Pages 4 & 5

1970 GENIUS OF GEORGE AND OTHER FOOTBALL GREATS

WHO was the greatest footballer of all time? It is a hotly-debated subject – but George Best is one of the few genuine contenders.

Before his life became a merry-go-round of alcoholic binges and life-or-death hospital treatment, Best spent his short career bewildering defences.

By the time he was 15, endless practice on the streets of the Cregagh estate in Belfast had equipped him with the sublime skill and the impudence to catch the eye of Manchester United scout Bob Bishop. Bishop sent a telegram back to manager Matt Busby simply saying: "I have found a genius."

Best helped United to the league championship in 1967 and drew a wider audience in the club's first European Cup triumph, against Benfica in 1968, scoring a trademark goal, walking the ball into the net. Superstar status beckoned and Best lapped up the attention. Living a pop-star lifestyle, he was dubbed the "fifth Beatle".

In the FA Cup 5th round in 1970, Best scored an astonishing six goals against Northampton Town, showcasing his mastery of all aspects of the game and sealing his status as a football genius.

He exited top-flight football at just 25 in favour of his other two passions, women and wine. Throughout the 1970s he showed only flashes of his brilliance with lower league clubs and in America where, playing for the San Jose Earthquakes, he scored one of best goals one is ever likely to see. Slowly but surely, the drink withered his skill, destroying his career and, more than two decades later, his life. Pele called Best "the greatest player of his generation".

"I was born for soccer, just as Beethoven was born for music." Pele played in four World Cups, scoring 12 goals.

SPORT SPOT

A hotel waiter, spotting wads of cash and Miss World on Best's bed, is said to have asked him: "George, where did it all go wrong?"

Right: Diego Maradona debuted for Argentina in 1977 aged 16 years 120 days.

But one must assume modesty got the better of him, for Pele himself is statistically the greatest player ever. He was a World Cup winner for Brazil in 1958 (aged 17 and scoring a hat-trick in the semi-final), 1962 and 1970 and the first and only player to score 1,000 goals in professional football. Aside from his eye for goal, Pele had extraordinary strength and athleticism. A long and successful career was rewarded when he was voted FIFA's Footballer of the Century and the IOC's Athlete of the Century.

As an aging Pele repaired to the North American soccer league in the late 1970s, so emerged the equally gifted Diego Maradona. Brought up in a shanty town on the outskirts of Buenos Aires, the diminutive Argentine rose to become the most feted player of

his generation, single-handedly leading his country to the 1986 World Cup.

At his best Maradona was probably the most complete footballer the world has known, combining strength, balance and

Above: Holland's Johan Cruyff had wonderful balance, deadly speed, vision and breathtaking ball control. Sports writer David Miller dubbed him "Pythagoras in boots".

amazing individual skill. His reputation was tarnished by two drug bans and the "Hand of God" cheating incident against England in 1986 - though that match, and his wonderful second goal, perfectly encapsulate his reputation as both genius and villain.

The Dutch star Johan Cruyff was European Footballer of the Year a record three times (1971, 1973 and 1974) and perfected a devil-

Eusebio was the top scorer at the 1966 World Cup with nine goals. In 46 appearances for Portugal he scored 38 times.

ish dummy known as the "Cruyff turn" – he would shape to cross the ball, only to drag it back behind his standing leg, leaving the hapless defender chasing his shadow. He scored 33 times in 48 internationals and was voted player of the tournament at the 1974 World Cup, helping Holland to the final.

Portugal's Eusebio scored 41 goals in 64 matches for his country. One of the most feared strikers in world football, he was part of the great Benfica side that won 11 Portuguese championships between 1961 and 1974.

FRONT PAGE NEWS

1969 Woodstock rock festival in U.S. becomes lasting symbol of hippie era

1969 Yasser Arafat becomes leader of the Palestine Liberation Organisation (PLO)

1969 Neil Armstrong is the first man on the moon

1969 Concorde's maiden voyage

1969 Sun newspaper launches as a tabloid

1969 BBC1 in colour for first time

1969 Harrier jump-jet, with vertical take-off, invented in Britain

NOW JUMP TO... ◆ MARADONA page 126 ◆ BECKHAM page 132 ◆ STANLEY MATTHEWS page 78

THE Sun

Monday, February 9, 1970 6d

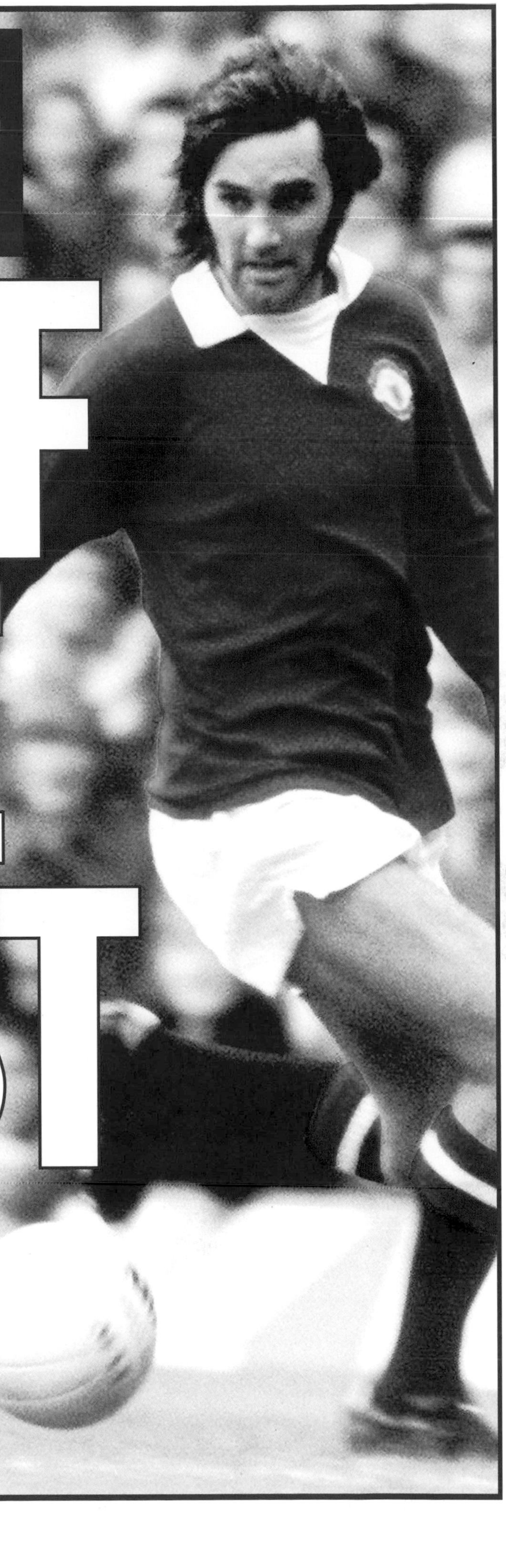

6 OF THE BEST

Genius George's double hat-trick stuns football

LIVE FOR A WEEK LIKE BESTIE

Fantastic Sun prize

GEORGE loves life's finer things, and you could too in a fantastic new Sun competition. We'll give the winner a week's cash to spend on birds and booze. The rest you can squander!

Details on Page 3

BOOZE

BIRDS

& CASH

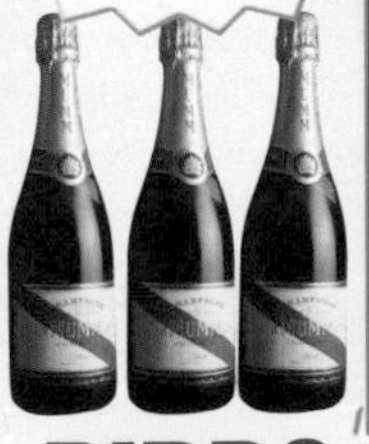

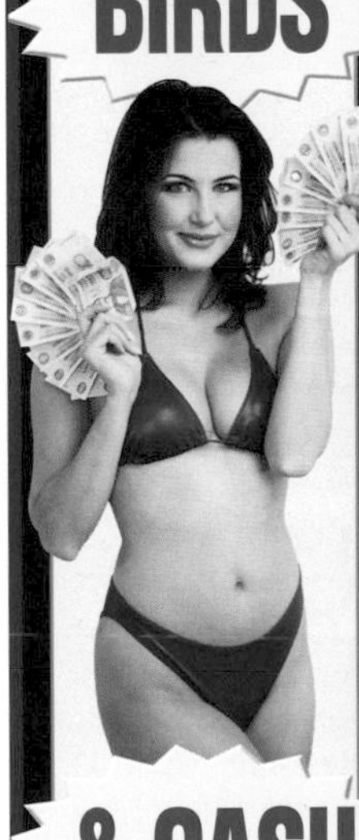

By IAN DANETTE, Football Correspondent

THE world of football was united in awe of George Best last night after his incredible SIX goals in one match at the weekend.

The 23-year-old superstar's masterclass of skill and strength single-handedly destroyed Northampton Town in the FA Cup, winning adulation from their fans as well as the Man Utd faithful.

One Northampton supporter said: "I feel privileged to have been there."

The Joy Of Six — Back Page

1970 JACKLIN AND OTHER BRITISH GOLF STARS

Left: Harry Vardon stills holds the record for most Open victories. He won the title six times, the last at Prestwick in 1914.
Below: Tony Jacklin accepts the Claret Jug after winning the 1969 Open at Royal Lytham and St Annes.

Above: Out of the wilderness. Faldo claims his first major at Muirfield in 1987. It marked the beginning of his dominance of world golf.

ALTHOUGH there has been no British winner of a Major championship since 1999, British golfers have a rich tradition of success in the Majors and have produced some of the world's greatest champions.

Harry Vardon dominated professional golf before World War One, winning six British Opens, and is regarded as the game's first international celebrity. Vardon, along with JH Taylor and James Braid (known collectively as the "Great Triumvirate") monopolised golf, winning the Open Championship no less than 16 times between them from 1894 to 1914.

It was left to Henry Cotton to inject some much-needed zest into British golf during the 1930s and 1940s. With the heroes of yesteryear long gone, Cotton emerged as one of the greatest players of his era, winning three Open Championships (1934, 1937 and 1948). He would have won more but for World War Two. Witty and urbane, Cotton raised the profile of British golf and championed the cause of its professionals. His success was built on endless practice and after he stopped playing in 1948 he went on to be-

Practice makes perfect. To strengthen his hands and wrists, the "Maestro" Henry Cotton would hit balls from the heavy rough until his hands blistered and bled.

come a highly-respected golf instructor.

Like Cotton, Tony Jacklin's rise to the top was during a period of American domination. He was one of only seven non-Americans to win a Major throughout the 1960s and 1970s. In 1969, Scunthorpe-born Jacklin became the first Briton since Max Faulkner in 1951 to win the British Open. His triumph at Royal Lytham and St Annes was followed a year later with a win at the U.S. Open. His victory at Hazeltine National Golf Club, Minnesota, by seven strokes – the fourth highest winning margin in its 112-year history – was the first for Britain since Ted Ray won in 1920. No Briton has won the event since.

Jacklin was only at the top of his game for six or seven years, but as non-playing captain of Europe's Ryder Cup team he created golfing history, masterminding the historic victories in 1985, the first over the U.S. in 28 years, and in 1987, Europe's first triumph on American soil.

After Jacklin's victory, 15 years went by without any British winners at a Major. But Scotland's Sandy Lyle then won the Open Championship at Sandwich, Kent, in 1985, and two years later became the first Briton to win the U.S. Masters, firing a magical seven iron to 6ft from a fairway bunker at the 18th. It hailed the beginning of an unmatched period for British golf. During the late 1980s

SPORT SPOT
Tony Jacklin hit the first hole-in-one to be televised live in Britain – at the 16th hole at Royal St George's in 1967.

and early 1990s Nick Faldo became the most successful British golfer of all time, securing six Major titles (three Open Championships, three U.S. Masters), and was by some distance the best golfer in the world. His transformation started in the mid-1980s, when a series of final round slumps in the Majors convinced Faldo he needed to reconstruct his swing. Enlisting the help of golf coach David Leadbetter, Faldo spent two years in the golfing wilderness before re-emerging as a world-beater.

Eighteen straight pars in the final round of the 1987 Open Championship at Muirfield secured his first Open title and was testament to his newfound fortitude. The most memorable of his three Masters titles came in 1996 when he carded a five-under final round 67, as his playing partner and tournament leader Greg Norman slumped to a final round 78. Faldo thrived on pressure, especially in the Ryder Cup. He appeared in a record 11 matches and has scored more points (25) than anyone in the history of the competition. He will captain the European team in 2008.

Sandy Lyle kisses the famous Claret Jug after his victory at Sandwich in 1985. His win at the US Masters three years later put European golf on the map

FRONT PAGE NEWS

1970	Conservative Ted Heath is elected Prime Minister
1970	Apollo 13 lands safely after crisis in space grips the world
1970	Boeing 747 jumbo jets are introduced
1970	Paul McCartney announces that the Beatles have split up
1970	Guitar legend Jimi Hendrix dies of overdose in London

SunSport US Open golf special

UNION JACK

Britain's hero Jacklin home with trophy

By ALBIE TROSS, Golf Correspondent

HATTABOY! Golf superstar Tony Jacklin brings the U.S. Open trophy home for Britain yesterday, then plants the lid on son Bradley's head.

Tony, 25, from Scunthorpe, is the first Briton to win the prestigious tournament in 50 years.

He was a whopping seven strokes ahead of his rivals at Hazeltine National Golf Club in Minnesota — just a year after his famous win at The Open.

Tony led the U.S. tournament from start to finish, putting himself well ahead of the pack with an amazing 71-shot opening round in 40mph winds.

He said: "Hazeltine was the best week of golf I've ever had — as near a perfect week as I have ever experienced."

The Eagle Has Landed — Page 76

My par . . . dad Tony with wife Vivien, son Bradley and trophy

1971 SHOW-JUMPING...AND HARVEY'S DEFIANT 'V'

Mark Todd riding his horse "Charisma" on the cross-country course at the 1984 Los Angeles Olympics. The New Zealander won gold.

EQUESTRIAN sports in Britain were traditionally the preserve of wealthy upper-classes – which is why when a blunt Yorkshire farmer thrust a V-sign at showjumping judges it caused a national scandal.

Horses had been trained for war for more than 1,000 years. But riding schools only emerged during the Renaissance (14th-16th Century). The first was founded in Naples in 1532 by Federigo Grisone, who also published the first instructional work "Ordini di cavalcare" ("the art of riding") in 1550.

The controlled exercise of a horse is known by the French term "dressage". It laid the foundations for the later jumping disciplines, though modern methods were only established in the 19th Century.

The early riding schools of Europe all concentrated on a backward seat when jumping – a rider leaned back and pulled the reins to force the horse's head up and back. That encouraged the animal to land on its hind legs, protecting the perceived fragility of its front ones.

But at the turn of the 20th Century an Italian instructor, Captain Federico Caprilli, promoted the forward seat position which allowed horses to follow their natural instincts and land on their front legs. Caprilli was fired for his unorthodoxy, though he was later recalled when it became obvious his methods made sense.

Caprilli demonstrated the new technique

Italian Federico Caprilli (1868-1907) revolutionised jumping with his "forward seat" position.

at the 1906 Olympics in Athens – and show-jumping took off (although an equestrian high jump and long jump were already on the programme at Paris in 1900).

The international horse show at Olympia, London, was launched in 1907 and by the 1912 Stockholm Olympics both individual and team three-day eventing competitions – dressage, cross-country and show jumping – had become a Games fixture. In 1921 eight nations founded the Fédération Equestre Internationale (FEI), which now has more than 100 members. Until the 1952 Olympics, only military officers were allowed to compete, but civilians were then allowed to take part too.

The early world leaders in three-day eventing were Sweden and the Netherlands. Ger-

many dominated the Berlin Olympics in 1936, while Britain topped the medal table for the first time at Mexico in 1968.

Three years later, at Hickstead, Sussex, Harvey Smith shattered show-jumping's genteel atmosphere by showing the V-sign to a line of judges after completing his winning round at the British Show Jumping Derby, an event he won seven times.

Smith had earlier had a heated row with a judge after neglecting to bring along the trophy, which he had won the year before. The judges believed he was arrogant enough to assume he would retain it – which, to his evident satisfaction, he then did.

Smith cheekily claimed he was evoking Churchill's "V for victory" sign but was stripped of his title and the £2,000 winners' cheque. There was a public outcry and amid huge popular support Smith's disqualification was reversed - although much later he admitted the V-sign WAS the defiant gesture everyone suspected. Doing a "Harvey Smith" became a recognised phrase which is still in some dictionaries.

Between them Smith and Princess Anne propelled show-jumping into the spotlight during 1971. Anne (who later competed at the 1976 Montreal Olympics) won the individual title at the European Eventing Championships at Burghley House, Lincolnshire, and was crowned BBC Sports Personality of the Year. Her daughter Zara won the same BBC award 35 years later after a spectacular display at the 2006 World Equestrian Games where she won the individual gold.

Without doubt the most revered rider on the eventing circuit was New Zealander Mark Todd, voted rider of the 20th Century by the FEI in 2000. Todd won the individual gold at both the 1984 and 1988 Olympics.

Below: Princess Anne at the Burghley Horse Trials at Stamford in 1981. **Right:** Her daughter Zara Phillips at the same jump 22 years later.

THE Sun

Monday, August 16, 1971　　6d

'Churchill did it too'

HARVEY insisted his V-sign simply meant "victory". He added: "Churchill used it throughout the war." But our picture shows the ex-PM's palm pointing AWAY from him, a crucial difference.

THAT TOLD 'EM HARVEE!

Show-jump fury as rider gives 'V' to judges on TV

Jumping a-fence . . . 'V' sign was seen by millions on BBC telly last night

By RAINE TUGGER, Equestrian Editor

TOP show-jumper Harvey Smith caused a storm last night by flicking a V-sign at judges on live TV.

The blunt Yorkshireman, 32, made his rude gesture moments after winning the British Show-Jumping Derby at Hickstead.

Judges branded him "disgusting" and axed his £2,000 winnings and title. Harvey earlier "forgot" to bring the trophy, which he won last year.

Judges said he did it deliberately because he was sure he would win again. They said he had "no chance".

Handy Guide To Offensive Gestures: Page 24

V funny . . . smirking Harvey rides away

1972 MUNICH MASSACRE: THE OLYMPICS' DARKEST DAY

THE murder of 11 Israeli athletes and staff by Palestinian terrorists at the Olympic village in Munich in 1972 was the bleakest day in the history of the modern Games.

The Olympics had returned to Germany for the first time since the Berlin Games of 1936, which Adolf Hitler used to showcase Nazi ideals. With that notorious event in mind, German officials were keen to promote openness and freedom in and around the Olympic village. It was a naive policy with disastrous consequences for security, and the Israeli team became easy prey.

At 4.30am on September 5th, eight members of the Palestinian terrorist group "Black September" – later confirmed as having links with Yasser Arafat's Palestine Liberation Organisation (PLO) – scaled the fence surrounding the Olympic village.

Wearing ski-masks and brandishing machine-guns they raided the Israeli team's apartments. Yossef Gutfreund, an Israeli wrestling judge, was woken by scratching at

The Israeli flag flies at half-mast among national flags at the Munich Olympic Stadium on 10 September 1972.

his apartment door. He immediately got up and threw himself against the door, allowing weightlifting coach Tuvia Sokolovsky time to escape. But in the ensuing struggle to prevent the terrorists capturing more members of the team, the wrestling coach Moshe Weinberg and weightlifter Yossef Romano were shot and killed.

At 6am, with two dead and nine Israeli hos-

tages seized, Black September issued a ransom note demanding the release of 236 political prisoners and safe passage out of Germany. Negotiations with German and Israeli officials lasted throughout the day, in the full gaze of the world as television screened the unfolding drama.

The live images handed the terrorists priceless publicity – and allowed them to watch German police positioning snipers on the roof.

Bizarrely, the Games continued throughout the morning and part of the afternoon, to the anger of Israeli officials. Only at 4pm were they suspended.

Israel's government resolutely refused to negotiate with the terrorists, and a plan was hastily hatched by German authorities. The terrorists had demanded a plane to Cairo and had agreed to be taken by helicopter to a NATO airbase at Fürstenfeldbruck where a Boeing 727 would be waiting.

During the transfer to the airport it became clear there were eight terrorists and not five as German police had first thought. Crucially, this undermined a planned ambush and rescue at the airport, where only five police snipers were in position.

At 10.30pm the captors and hostages arrived at the airport. Two terrorists inspected the Boeing and, finding the cabin empty of flight-crew, realised they had been duped and ran back to the helicopters.

At 11pm German police gave the order for their marksmen to fire. In the ensuing gun battle two kidnappers and one policeman were killed. The

SPORT SPOT

After the security shambles that left the Israelis exposed, Canada spent $100million ensuring the safety of athletes and spectators at the 1976 Montreal Games.

Six of the eleven Israeli Olympic team members who were killed in the Palestinian terrorist attack. L-R: (top) trainer Moshe Weinberg and officials Kehat Schur and Yakov Springer, (bottom) official Yosef Gottfreund, wrestler Eliezaar Halfen, and official Amitzur Shapira.

hostages were still tied up in the helicopters and a stalemate developed as the remaining terrorists fired sporadically at the airport building.

A short time after midnight the terrorists, realising the futility of their situation, began their final act. They shot four of the hostages in one helicopter and then tossed a grenade into the other.

In all 11 Israeli team members were killed. The German rescue had been a disaster.

Three of the eight terrorists escaped death that night, and amazingly, were all released the following month when the German government caved into demands for their release following the hijacking of a Lufthansa jet by Islamic terrorists.

Two were later assassinated by the Israeli secret service. One, Jamal Al-Gashey, is still alive and living in North Africa.

Below: An armed German policeman, dressed as an athlete, stands around the corner from the balcony of the apartments where members of the Black September terrorist group held the Israeli athletes hostage.

FRONT PAGE NEWS

1971	The floppy disk is introduced for portable data storage
1972	Bloody Sunday: Army kills 13 Catholic civil rights marchers in Northern Ireland
1972	First scientific hand-held calculator, the HP-35, is introduced costing $400
1972	The Godfather – still topping "greatest film" polls today – is released in the USA

THE Sun

Wednesday, September 6, 1972   3p

3AM EDITION

Hooded assassin . . . terrorist in Olympic village

After the horror . . . helicopters at NATO airbase following disastrous rescue mission last night

MASSACRE AT THE GAMES

By SUN FOREIGN DESK

NINE Israeli Olympic athletes were shot dead early today in a gun battle between police and Arab terrorists.

They were killed when West German police marksmen opened fire on the Palestinians, who had held the athletes for 18 hours.

Five terrorists were killed and three captured. The massacre at the Fürstenfeldbruck air base, a few miles from the Olympic Village at Munich, was a catastrophic end to the crisis that gripped the world yesterday.

The terrorists and the hostages they snatched in the Olympic Village had been flown there by helicopters to board a jet to Cairo, Egypt.

But the Germans botched a planned ambush — and just after midnight the Arabs executed four Israelis before blowing five more up with a grenade.

Terrorists slaughter 9 Israeli athletes

Disaster — Pages 4 & 5

1974 RUGBY'S BRITISH LIONS & THE BLOODY TOUR OF '74

Above: The 1955 Lions. South Africa were acknowledged as the best side in the world and were a daunting prospect, but the four match Test series was drawn 2-2 and the Lions were acclaimed for their running rugby.

THE British Lions have toured the southern hemisphere for almost 120 years. Their performances, never dull, have ranged from exhilarating highs to dismal lows. The 1974 trip to South Africa was their most successful – and their most notoriously bloody.

In March 1888, in the wake of successful English cricket tours to Australia, the first unofficial British Isles rugby team comprising English, Scottish and Welsh players set sail for Australasia. A 21-man squad played 35 matches against club sides in New Zealand and Australia, winning 27. Three years later, in 1891, they played their first Test matches against South Africa and returned home unbeaten having conceded just one point in 20 matches. It was not until 1910 that a committee representing all four home nations selected the first official touring team.

Welsh fly-half Phil Bennett scored 103 points on tour and was the Lions' star player in 1974. His 50-yard try in the 28-9 second Test victory in Pretoria remains one of the most sublime examples of individual brilliance on a rugby pitch.

FRONT PAGE NEWS

1972 **Miners' strike causes power cuts in Britain**
1973 **America pulls troops out of Vietnam**
1973 **New York's World Trade Center completed**
1973 **Britain joins the European Economic Community**
1973 **Spanish painter Pablo Picasso dies aged 91**
1974 **President Nixon quits over Watergate**

"The Invincibles". Led by Irish lock "Willie John" McBride, the Lions averaged more than 30 points and almost five tries a match. They compiled 729 points and conceded only 207 in their 22-match tour of South Africa in 1974.

The resulting trip to South Africa was moderately successful, though the Springboks won the Test series 2-1.

On the 1924 tour to South Africa the team officially adopted the name British Lions, inspired by the heraldic emblem on their tour ties. Their famous red jerseys appeared in 1950.

The 1950s saw the Lions' attacking style take root. Captained by the gifted Welsh fly-half Cliff Morgan, the 1955 South Africa tour exemplified the new spirit. The tour produced some sparkling rugby with uncapped English scrum-half Dickie Jeeps feeding Morgan. English centres Jeff Butterfield and Phil Davies worked their magic in midfield, while 19-year-old Irish winger Tony O'Reilly scored a record 16 tries.

The Lions toiled hard in the 1960s without much reward. The decade produced just one series win, against Australia in 1966 (2-0), though the rest of that tour, in New Zealand, ended with a 4-0 defeat to the All Blacks.

The 1970s began with a first series win over New Zealand in 1971.

Then in 1974, the Lions, led by Irish lock Willie John McBride, toured South Africa and returned home unbeaten, having won 21 out of 22 matches. The other was drawn.

The back-line was blessed with Welsh flair. Half-backs Gareth Edwards and Phil Bennett – who became the star of the tour, befuddling opponents with sidesteps and dummies – were assisted by JJ and JPR Williams. The forwards were perhaps the greatest the Lions have ever assembled. And they needed to be when the Springboks, aiming to disrupt

the Lions, began trying to punch their way out of a corner. Fed up with the Boks' brutality, captain McBride invoked his famous "99" call, the signal (based on the 999 emergency number) for all his players to wade in when trouble flared up. The Springboks were humiliated and only the referee saved them from being whitewashed 4-0 in the series when he disallowed a legitimate Lions try.

It would be 15 years before the Lions completed another series win, this time against Australia in 1989. Their last Test series triumph (2-1) was in 1997 against South Africa when Jeremy Guscott slotted a drop-goal in the dying seconds of the second Test at Durban to win 18-15 and give them an unassailable 2-0 lead.

On the most recent tour, to New Zealand in 2005, the British and Irish Lions – as they are now known – suffered some of their heaviest ever defeats and lost the Test series 3-0. In 2009 they will make the journey to South Africa hoping to add a happier chapter to their proud history.

SPORT SPOT

When the 1974 Lions trashed a hotel in Port Elizabeth, the manager told McBride he had called the police. McBride said: "Will there be many of them?"

Jeremy Guscott played on three Lions tours (1989, '93 & '97) and with eight Test appearances is, along with Mike Gibson, the Lions' most capped centre.

SunSport roars on our boys

YOU POOR DEERS

Lions maul Springboks
in new tour bloodbath

From NIALL ASIAN in Port Elizabeth

THE majestic British Lions ate South Africa's Springboks alive here in the bloodiest rugby match ever witnessed.

The 'Boks picked a team of hard-men for the Third Test at the Boet Erasmus Stadium hoping to halt the Lions, who have won ALL 17 tour matches.

But they were trampled under-foot as the Lions, led heroically by Ulster's Willie John McBride, won 26-9. Several times he gave his infamous "99" call for his men to wade into the 'Boks.

Springbok Moaner van Heerden was pummelled after booting a Lion. The second half saw a string of fights, with McBride punching like Joe Frazier.

Now 3-0 up in the Tests, the Lions are heroes to South Africa's blacks. One student said: "We are made to believe Afrikaners are perfect. But they're being humiliated."

BRITISH LIONS

HERE COMES McBRIDE
PAGES 68 AND 69

1974

MUHAMMAD ALI: THE NO1 ATHLETE OF 20TH CENTURY

"I done wrestled with an alligator, I done tussled with a whale; handcuffed lightning, thrown thunder in jail; only last week, I murdered a rock, injured a stone, hospitalised a brick; I'm so mean I make medicine sick."

AT 4.45am on October 30th 1974, Muhammad Ali delivered the punch that secured him sporting immortality. The brilliant, turbulent career of the man later voted the greatest athlete of the 20th Century reached its zenith on a sweltering African night.

Ten years earlier, in February 1964, Ali, from Louisville, Kentucky, confounded critics and bookmakers to defeat Sonny Liston – "the ugly old bear", as Ali liked to call him. The 7-1 rank outsider was world heavyweight champion at 22 and had finally delivered on his boast of being 'the Greatest'.

Ali joined the Nation of Islam, a religious separatist group founded in 1930 to improve the lot of black Americans, changed his name from Cassius Clay and provoked controversy wherever he went.

Between 1965 and 1967, Ali defended his title nine times before being drafted into the military. But he refused to serve in Vietnam. "I ain't got no quarrel with those Vietcong," he protested. "No Vietcong ever called me a nigger."

Ali was stripped of his title, his boxing licence and convicted of draft evasion. He was handed a suspended jail sentence, fined $10,000 and banned from leaving America.

Re-granted his licence in 1970, Ali suffered his first professional defeat, to Joe Frazier, in 1971. He also lost to Ken Norton two years later and had his jaw broken. But his rematch and victory over Frazier in January 1974 set up a $10million world title fight, the so-called "Rumble in the Jungle", with George Foreman in Kinshasa, Zaire.

Foreman was a brutal puncher. His 40 fights had produced 37 knockouts. But during the build-up, Ali mocked Foreman, calling him "The Mummy",

SPORT SPOT

Laila, (born 1977), daughter of Ali and his third wife Veronica Porsche, is an undefeated world female super middleweight champion boxer.

while reminding everyone he would "float like a butterfly, sting like a bee".

Boxing journalists agreed that Ali would have to dance around the ring to make Foreman miss, but Ali had other ideas. He set to work on *his* plan and revealed it to no one.

In round one, Ali took the attack to Foreman, landing with 12 right-hand leads – an unconventional and dangerous strategy which infuriated Foreman.

But in round two Ali retreated to the ropes and let Foreman pummel him. "You don't hit as hard as I thought you would, George," Ali taunted. "Is that all you got, George?" The jibes only made Foreman punch harder, but Ali soaked them up. After five rounds of what Ali later dubbed his "rope-a-dope" tactic, Foreman was exhausted.

His punches grew weaker and weaker. In the eighth round, Ali sniffed his chance. Suddenly, from his position on the ropes, he knocked Foreman out to reclaim his title. No one could

quite believe it, least of all TV commentator Harry Carpenter:

"Oh, he's got him with a right hand! He's got him! Oh you can't believe it...and I don't think Foreman's going to get up... and he's out! Oh my God, he's won the title back at 32! Muhammad Ali!"

The Thrilla in Manila followed in 1975, another epic battle with Ali gaining revenge on Joe Frazier with a 14th round stoppage. But Ali was now 33 and his powers in decline. He held on to his title until 1978, when Leon Spinks beat him. But a rematch saw Ali regain the title yet again.

He announced his retirement, but it was short-lived and an ill-advised comeback fight against world champion Larry Holmes in October 1980 ended in defeat.

The following year he lost to Trevor Berbick, 12 years Ali's junior, and his career was over.

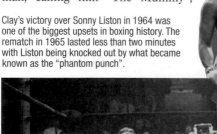

Clay's victory over Sonny Liston in 1964 was one of the biggest upsets in boxing history. The rematch in 1965 lasted less than two minutes with Liston being knocked out by what became known as the "phantom punch".

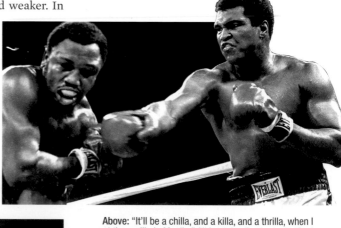

Above: "It'll be a chilla, and a killa, and a thrilla, when I get the gorilla in Manila." Ali beat Joe Frazier in the final round at the Araneta Coliseum on October 1st 1975. Frazier had inflicted one of only five losses (in 61 bouts) on Ali at Madison Square Gardens in 1971

FRONT PAGE NEWS

1974	Mental patient Ian Ball fails to kidnap Princess Anne in The Mall
1974	Lord Lucan disappears after his children's nanny murdered in the family home
1974	USA and Soviet Union sign Strategic Arms Limitation Treaty (SALT)
1974	IRA's Guildford pub bombings kill five people, leading to wrongful imprisonment of the Guildford Four

NOW JUMP TO... ↻ GEORGE FOREMAN page 130

THE Sun

Thursday, October 31, 1974   10p

Crafty Ali crowned champ again at 32

MUHAMMAD Ali won back his heavyweight crown last night after bamboozling George Foreman with magical cunning and skill.

The 32-year-old legend knocked out the 25-year-old favourite in the eighth round of the "Rumble in the Jungle" in Kinshasa, Zaire.

Ali's tactics confused Foreman from the off. Instead

By NOAH DAMEANARRY

of dancing around to avoid the heavy-hitting champion, he came straight at him.

Then, in the second round, he retreated to the ropes and soaked up punch after punch deliberately to wear Foreman down.

After seven rounds – during which Ali goaded him by saying "That all you got, George?" – Foreman was exhausted. Ali then decked him with a ferocious flurry of punches in the eighth.

I'm Still Greatest — Pages 4 & 5

Bye, George . . . duped Foreman's out for count

KING OF THE JUNGLE

'Never again make me the underdog' . . . Ali sounding off last night

It looks ropey . . . but Ali's bizarre defensive tactic was pure genius

STILL
Defiant Ali orders critics: Don't write me off till I'm 50

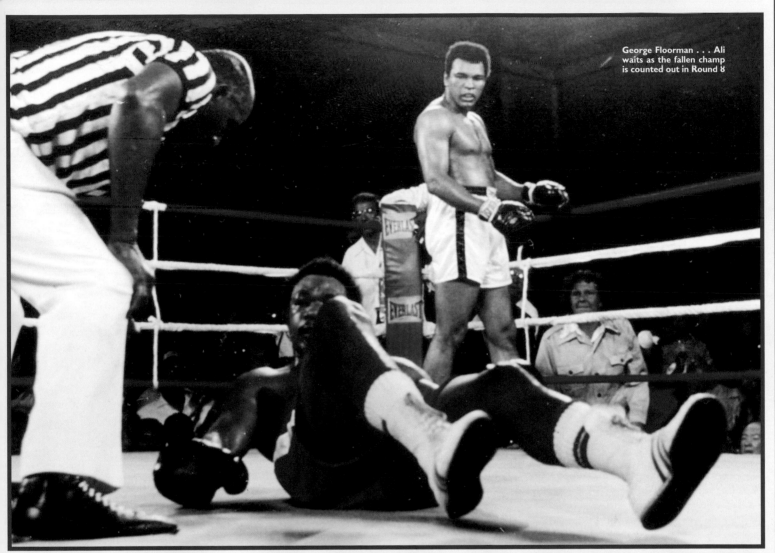

George Floorman . . . Ali waits as the fallen champ is counted out in Round 8

THE GREATEST

MUHAMMAD Ali declared "I am STILL the greatest" last night — and no one could argue with him.

In an amazing interview with TV's David Frost minutes after winning back the world title, he told how he meticulously planned how to beat big-hitter George Foreman.

And he gave both barrels to critics who said that, at 32, he had no chance.

Ali said: "Never again say I

By BOB ANWEEV in Kinshasa, Zaire

am going to be defeated. Never again make me the underdog until I am about 50 years old. Then you might get me!

"I told you all, all my critics, that I was the greatest of all time when I beat Sonny Liston. I am still the greatest of all time."

The fighter then explained his bizarre tactic of leaning on the ropes, soaking up punch after punch for round after round, exhausting Foreman, 25, in the process.

Before the fight in Kinshasa, Zaire, Ali claimed he

would dance around the ring to evade the champion's notoriously powerful punches. It would be a case of "now you see me, now you don't. George thinks he will, but I know he won't".

It was a bluff — Ali had decided on another plan which he kept secret even from his corner. He flew at Foreman in the first round, then retreated to the ropes for the rest of the fight.

He said: "I didn't dance for a reason. I wanted to make him lose all his power. He couldn't hit, he was swinging like a cissy. When I stay on the ropes you think I'm doing bad. But staying on

the ropes is a beautiful thing for a heavyweight when you make him shoot his best shots and you know he's not hitting you."

Ali, a Muslim, claimed Allah helped him win.

"Allah has power over all things. If you believe in him even George Foreman will look like a baby," he said.

Ali admitted he spent the entire fight taunting Foreman. He said: "I was saying, 'Come on, champ, you can do better than that. They told me you were a big hitter'."

Confused and enraged, Foreman tried harder and harder to pummel Ali, but the genius of the ring saw every

punch coming. In the eighth round, the moment Ali had planned for all along finally arrived. Foreman aimed one more tired punch at him and staggered forward with its momentum.

Ali leapt off the ropes, landed two right-handers, a left hook and a final knock-out right-hand.

Foreman pirouetted slowly and fell. He was counted out and his reign as champion was over.

Ali, the 6ft 3ins boy from Kentucky, first became undisputed heavyweight champion of the world in 1964 and won the crown again in 1967.

Now it is his once more.

1976 A SHORT HISTORY OF THE IGNOBLE ART OF CHEATING

Rosie's ruse: Rosie Ruiz staggers home after allegedly completing less than one mile of the Boston Marathon in 1980.

CHEATING is as old as sport itself. The many examples – ingenious, humorous, tragic or downright despicable – could fill a book of their own.

The Olympics have attracted some of the most brazen attempts. In front of a home crowd at the 1904 Games in St Louis, Missouri, Fred Lorz came home first in the marathon, accepting rapturous applause and a laurel wreath from President Roosevelt's daughter Alice. That was before he was rumbled for hitching a lift.

Lorz had exhausted himself after running just nine miles in 90 degree heat, so his manager bundled him into his car and set off towards the stadium. Five miles from the finish, a revitalised Lorz rejoined the race, coming home first. News of his deception spread around the stadium as he took the plaudits, and cheers turned to boos. Lorz tried to pass off his cheating as a joke, but received a one-year ban.

At the Boston marathon 76 years later an equally bizarre episode took place. In 1980 amateur runner Rosie Ruiz came home first in the then third best women's marathon time in history (2hrs, 31mins, 56secs). But she is said to have joined the race by jumping the crowd barriers half a mile from the finish line, cruising home way ahead of other competitors. Officials smelt a rat because she was hardly sweating and could remember none of the course landmarks. After a week she was disqualified, but

SPORT SPOT

Robin Knox-Johnston won the Sunday Times Golden Globe Race which Crowhurst entered – and gave his £5,000 winner's cheque to Crowhurst's widow.

Below: Ben Johnson wins the 100m at the Seoul Olympics. Three days later he was stripped of his medal and his world record of 9.79secs.

protests her innocence to this day.

At the 1976 Montreal Olympics, Ukrainian army officer Boris Onishchenko was disqualified from the modern pentathlon for cheating in the fencing. Onishchenko – later dubbed 'Disonishchenko' by some newspapers – had wired up his epee to register hits without touching his opponent. A tiny button he installed in the sword's grip would trigger the electronic scoring system when pressed. British captain Jim Fox became suspicious when he faced the Soviet, and reported him. Officials examined the sword and Onishchenko was sent home in disgrace. Stripped of his medals, he later became a taxi driver.

Canadian sprinter Ben Johnson is the most infamous cheat in all sport. At the 1988 Seoul Olympics he went from hero to zero in two days. Having won the 100m final in a world record 9.79secs, it was thought he had categorically proved he and not his American arch-rival Carl Lewis was the fastest man on Earth. Afterwards he said "no one can take the gold medal away from me." But 72 hours later Olympic officials did just that, after his urine sample was found to contain a banned steroid, stanozolol. The world was stunned and Johnson's career effectively ended.

Perhaps the most tragic deception of all was committed by Donald Crowhurst, whose attempt to sail non-stop around the world in 1968 ended in his death. Enticed by a prize of £5,000, Crowhurst built a 40ft trimaran, but was at best a part-time sailing enthusiast and

woefully underprepared for the 27,000-mile race. He quickly fell behind schedule but persisted in sending radio and telegram messages informing the national Press and his many supporters back home that he was making excellent progress. In truth he was lying low around Cape Horn, hoping to rejoin the race when other boats passed by on the return leg.

The guilt of his epic lie and the undeserved hero's welcome that awaited him proved too much for Crowhurst, who detailed his shame in a series of taped confessions and logs from the boat's cabin. His empty trimaran was finally found a year later in July 1969. His body was never recovered.

FRONT PAGE NEWS

1975	End of the Vietnam War
1975	Spain becomes democracy after death of Franco
1975	Margaret Thatcher becomes leader of the Conservative Party
1975	Moorgate Tube disaster in London leaves 41 dead
1976	Concorde begins its first commercial transatlantic flights

Donald Crowhurst making final preparations to his boat, Teignmouth Electron, before setting sail on his ill-fated voyage in 1968.

NOW JUMP TO... ❍ **MARADONA page 106** ❍ **MICHAEL SCHUMACHER page 130**

THE Sun

Tuesday, July 20, 1976   10p

SKIPPER: I DOBBED IN BORIS THE BENT

BRITISH team captain Jim Fox told last night how he knew Onischenko was dodgy.

Jim, 36, noticed that the Soviet cheat seemed to score against Brit Adrian Parker without touching him. Jim then faced him and deliberately swayed far out of his reach — but the rigged sword **STILL** registered a hit.

Jim *(left)*, who has become friendly with Onischenko at past competitions, said: "He passed me later and said, 'Jim, I'm sorry'. I knew then something was up."

The sword of truth . . . officials examine weapon

Red and buried . . . downcast Boris is out

FOILED

Brits get cheating Soviet fencer

Olympic ban over sword gizmo

A TOP Soviet fencer has been banned from the Olympics for CHEATING against the British. Boris Onischenko, 38, dubbed "Disonischenko",

By **DEE CEEVER** in Montreal, Canada

rigged up an electronic gadget in his foil to register a "hit" even if it made no contact with his opponent. The

KGB Colonel was busted when our Modern Pentathlon stars reported him. Officials in Montreal examined his sword and disqualified his Soviet team.

OFF TO THE SALT MINES: PAGES 4&5

1976 HISTORY OF GYMNASTICS AND NADIA'S PERFECT 10

The Gymnasion at the site of the ancient Olympic Games at Olympia in Greece.

Romanian Nadia Comaneci, aged 14, celebrates winning gold in the women's uneven bars at Montreal in 1976. She won nine Olympic medals during her career.

GYMNASTICS is among the oldest Olympic sports, and was practised widely throughout the ancient world. It was one of the few sports reintroduced when the Games were revived in 1896. The Romanian Nadia Comaneci was the first gymnast judged to have achieved perfection.

The Greeks were passionate about exercise and each city had at least one area set aside for it. They called them "gymnasion", a word taking its root from "gymnos", literally meaning naked. Men regularly competed in the nude. A gymnasion was a place to exercise the body and the mind – it doubled as a meeting point for those wishing to discuss philosophy and art.

The abolition of the Olympics and other sporting festivals in 393AD virtually ended gymnastics for 1,400 years, until two competing forms were devised. They eventually combined to give us the sport we know today.

In the late 18th and early 19th centuries, gymnastics flourished in Germany mainly due to the PE teacher Friedrich Ludwig Jahn. Considered the "father of modern gymnastics", he devised various apparatus – the side bar, the horizontal bar, the parallel bars and the balance beam – still in use today. Jahn opened a series of gymnastics schools, the first in Berlin in 1811. Soon clubs formed across Europe.

In Sweden, Pehr Henrik Ling developed a more rhythmic regime promoting better health and poise without apparatus. The Olympic floor exercises are a direct result. A dance performed with a hoop, ball or ribbon was introduced as an Olympic sport at Los Angeles in 1984.

Men's gymnastics, the German way, was on the schedule of the first modern Olympics in 1896. Unsurprisingly Germany won five of the eight medals. Rope climbing was an Olympic discipline in the first Games and remained so until 1932.

Competitive gymnastics for women began only in 1936 at Berlin, when Germany won the team event. An individual contest was introduced at Helsinki in 1952. Twenty years later, at the Munich Olympics, gymnastics entered its most important and popular era. Olga Korbut, of the Soviet Union, won two golds in the balance beam and the floor exercise. She was the first gymnast to complete a backward somersault on the balance beam.

But the performances of Nadia Comaneci at Montreal in 1976 were undoubtedly the most famous and enduring spectacle seen in a gymnastic arena. The 14-year-old Romanian achieved a perfect 10.0 – an unprecedented score which proved too much for the electronic scoreboard.

Her first of seven perfect 10s came on the asymmetric bars during the team competition in which she won silver. But Comaneci went on to take three individual golds in the all-round competition, the uneven bars and the balance beam. She became a global superstar, making the cover of America's prestigious *Time* magazine.

Britain had always failed to make any impact at the highest level in gymnastics until Beth Tweddle became our first ever world champion, on the uneven bars in 2006.

> ## SPORT SPOT
> **While Comaneci was the youngest gymnastics gold medallist, Agne Kelleti of Hungary was nearly 36 when she won golds on floor, beam and uneven bars in 1956.**

Bust of Pehr Henrik Ling. He is responsible for the development of natural gymnastics. In 1813, Ling founded the Royal Gymnastics Central Institute in Stockholm. Ling devised and taught a system of gymnastic exercises designed to produce medical benefits for the athlete.

Russian Olga Korbut, 15, displays one of the three gold medals (floor exercise, balance beam and team competition) she won during the 1972 Munich Olympics.

FRONT PAGE NEWS

1976 Computer firm Microsoft is officially registered with the Office of the Secretary of the State of New Mexico

1976 Former peanut farmer Jimmy Carter elected US President

1976 Chairman Mao Tse-tung, leader of Communist China, dies aged 82

1976 The Sex Pistols swear on live TV and punk rock explodes in Britain

1976 Novelist Agatha Christie dies aged 85

NOW JUMP TO... ➲ COE & OVETT page 112

THE Sun

Saturday, July 24, 1976   10p

Score blimey . . . Nadia's '1.00'

SCOREBOARD IS STUMPED!

NADIA'S perfect marks even confused the new digital scoreboards. No one ever thought a gymnast could score ten, so they were only designed to go up to 9.99. In the end they displayed her 10s as 1.00.

Amazing grace . . . camera wizardry shows teenager's flawless beam performance

TEENAGE gymnastics star Nadia Comaneci bagged three Olympic golds last night after SEVEN historic "perfect 10" scores.

The tiny 14-year-old Romanian stunned the world with the first ever Olympic "ten", on the uneven bars in Montreal last Sunday.

She repeated the trick twice on Monday, on beam and bars, and did the same again on Wednesday.

Yesterday she pulled it off twice more — and walked away with golds for beam, bars and all-round performance. She also won a team silver, plus bronze on the floor exercise.

An estimated one billion people watched her scintillating performances on TV — and Nadia is set

From JIM NASIUM in Montreal

for global superstardom. In one week she has eclipsed the Soviet star Olga Korbut, who captivated the world at Munich four years ago, as the No1 draw in gymnastics.

Fans had hoped their first competitive meeting would be a clash of the titans — but it wasn't even close.

Nadia, just 4ft 11ins and 6st 2lb, was amazingly cool last night about her achievements.

At a press conference she said: "I've had 19 tens in my career. It's nothing new."

The car mechanic's daughter was discovered at the age of six and put through a daily four-hour gym training regime on top of normal lessons.

She is known for her unsmiling image. But Nadia insisted: "I can smile. I just don't care to."

Ten Things You Didn't Know About 'Perfect Ten' Girl — See Page 10

VAULTLESS
Gymnast Nadia scores seven 'perfect 10s'

1977

RUMMY...AND BRITAIN'S BEST-KNOWN RACEHORSES

FRONT PAGE NEWS

1977 Elvis Presley dies aged 42
1977 Queen celebrates her Silver Jubilee
1977 Freddie Laker begins budget flights to the USA
1977 South African anti-apartheid activist Steve Biko dies in police custody
1977 Worst air crash in history, as two jumbo jets collide at Tenerife Airport, kills 574

TAKING his name from the last three letters of his mother Mared and father Quorum, Red Rum was, and still is, Britain's most famous horse. His performances at the Grand National from 1973 to 1977 are unlikely to be bettered.

His achievements are all the more remarkable considering he suffered for most of his life from pedal osteitis, a debilitating bone disease in the hoof. To alleviate the pain when exercising, his trainer 'Ginger' McCain took him to Southport beach on Merseyside, galloping him in the shallow salt water.

Red Rum, born in 1965, started his association with Aintree on April 7th 1967 when, in his debut race the Thursby Plate he finished first in a dead heat with Curlicue.

Six years later he would win one of the most dramatic Nationals in history. Australian horse 'Crisp' was 15 lengths clear when he cleared the final jump, but he tired dramatically and 'Rummy', as he became affectionately known, snatched victory by three-quarters of a length.

In 1974 he repeated the feat, beating L'Escargot by seven lengths, and becoming the first horse since Reynoldstown in 1935 and 1936 to win back-to-back Nationals. Three weeks later he completed a unique double, winning the Scottish Grand National at Ayr.

He raced in the National again in 1975 and 1976 and finished second both times, losing to L'Escargot and Rag Trade.

But he returned the following year and crossed the line 25 lengths ahead of his nearest rival Churchtown Boy to seal a place in racing history and the nation's hearts. It was a fairytale finish for a horse considered by many too old to compete in such a challenging race. Like Red Rum, Desert Orchid's fame reached far beyond racing circles. His distinctive grey coat was easily recognisable by race-going novices. 'Dessie' was a brave front runner and the only horse to have won the King George IV Chase four times, but his career highlight came in 1989.

Against all the odds – racing in heavy conditions and on a left-handed course – he overhauled the mud-loving Yahoo to win the Cheltenham Gold Cup.

The Irish steeplechaser Arkle is regarded by many to be the greatest horse of all time. He won consecutive Gold Cups from 1964 to 66 – his first against arch rival Mill House. He went on to record 27 wins in 34 races and was far and away the most famous racehorse of his day.

Apocryphal tales abounded of Arkle swigging Guinness twice a day. Tourists are said to have wanted to visit his stable at Greenogue more than to kiss the Blarney Stone. Someone scrawled 'Arkle for President' on a Dublin wall. Another racing great was Nijinsky, named after the Russian ballet dancer, who became in 1970 the first horse in 35 years to win the Triple Crown: the Two Thousand Guineas at Newmarket, the Epsom Derby and the St Leger Stakes.

The jockey Lester Piggott said of him: "Nijinsky possessed more natural ability than any horse I ever rode."

> ## SPORT SPOT
> The greatest number of Grand National finishers was 23 in 1984, with the fewest being just two in 1928.

The Nation's favourite horse: Desert Orchid raced from 1983 to 1991, winning 34 of his 71 races.

Left: Not once did Arkle fall over fences. As well as his Cheltenham treble, he won the King George VI Chase, the Irish Grand National and two Hennessy Gold Cups.

Above: Trained by the legendary Irishman Vincent O'Brien, Nijinsky went on to sire 1982 Derby winner Golden Fleece.

1973 **1974**

1977

Won, 2, 3 . . . Rummy wins Grand National again as fans go barmy

TRIPLE RUM!

Britain's fave horse wins THIRD National

THIS was the magical moment as Red Rum galloped into racing legend by winning the National for a record THIRD time.

Rummy first won Britain's greatest race in 1973. He did it again in 1974 and came second

From GEE UP at Aintree

in 1975 and last year. On Saturday he took the lead at Becher's Brook on the second circuit and never looked like being caught, finally romping home by 25 lengths before being

engulfed by a delirious mob. Some pundits wrote the 12-year-old off as too old to win the gruelling race again.

But jockey Tommy Stack said: "He made his intelligence count."

Britain's Biggest Star — Page 7

1980
COE'S GREAT TRIUMPH... & BRIT OLYMPIC HEROES

SEBASTIAN Coe's 1500m triumph at the Moscow Olympics in 1980 was redemption from the "cardinal sins" he admitted making in losing the 800m final to his greatest rival Steve Ovett days earlier. It was also a stunning act of vengeance for that shock defeat.

The outcome of both races had seemed entirely predictable. On paper, Coe was fastest over 800m and Ovett undefeated over 1500m in 42 races. But the pair had not raced each other for more than two years – they did so only seven times in all – which made their Moscow duel one of athletics' most eagerly anticipated clashes.

The two characters were poles apart, their contrasting backgrounds spicing up the rivalry. Coe, born into middle-class comfort, was the golden boy of British athletics and enjoyed the media attention. Ovett, a market trader's son, was less at ease in the spotlight and at times appeared aloof.

But it was Ovett, unfancied for the 800m, who drew first blood. The slow and untidy race did not suit Coe, who fell hopelessly out of position and became mired in the middle of the pack. Ovett had steered clear of trouble and with 200m to go began to kick for the tape – "Ovett in fourth place, those blue eyes like chips of ice", commentator David Coleman memorably remarked.

Coe was left with too much to do and Ovett sped away, even finding time to raise his arm triumphantly before crossing the line to take gold. Coe's extraordinary speed in the home straight saw him pass Nikolay Kirov of Russia to take silver – an amazing achievement considering he ran such a poor race.

Berated by his father and coach Peter for

SPORT SPOT
Seb Coe first ran against arch-rival Steve Ovett in a schoolboys' cross-country race in 1972. Neither of them won.

tactical ineptitude, Coe quickly regrouped. He was lucky, he told himself. He had a chance to put things right in the 1500m. Six days later he did just that, running a textbook race. Tucked in behind the leader on the final bend, Coe struck decisively for home. He hit the tape with his arms outstretched in one of athletics' most famous photos. Ovett could only finish third in his best event.

The Moscow Olympics were notable for the triumphs of other greats of British athletics besides Coe and Ovett. Allan Wells made the most of the USA team's boycott by winning gold in the 100m and beating Cuban favourite Silvio Leonard. The Scot, who also took silver in the 200m, remains the last white athlete to win the men's 100m.

During his career, Daley Thompson won eight gold medals including two consecutive Olympic golds (in 1980 and 1984) and broke the decathlon world record four times. He was unbeaten in major competitions for

Mary Peters was made a Dame Commander of the Order of the British Empire in the 2000 Queen's Birthday Honours List for her services to sport.

FRONT PAGE NEWS
1977 Star Wars released at cinemas
1978 Anna Ford becomes Britain's first female newsreader
1978 Space Invaders arcade game sweeps world
1979 Margaret Thatcher becomes first woman Prime Minister
1979 Soviet invasion of Afghanistan
1979 Debut of the Sony Walkman

Daley Thompson finishes the 1500m to take gold and a new decathlon world record at the European Athletic Championships in 1982.

nine years from 1979 to 1987. Only injury denied him an unprecedented third decathlon gold at Seoul in 1988. Even 15 years after his retirement, Thompson is regarded as the greatest ever all-round athlete.

Mary Peters not only won the pentathlon gold at Munich in 1972, she posted a world record score of 4,801 points. She remains the oldest woman, at 33, to win the pentathlon or its successor, the heptathlon, which Britain's Denise Lewis won at Sydney in 2000.

Rower Steve Redgrave sealed his title as Britain's greatest Olympian when he won his fifth consecutive gold at Sydney in 2000. He first won gold back in 1984 in the coxed fours in Los Angeles. He switched to the coxless pairs at Seoul in 1988 and won with partner Andy Holmes. The Barcelona Games of 1992 marked the beginning of his partnership with Matthew Pinsent, which saw them win there and in Atlanta in 1996. In 2000, Redgrave triumphed again in the coxless fours.

One of the greatest achievements ever by a British athlete came in 2004 at the Athens Olympics. After years of injury setbacks and with only a clutch of silver and bronze medals to show for her efforts, Kelly Holmes finally made the step up from good to great with two inspired runs to win gold in both the 800m and 1500m.

Left to right: Ovett, Cram and Coe, three of the greatest British middle-distance athletes ever, running in the 1500m Olympic final in Moscow.

Years of toil and injury melt away as Kelly Holmes becomes only the third woman in history to complete the 800m and 1500m Olympic double.

THE Sun

Saturday, August 2, 1980   12p

SIX DAYS AFTER THIS...

Done him . . Ovett wins the 800m

REVENGE

Moscow thriller as Seb nicks Steve's gold in the 1500m

By EVE ENSTEVEN, Athletics Correspondent

SEB Coe stormed to Olympic gold yesterday in a sensational act of revenge over Steve Ovett. The 23-year-old star won the 1500 metres in Moscow five days after Steve's stunning victory in Seb's best event, the 800 metres.

Steve, 24, the 1500m favourite and unbeaten for 42 races, could only manage bronze. Seb's victory vindicated his steely remark after losing in the 800m: "Tomorrow is another day. There will be another battle."

So Who's The Greatest — Back Page

1981 THE MODERN LEGENDS WHO DOMINATED TENNIS

FRONT PAGE NEWS

1980 John Lennon assassinated by Mark Chapman in New York

1980 "Psycho" film director Alfred Hitchcock dies aged 80

1980 Mount St Helens erupts in Washington, USA

1981 Race riots engulf British cities

1981 IRA prisoner Bobby Sands dies after a 66-day hunger strike

JOHN McEnroe's outbursts throughout the Wimbledon Championships of 1981 sealed his reputation as the enfant terrible of the tennis world. He is also one of the game's greatest players.

In defeating Bjorn Borg in the final 4-6, 7-6, 7-6, 6-4, McEnroe ended the Swede's record-breaking winning streak of 41 matches at the All-England Club and avenged the defeat he suffered a year earlier when Borg achieved his fifth consecutive Wimbledon title.

The 1981 season was a changing of the guard in world tennis. Borg had won his sixth and final French Open two months earlier – but he would never add to his tally of 11 Grand Slam titles and surprised everyone when he ended his nine-year career in 1983 at the age of 26.

For McEnroe it was the beginning of his reign as the world's best player. He won the US Open title later in 1981 and was the undisputed world No1 for just over a year.

But for all his successes McEnroe is still regarded by many tennis pundits to have underachieved. His tally of three Wimbledon and four US Open titles belied his supreme natural talent. When he wasn't arguing with an umpire, or chastising line judges or members of the crowd, he was capable of breathtaking tennis. McEnroe had it all: cross-court winners, backhand drives and a silky touch around the net. He preferred to play rather than practise, collecting a further nine major titles with doubles partner Peter Fleming and latterly Michael Stich.

McEnroe lost his Wimbledon title in 1982 to fellow American Jimmy Connors, the latter's second Wimbledon title and his sixth major title overall.

Connors had been world No1 from July 1974 to August 1977. His great strength was his competitiveness – he

Above: Bjorn Borg sinks to his knees after defeating John McEnroe in the 1980 Wimbledon final – his fifth successive win.
Right: Still in his 20s, Roger Federer has the chance to become the greatest player of any era.

liked nothing better than a scrap. He wasn't the most powerful or elegant player on the circuit, but he was probably the fittest ... he won his fifth US Open title in 1983 aged 31. Connors' rise in the early 1970s coincided with a general boom in the popularity of tennis, and his jovial asides and willingness to engage with the crowd won him many fans.

As McEnroe and Connors faded, their place was taken by 17-year-old German Boris Becker who became the youngest person and the first unseeded player to win Wimbledon. Nicknamed "boom boom" on account of a ferocious serve, Becker was equally at home in at the net, leaping and diving acrobatically. In all he won six Grand Slam titles – three Wimbledons, two Australian Opens and one US Open. Becker's last win at Wimbledon came in 1989.

The 1990s were dominated by the American Pete Sampras, who won 12 of his 14 Grand

Slam titles during that decade. Sampras took grass court tennis to a new level, combining the old and new styles, sometimes powering his way to points from the baseline, other times playing a serve-and-volley game. It was an irresistible combination which won him a record seven Wimbledon titles. In his quest to win an eighth and fifth consecutive Wimbledon title in 2001, Sampras was beaten in the fourth round by Roger Federer, from Switzerland, who has since cemented his place as an all-time great, having won 10 Grand Slam titles in just 31 appearances. He is one of the most elegant players of any era.

From the late 1970s, the women's game was dominated by Martina Navratilova, a Czech-born US citizen. Her record of nine Wimbledon singles titles – including six straight victories from 1982-87 – confirmed her place as the greatest grass court women's player of all time. She won a total of 18 Grand Slam singles and 31 doubles titles. It appeared inconceivable that her singles record would ever be broken. But along came the German Steffi Graf, who won 22 career Grand Slam finals – seven Wimbledons, six French Opens, five US Opens and four Australian Opens.

SPORT SPOT

American Jeff Tarango stormed off court at Wimbledon in 1995, calling the umpire "corrupt". Tarango's wife Benedicte slapped the hapless official for good measure.

Jimmy Connors won eight Grand Slam titles and was World No1 for three years consecutively from 1974 to 1977.

Left: In addition to her 18 Grand Slam singles titles, Martina Navratilova won 31 doubles finals during a 34-year career.
Below: Steffi Graf completed the Grand Slam and won tennis gold at the Seoul Olympics in 1988.

Becker makes a characteristic dive for a volley at Wimbledon in 1993.

THE Sun

Tuesday, June 23, 1981   12p

Volley of abuse . . . McEnroe yells 'You cannot be serious'

Got the 'ump . . . Brat brands Ted 'pits'

By RUUD GITT

TENNIS "superbrat" John McEnroe disgraced Wimbledon yesterday with an obscene on-court rant at officials.

The spoiled Yank branded umpire Ted James "the pits of the world" when a line call went against him.

He screamed: "You cannot be serious!" and smashed his racquet.

He then called tournament ref Fred Hoyles "a ****". McEnroe, 22, a finalist last year, faces a big fine.

That Disgusting Rant In Full — Page 9

What a racket!

SUPERBRAT'S VILE RANT

1981 ASHES GLORY THAT MADE BEEFY BOTHAM IMMORTAL

"IT was the summer of summers for England," said cricket commentator Richie Benaud of the 1981 "Botham's Ashes" series against Australia. Rarely has cricket, and in particular one player, captured English hearts so emphatically.

The summer's gloomy start made for its fairytale ending. The winter tour to the West Indies had been long, difficult and controversial. Ian Botham returned home exhausted and unsure of his future as captain. His appointment on a match-to-match basis merely heaped on the pressure.

England lost the first Test at Trent Bridge by six wickets and drew the second at Lords. It was Botham's final match as captain. When Australian spinner Ray Bright bowled him around his legs to complete a pair of ducks, he returned to the pavilion in near silence. At the end of the match Botham announced he was stepping down and suggested Mike Brearley replace him.

The Middlesex captain was duly installed. The hope was that Botham, England's greatest ever all-rounder, would return to form once unburdened of leadership duties.

Brearley's genius for man management - he is now a psychoanalyst - brought out the best in "Beefy" Botham, who began to show signs of his old self. He took six wickets for 95 in Australia's first innings 401 at Headingley, then smashed 50 in England's paltry reply of 174. Australia enforced the follow-on.

Requiring 222 to avoid an innings defeat,

Above: England were given odds of 500-1 after being made to follow-on in the Test at Headingley which England won by 18 runs. Australians Dennis Lillee and Rodney Marsh bet on England.

England were given odds of 500-1 to win the match. When they collapsed again to 135 for 7, it was as good as over.

Botham was joined at the crease by tailender Graham Dilley, and suggested they "give it a whack and see what happens". In just over an hour they blazed a 100 partnership. Dilley departed for 56, but Botham continued peppering all corners of the ground with fours and sixes. "That's gone straight into the confectionary stall and out again," Benaud told BBC TV viewers. Botham's pyrotechnics gave England a lead of 130 and a sniff of the most improbable victory.

The next morning England fast bowler Bob Willis ran in like a man possessed, taking wicket after wicket to post career-best figures of 8 for 43. Australia were skittled for 111. "It is one of the most fantastic victories ever known in Test cricket history," said the astonished Benaud, a former Australian captain. The defeat did lasting damage to the Australians, who were for years vulnerable chasing small targets.

Botham repeated his magic in the next

Above: Ian Botham yorks Terry Alderman, sealing victory and another sensational turnaround for England in the fourth Test at Edgbaston.

Test at Edgbaston. By the fourth day Australia needed 151 to win and were edging their way towards their target at 105 for 5. Botham seized the ball and in front of a delirious crowd took 5 wickets for 1 run off 28 deliveries. With Terry Alderman clean bowled and Australia all out for 121, Botham raised a stump in triumph and charged off the pitch before the joyous crowd could engulf him.

Botham was still not done. On the Saturday

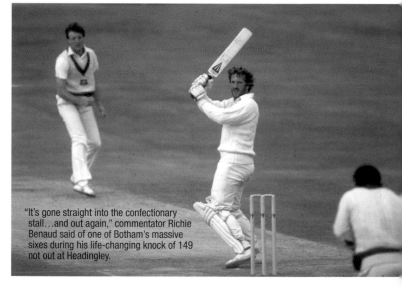

"It's gone straight into the confectionary stall…and out again," commentator Richie Benaud said of one of Botham's massive sixes during his life-changing knock of 149 not out at Headingley.

afternoon of the fifth Test at Old Trafford, he strode to the crease with England on a precarious 104 for 5. Just 86 balls later he had smashed another glorious hundred, which the commentator Jim Laker described as "the most spectacular Test match hundred I have ever seen".

The Aussies were vanquished 3-1, and Botham's hero status was secure forever. It took 26 years – and millions of pounds raised for charity – before "Beefy" was knighted. But there are those who would have handed it to him there and then, in the late summer of 1981.

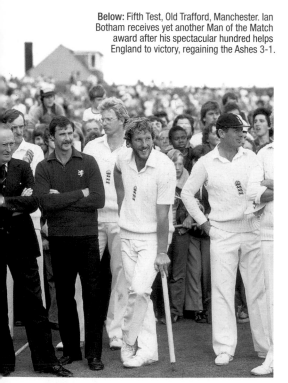

Below: Fifth Test, Old Trafford, Manchester. Ian Botham receives yet another Man of the Match award after his spectacular hundred helps England to victory, regaining the Ashes 3-1.

NOW JUMP TO... ○ SHANE WARNE page 128 ○ GARRY SOBERS page 88

SunSport sees Headingley miracle

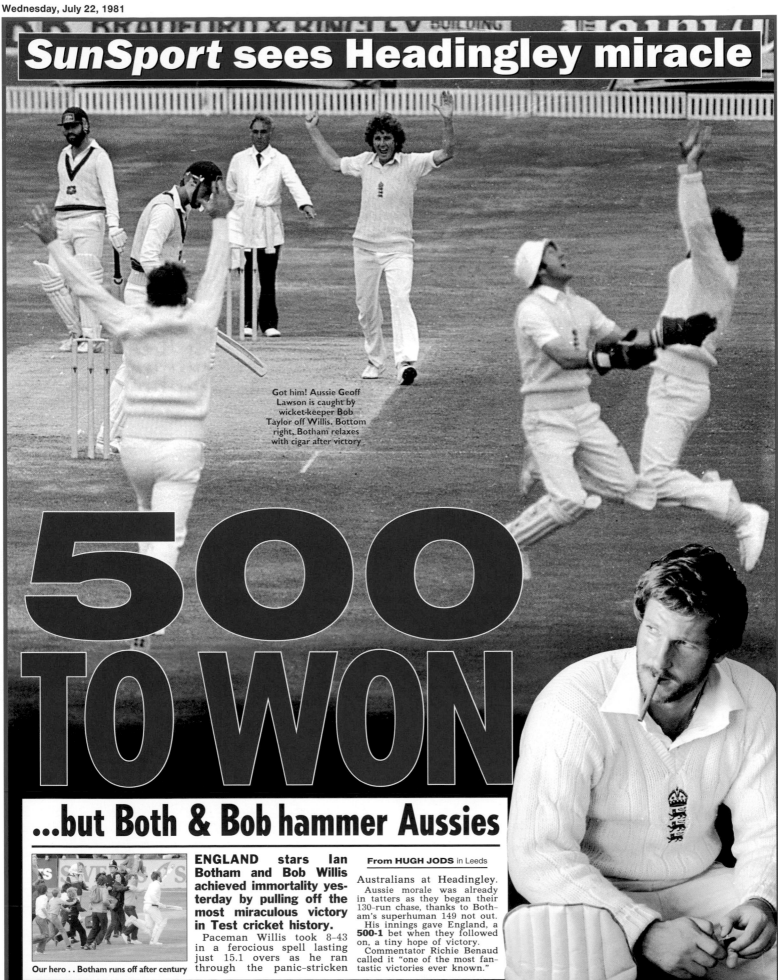

Got him! Aussie Geoff Lawson is caught by wicket-keeper Bob Taylor off Willis. Bottom right, Botham relaxes with cigar after victory

500 TO WON

...but Both & Bob hammer Aussies

Our hero .. Botham runs off after century

ENGLAND stars Ian Botham and Bob Willis achieved immortality yesterday by pulling off the most miraculous victory in Test cricket history.

Paceman Willis took 8-43 in a ferocious spell lasting just 15.1 overs as he ran through the panic-stricken

From HUGH JODS in Leeds

Australians at Headingley.

Aussie morale was already in tatters as they began their 130-run chase, thanks to Botham's superhuman 149 not out.

His innings gave England, a **500-1** bet when they followed on, a tiny hope of victory.

Commentator Richie Benaud called it "one of the most fantastic victories ever known."

GIVE 'EM A KNIGHTHOOD: PAGES 74-75

1982 DARTS: FROM PUB GAME TO TV PHENOMENON

Darts became popular in British pubs in the early 20th Century. This picture was taken in a Sheffield working men's club in 1961

Eric Bristow was the dominant player and character in darts during the 1980s and raised the profile of the game.

DARTS has a longer association with drinking than you might think. The first games were played by soldiers in the Middle Ages who, to alleviate boredom, threw arrows at upturned beer barrels.

Soon cross-sections of trees were used as targets, their concentric rings making the task of determining a winner much easier. The game became popular with the nobility and it is said that in 1530 Anne Boleyn presented Henry VIII – a man with the physique of a darts player – with an ornate set of darts.

Darts as we know it took off in the late part of the 19th Century. The numbering system on the board was invented by Brian Gamlin, a carpenter from Bury, in 1896. The paper flight was patented by the turn of the century.

The origin of the throwing distance and the word "oche" is debatable. The story goes that a brewery, Hockey and Sons, based in south-west England, established the accepted throwing distance of 8ft by placing four 2ft beer crates end to end. Over time "Hockey" was shortened to "oc-kee" and eventually to "oche". It is a neat and convenient history, but almost certainly apocryphal. In truth no one is really sure where the term comes from. In any case, the standard international throwing distance is 7ft 9¼ inches. Darts quickly became synonymous with the pub, but it was considered by some local authorities to be a game of chance, not skill, and was banned on the basis that it encouraged gambling.

In 1908 Jim Garside, landlord of The Adelphi pub in Leeds, was taken to court for allowing darts. He argued it was a game of skill and arrived at the hearing with a dartboard and the best player he could find, William "Bigfoot" Annakin. By hitting a selection of the numbered segments chosen by the judge, Annakin convinced him darts did indeed require skill, and it was allowed to continue at The Adelphi.

Phil Taylor, the greatest darts player ever, only took the game up aged 25.

Once, almost every pub in the land had a dartboard but today, with the rise of the gastro pub, the figure has dropped to around 50 per cent.

Darts thrived in the early 20th Century. The News of the World tournament, launched in 1927, quickly became the one every player wanted to win. By 1947 it was attracting nearly 300,000 entrants.

But it wasn't until the 1970s that darts' profile was raised through TV. The British Darts Organisation (BDO) was established in 1973 and matches began to be televised with the now customary split-screen. The first world championship was held in 1978 and won by Leighton Rees. In 1985 it moved to Lakeside, near Camberley in Surrey. Millions tuned in to watch the "Crafty Cockney" Eric Bristow dominate the championship, claiming five world titles.

Bristow, Jocky Wilson and John Lowe dominated darts in 1980s and became household names.

In 1990, Phil "The Power" Taylor took over as the undisputed master, winning the first of his 13 world championships and beating his mentor Bristow 6-1 in the final. In 1992, with other top players, he broke away from the BDO to join the newly-created Professional Darts Corporation (PDC). Darts has not looked back.

FRONT PAGE NEWS

1982	Britain beats Argentina in war over the Falklands
1982	Princess Grace of Monaco (film actress Grace Kelly) is killed in a car crash
1982	The compact disc goes on sale for the first time
1982	Michael Fagan breaks into the Queen's bedroom at Buckingham Palace
1982	Channel 4 is launched
1982	ET is massive movie hit

THE Sun

Monday, January 18, 1982   14p

TREBLE TOP
DOUBLE TOP
LAGER TOP
501 essential darts phrases —
Page One Hundred and Eighty

Booze a clever boy, then . . .
Jocky is darts king of world

WINNER ON PINTS
Boozy Jocky is world darts champ

Jocky on oche
. . . he throws

LEGENDARY boozer Jocky Wilson was the King of Darts last night — as the new world champion.

The 20-stone Scot, who calms his nerves with pints of lager plus "seven or eight" vodkas, beat

By BILL SYE, Darts Correspondent

John Lowe 5-3 at the Jollees Cabaret Club in Stoke. Jocky, 31, whose last tooth fell out at 28 through eating sweets, intends to

spend some of his £6,500 winnings on DENTURES. The ex-miner from Fife once said: "I'm short and fat. So what? That's life!"

Last night he said only this of his triumph: "I've done it!"

SUPER, SMASHING, LOVELY: BACK PAGE

1983 SHERGAR: WHEN SPORT AND POLITICS COLLIDE

POLITICS and sport have often collided with explosive results. The kidnapping of Shergar is one of the most notorious examples.

Nicknamed "the wonderhorse", Shergar was the finest flat racer of his day. In 1981 he won the Epsom Derby by a massive ten lengths and then claimed the Irish Derby, King George VI stakes and the Queen Elizabeth stakes before being put out to stud.

His kidnapping came after only one breeding season. On the night of February 8th, 1983, his abductors, almost certainly the IRA, raided the house of Shergar's groom Jim Fitzgerald at the Aga Khan's Ballymany Stud Farm in County Kildare, Ireland.

Shergar was taken from his stable and driven away in a horsebox. A £2million ransom demand was received hours later. The Aga Khan hired an ex-SAS soldier to negotiate with the kidnappers, but after four days contact was lost. It is thought this was when Shergar was killed.

Tales of the horse's fate abounded for years, with theories implicating the Mafia or even Colonel Gadaffi's Libya. Former IRA member turned informer Sean O'Callaghan later claimed Shergar was killed by his IRA abductors soon after he was taken because they could not handle him.

The controversy over cricketer Basil D'Oliveira had profound international consequences. He first came to England from South Africa in 1960, where under apartheid he was barred from first-class cricket. By 1964 he had joined Worcestershire and in 1966, after becoming a British citizen, he played his first game for England.

A talented all-rounder, D'Oliveira scored 158 in the final Test of the summer against the Australians in 1968 and was a shoo-in for selection for the forthcoming tour to South

Left: "I am not saying anything, I am just trying to play cricket with the best in the world." Basil D'Oliveira maintained a dignified silence throughout the South Africa tour debacle in 1968 and helped show the outside world what apartheid really was.

Africa. But the MCC didn't pick him, citing the limp excuse that his bowling was ill-suited to South African pitches. In reality, the MCC had been pressurised by the South African government to omit D'Oliveira because non-whites were banned from professional sport there.

Three weeks later D'Oliveira was drafted into the squad when another bowler was injured. South Africa protested and the tour was eventually scrapped. But the affair had positive consequences. It highlighted the barbaric nature of white rule in South Africa and led to a worldwide sporting boycott of the country which was only lifted in 1991 at the end of apartheid.

One of the most powerful political gestures in sporting history came at the 1968 Mexico Olympics when black American athletes Tommie Smith and John Carlos gave their famous "black power" salute.

Discrimination and segregation were still widespread in America. In April that year riots had erupted when civil rights leader Martin Luther King was murdered in Memphis. Having won gold and bronze in the 200 metres, Smith and Carlos took to the victory podium dressed in black,

SPORT SPOT
Insurers never paid out to Shergar's owners, claiming the horse could still have been alive after the policy expired.

each with a black scarf, black socks and a single black glove. As the national anthem started, they raised their fists in a silent salute to the black citizens of America. The International Olympic Committee made the bewildering decision to expel them from the games.

The most famous demonstration by the suffragette movement came at a race meeting. Emily Davison was a militant member of the Women's Social and Political Union, founded by Emmeline Pankhurst, which campaigned to give women the vote. In 1913 Davison was killed throwing herself in front of King George V's horse Amner at the Epsom Derby. Women were granted full voting rights in 1928.

Above: "The best racehorse I ever rode" said Walter Swinburn, who rode Shergar in the record-breaking win at the Epsom Derby in 1981.

Tommie Smith and John Carlos on the podium at the 1968 Olympics. The pair were roundly condemned for the "silent gesture". Smith would later comment: "We were not Antichrists. We were just human beings who saw a need to be recognised."

Above: Suffragette Emily Davison (far left) is fatally injured when she runs in front of Amner – a horse owned by King George V – during the 1913 Epsom Derby.

FRONT PAGE NEWS

THE Sun

RUNNERS AND RIDERS
1. THE IRA
2. GADAFFI
3. THE MOB
4. LORD LUCAN

Wednesday, February 9, 1983   15p

Hoofdunnit?

£2M RANSOM   BID FOR SHERGAR

By KIT NAPPER

TOP racehorse Shergar was **KIDNAPPED** last night by six masked gunmen demanding a ransom of £2million.

The runaway winner of the 1981 Epsom Derby was abducted from a stud farm in Ireland.

The gang held head groom James Fitzgerald at gunpoint and made him load Shergar into a horse box attached to a Ford Granada.

Fitzgerald was also taken hostage, then freed four hours later with a ransom note.

Last night fingers were pointing at the IRA as the culprits.

But Chief Superintendent Jim Murphy, leading the investigation, admitted: "A clue . . . that is what we haven't got."

Race To Find Him — Pages 4 & 5

Legend of the track . . . Shergar in action

He's bolted . . . empty stable

1985 SNOOKER: ARMY GAME TO KEEP MILLIONS ENGROSSED

FRONT PAGE NEWS

1984 Indian Prime Minister Indira Gandhi assassinated

1984 IRA bombs Grand Hotel, Brighton, narrowly missing PM Margaret Thatcher

1984 Leak of toxic gas from insecticide plant at Bhopal, India, kills 2,500

1985 Mikhail Gorbachev takes power in the USSR

1985 Live Aid concerts in London and Philadelphia raise more than £40m for Africa

IT took snooker a little more than a century to evolve from a game thought up at a British Army station in southern India to a national obsession which has enthralled colossal TV audiences.

In 1875, a British colonel stationed in the Nilgiri Hills, Sir Neville Bowes Chamberlain, merged two games. They were Pyramids – played with a triangle of 15 reds – and Life Pool – a multi-player game using a variety of coloured balls. The result was "Snooker's Pool".

The name derived from its popularity with new Army cadets – "snookers" in military slang. The game soon caught on back home, with snooker sets produced by the John Roberts Billiard Supply Company. The first rules were written by the Billiards Association in 1900 and by 1916 the first Amateur English Championship was under way.

The first professional championship was held in 1927. Joe Davis beat Tom Dennis 20-11 in the final and went on to win every world championship until he retired in 1946. He, more than anyone, popularised the game among players and spectators.

Joe's younger brother Fred won the championship three times in 1948, 1949 and 1951.

Disputes between the players and the governing body – the Billiards Association and Control Council – led to the world championship not being staged between 1958-63. But the introduction of colour TV in the late

Billiards was a popular activity among British Army officers stationed in India and variations on the game were devised.

1960s provided snooker with a much-needed shot in the arm. The BBC launched the TV programme 'Pot Black', which proved hugely popular and snooker began to flourish. Ray Reardon dominated the sport in the 1970s, winning six world titles.

In 1977, the world championship found a permanent home at the Crucible Theatre in Sheffield, which has staged it ever since.

Snooker audiences grew and grew in the 1980s, with Steve Davis equalling Reardon's record of six world titles. Canada's Cliff Thorburn, who won the title in 1980, recorded the Crucible's first 147 maximum break in 1983.

Flair players like Alex Higgins (two world titles) and Jimmy White (famously no world titles from six finals) did much to attract viewers. Higgins' masterful match-saving break of 69 against White in the 1982 world

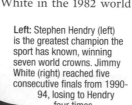
Above: Joe Davis, snooker's first real superstar, also won four world professional billiards titles.

SPORT SPOT

The longest match in Crucible history lasted 13 hours. Cliff Thorburn and Terry Griffiths finished their second-round match at 3.51am. Thorburn won 13-12.

championship semi-final is one of snooker's most memorable moments.

But it was the 1985 final that will always be remembered as the greatest match in world championship history.

Never were the whispered tones of veteran snooker commentator Ted Lowe heard by so many as more than 18.5 million viewers stayed up until 12.30am to watch Northern Ireland's Dennis Taylor sink the final black and complete a match that had lasted nearly 15 hours. Taylor had trailed 8-0 after the first session, but fought back to level the scores at 17 frames apiece before taking the electrifying decider. Davis was devastated but continued to dominate the game until Scotland's Stephen Hendry emerged. So far Hendry has won a record seven world titles and compiled more than 700 competitive century breaks.

The game has recently seen an influx of highly talented young players, such that no one player has been able to dominate. There have been five different world champions since 2000, with Ronnie O'Sullivan – arguably the most gifted snooker player ever – emerging as the biggest draw.

Left: Stephen Hendry (left) is the greatest champion the sport has known, winning seven world crowns. Jimmy White (right) reached five consecutive finals from 1990-94, losing to Hendry four times.

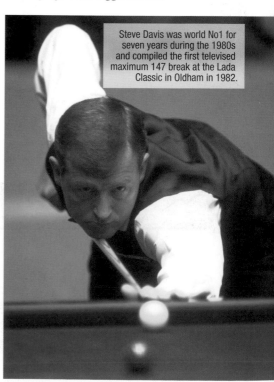
Steve Davis was world No1 for seven years during the 1980s and compiled the first televised maximum 147 break at the Lada Classic in Oldham in 1982.

SunSport special from Crucible

SNOOKER DROOPY!

19m bleary-eyed after Taylor grabs title in early hours

By MAX BREAK

BRITAIN is waking up bleary-eyed today after staying up past midnight to witness snooker's greatest thriller ever.

Almost 19million people watched on BBC2 at 12.19am as Dennis Taylor snatched the world title from Steve Davis.

Taylor, 35, won by 18 frames to 17 after potting the black in the nail-biting decider at the Crucible in Sheffield.

It crowned his stunning comeback from 8-0 down. Davis (below) said only: "It was all there in black and white."

I've Den It — See Pages 76-77

Cue celebrations.. after deciding pot

Taylor made for me . . . with trophy

1986 GOLF'S GREATEST PLAYER & HIS YOUNG CHALLENGER

Named "Rookie of the Year" in 1962, Nicklaus not only claimed the US Open but also the then prestigious World Series of Golf title.

Nicklaus celebrates his third and final Open victory in 1978 at St Andrews. The win also gave him the triple career slam.

IT had been six years since Jack Nicklaus had won a Major title (the 1980 USPGA) and at 46 nobody expected him to win another. No one except Nicklaus.

His sixth US Masters title and his 18th Major Championship win was the fairytale ending to an unparalleled golfing career.

Nicklaus was born on January 21st 1940 in Columbus, Ohio. His father introduced him to sports and he learned his golf at the Scioto Country Club. As an amateur, Nicklaus was clearly a prodigy and in 1959, aged 19, he won the U.S. Amateur title. He regained it at Pebble Beach in 1961 and in between tied for second place at the 1960 US Open – one of 19 occasions when Nicklaus finished second in major championships.

By the time he turned pro in 1962, Nicklaus had mastered all the technical aspects of the game. Capable of explosive shot-making as well as unerring discipline, Nicklaus allied this natural talent to a rock solid temperament that allowed him to adjust quickly and decisively at pivotal moments during a round.

His first Major win came at the 1962 US Open at the Oakmont Country Club. By 1967, he had won six more – winning all four Majors at least once. The 1970s yielded a further eight titles. But after winning two more majors in 1980, it was thought time was running out for 40-year-old Nicklaus to add to his tally, which then stood at five Masters, four US Opens, three British Opens and five USPGAs.

And so it proved for six more years until the 1986 Masters, where he confounded the rule that Augusta National was a golf course for young players.

His physical powers may have been on the wane, but mentally Nicklaus was as fresh as ever. In carding a final round 65, Nicklaus put together a scintillating back nine to win his sixth Masters by one stroke, beating the likes of Seve Ballesteros and Greg Norman. He described his 18th major victory as "by far the

SPORT SPOT

Tiger Woods was just 11 months old when he first started swinging a sawn-off golf club in his dad's garage in California.

Jack Nicklaus waving farewell to major championship golf from the Swilken Bridge at St Andrews in 2005. He played in 163 majors over 46 years.

most fulfilling achievement of my career". It was one of the greatest swansongs in sport and reconfirmed Nicklaus as the finest player of them all. No one would ever get close to the achievements of the "Golden Bear", it seemed. But then along came Tiger.

Eleven years after Nicklaus made history at the Masters, 21-year-old Tiger Woods sent out a clarion call marking his arrival on the golf scene. He was the youngest ever Masters champion and won by 12 shots with the lowest 72-hole score in Masters history. His fellow professionals shuddered at having to compete with him. Even Nicklaus conceded that Woods, with his power off the tee and his touch around the greens, could win ten times at Augusta.

On the back of that stunning victory in 1997 it was predicted Woods would win Major titles at a canter. That proved wide of the mark, as he took time to settle and mature into the role of the world's most famous sportsman. His second Major victory – the USPGA – came 2½ years later in 1999.

Since 2000, however, his record has been a staggering 11 wins in 29 starts, winning each of the four Majors at least twice. Only the great amateur Bobby Jones had a better winning ratio. In 2006, Woods surpassed Walter Hagen's total of 11 Majors when he won his third USPGA. He won his 13th in August 2007. Only Nicklaus remains ahead of him.

The next ten years will tell if Tiger can track down the Golden Bear to become the greatest golfer the world has ever seen.

Tiger Woods holes out on the 18th green to win the 2005 US Masters. Moments earlier, on the par 3 16th, he played perhaps the greatest chip shot in Masters history.

Tiger in 2004 with father Earl, who spotted and nurtured his talent when he was just a toddler. The retired U.S. Army lieutenant colonel died in 2006

FRONT PAGE NEWS

1985 Reductions of up to 70 per cent in the ozone layer observed over Antarctica

1985 Crush during Liverpool football match at Heysel Stadium, Brussels, kills 39

1985 Blaze at Bradford City football ground kills 56

1985 EastEnders launches on the BBC

1985 Sir Clive Sinclair launches his C5 buggy

1986 Chernobyl nuclear power disaster kills thousands in Soviet Union

THE Sun

Monday, April 14, 1986   16p

UNDISPUTED MASTER

Nicklaus crowns comeback
with his 18th Major...at 46

By DON RITEMIOFF

JACK Nicklaus, the greatest golfer of all time, sealed his fairytale comeback yesterday by winning the US Masters aged 46.

The American veteran began the day four shots adrift of the leader, Australia's Greg Norman.

But he completed the last nine holes at Augusta, Georgia, in just 30 shots to finish seven under par, pipping Norman by one stroke. It is his sixth Masters victory and the 18th Major title of an amazing career that began with a US Open victory back in 1962.

Nicklaus, from Columbus, Ohio, had not won a Major since 1980. And he admitted he was spurred on when a journalist recently branded him "washed-up".

Nicklaus said last night: "I kept thinking all week, 'Washed-up, huh? I've played too well for too long to let a shorter period of bad golf be my last'."

Yes! Nicklaus celebrates a birdie at the 17th hole

I did it . . . in winner's jacket, with ex-champ Bernhard Langer

I'M IN GOOD NICK: BACK PAGE

1986 THE HAND OF GOD...AND OTHER FOOTBALL CHEATS

FOUR minutes apart, at the Azteca Stadium in Mexico City in 1986, Diego Maradona scored two of the most memorable goals of all time: One, a blatant and forever infamous act of cheating. The other, now acknowledged as the greatest in World Cup history.

England's World Cup campaign under Bobby Robson had started badly. A surprise 1-0 loss to Portugal in the first group game was followed by a goalless draw against Morocco. But two 3-0 wins against Poland and Paraguay sent expectations soaring before the fateful quarter-final with Argentina.

In blisteringly hot noon sunshine Argentina made the stronger start, but a quiet first half ended goalless. The second half was only six minutes old when 25-year-old Maradona

so the Argentine stuck out his left arm and punched the ball into the open goal. To the horror of England's players, the Tunisian referee Ali Bennaceur awarded the goal. Maradona couldn't believe his luck.

The indignation of English players, fans and even commentators was nullified minutes later. Ten yards inside his own half, Maradona danced and spun out of two challenges and began his charge towards England's penalty area. He went past Peter Reid, Terry Butcher and Terry Fenwick before showing the ball to an advancing Shilton, only to drag it past him. Butcher's despairing tackle was too late and Maradona side-footed the

Brazilian Rivaldo clutches his face in what is by common consent the worst dive in football history. Hit on the legs by a ball passed to him by Hakan Unsal of Turkey during the 2002 World Cup, Rivaldo pretended it had hit him in the face and fell to the ground. Unsal was sent off.

SPORT SPOT

After a decade of cocaine and drink addiction, and surgery to combat morbid obesity, a svelte Maradona announced in 2007 he had quit alcohol and drugs.

notorious act of cheating in football history, but there are plenty of rivals.

Trailing a rampant Brazil in a World Cup qualifier in 1989, Chilean goalkeeper Roberto Rojas hurled himself at a smoking firework thrown on to the pitch by Brazilian fans and lying near his goal. He writhed on the ground, clutching his face and pretending the firework had hit him, then gashed his own head for extra effect using a razor blade he had hidden in his glove. The idea was to get the game abandoned and force a replay or Brazil's disqualification. It almost worked, but video evidence exposed him as a cheat.

Tales of football skulduggery wouldn't be complete without a mention of the now widespread art of diving. The most prolific modern exponent was Tottenham Hotspur's German star Jurgen Klinsmann, who even made fun of himself by incorporating a dive into his goal celebrations.

Probably the most appalling dive ever came from the Brazilian Rivaldo at a World Cup match against Turkey in 2002 in front of millions of TV viewers. He got an opponent sent off by collapsing, clutching his face as though shot, after a ball hit him in the shin.

Above: Having cut through England's defence Diego Maradona prepares to round goalkeeper Peter Shilton and score one of the greatest goals of all time.

performed his first trick. England defender Steve Hodge sliced a looping pass back to goalkeeper Peter Shilton, forcing him to run out and punch it clear.

Maradona ran forward and leapt in the air. He was just over 5ft 5ins, his head no threat to the outstretched fist of 6ft 1ins Shilton,

ball into the net. In an instant, disgust at Maradona's dishonesty was transformed into a grudging respect for his genius. TV's Barry Davies summed it up: "Oh! You have to say that's magnificent," he said.

Gary Lineker scored later, but England were beaten 2-1 and out of the World Cup. At a press conference, Maradona said his first goal was scored 'un poco con la cabeza de Maradona y otro poco con la mano de Dios' (a little with the head of Maradona and a little with the hand of God).

It is without doubt the most

Airborne, left: Jurgen Klinsmann – the worst serial diver of all time.

FRONT PAGE NEWS

1986 Halley's Comet visible from Earth for the first time in 76 years

1986 Space shuttle Challenger explodes 72 seconds after take-off from Florida, killing all seven crew

1986 Pop artist Andy Warhol dies shortly after a routine gall-bladder operation

1986 London Stock Exchange experiences "Big Bang" as Government implements deregulation of financial markets

1986 Clint Eastwood elected Mayor of Carmel, California

1986 Mike Tyson becomes youngest world heavyweight champ at 20

NOW JUMP TO... ◐ SPORTING CHEATS page 106 ◐ WG GRACE page 42

SunSport: ARGENTINA 2 ENGLAND 1

GOTTA HAND IT TO HIM

51mins: Cheating Maradona punches ball into our net...
55mins: He scores greatest goal ever

DIRTY Diego Maradona dumped England out of the World Cup yesterday with his HAND.

The cheating Argie, 25, then had the brass neck to claim his "goal" was scored by the "Hand of God".

But the little striker also scored possibly the finest **REAL** goal ever.

The handball came six minutes into the quarter-

From ROB DUSS in Mexico City

final's second half. Maradona leapt above goalie Peter Shilton and punched the ball into the net. Incredibly the Tunisian ref let it stand.

Four minutes later Maradona won the ball in his own half and spun past or dodged most of our team before kicking the ball ten yards into the net.

England boss Bobby Robson said after our 2-1 defeat: "That first goal was dubious. The second one was a miracle."

BOBBY: WE WUZ ROBBED, SON: PAGES 66-67

Sleight of hand . . . he fists ball past Shilton and it's 1-0

Dodgy character . . . Maradona weaves past England stars including Gary Lineker before scoring for 2-0

1993 WARNEY: PHENOMENON OF MODERN-DAY CRICKET

FRONT PAGE NEWS

1987 Herald of Free Enterprise ferry capsizes off Belgium, killing 193

1988 Lockerbie disaster kills 270 as terrorists bomb Boeing 747 in mid-air

1989 Hillsborough disaster leaves 95 dead

1989 Fall of Berlin Wall paves way for German reunification

1990 Nelson Mandela is released after 27 years in prison in South Africa

1991 First Gulf War begins

1993 Division of Czechoslovakia into Czech and Slovak Republics

FROM the moment he delivered the "ball of the century" to a dumbstruck Mike Gatting at Old Trafford in June 1993, Shane Warne cast a spell over Test batsmen the world over.

His dominance would last 14 years and establish him as probably the greatest bowler in history. The spiky blonde Australian single-handedly revived the dying art of leg-spin and inspired countless youngsters to take up the game.

Only the start of Warne's Test career could be described as ordinary. On his debut against India in 1992, he returned figures of 45-7-150-1, and took an unremarkable 25 wickets in his first ten Tests.

His transformation from a good young prospect into a superstar happened overnight. The ball to Gatting was the first he had delivered against England. It drifted in the air, pitching about 18 inches outside leg stump, before turning sharply, evading Gatting's outstretched pad and bat and clipping the top of his off stump. Gatting was one of the world's best players of spin. His astonished expression memorably conveyed both his shock and that of everyone watching. He looked like someone had stolen his lunch, England legend Graham Gooch said later.

Warne belied his appearance as an Aussie beach bum. Beneath his peroxide blonde hair, he possessed an acutely sharp cricketing brain. He is often mentioned as the best cap-

Above: "Sledging is an acceptable part of gamesmanship and I think I'm pretty good at it," Warne once remarked. He was also an highly exuberant appealer.

SPORT SPOT

When he was eight, Warne broke both legs and was on crutches for a year, something he believes contributed to his strong shoulders and wrists.

tain Australia never had. His skill with a ball was unrivalled. He could extract prodigious turn from the most unhelpful of surfaces and had a variety of equally confusing deliveries: The flipper, the googly, the top-spinner and the slider.

Warne's great technical skill was allied to a fiercely competitive nature, making his prolonged spells of bowling a spectacle in their own right. If he wasn't making animated appeals for an lbw or a catch, he was chirping away at the batsmen to break their concentration. He would quiz umpires about lbws, move fielders, consult his captain. He was always in the thick of it.

Warne was also a great survi-

Below: Warne bowling in the first Test at Lords in the 2005 Ashes series – his last in England. Warne finished it with 40 wickets at an average of 19.92.

vor. In his private life, he weathered a series of lurid scandals. He also had reconstructive surgery on his right shoulder in 2000 and dislocated it two years later against England. He broke one of his spinning fingers in 2000 and received a one-year ban in February 2003 for taking the banned diuretic drug Moduretic. Each time, he returned stronger, hungrier and often fitter. Even a fine for receiving money from a bookmaker during the 1994-95 tour to Pakistan and Sri Lanka failed to dent his reputation.

Warne was a useful lower-order batsman too. He mixed orthodox shot-making with unashamed slogging, infuriating the bowling side and rubbing salt into wounds that, more often than not, he himself had inflicted with the ball. He holds the record for scoring the most runs in Test cricket (3,154 at an average of 17.2) without a century – his highest score of 99 was against New Zealand in 2001.

Warne completed his career, aged 37, after the Ashes in January 2007, finishing with 708 wickets at an average of 25.41. Ashes battles seemed to bring out the best in him. In all he took 195 wickets in 36 matches, recording his best Test figures of 8-71 at Brisbane in 1994.

Many English cricket fans had mixed feelings about Warne's retirement from Tests. English batsmen, and those of all Test-playing nations, were glad to see the back of him.

Below: Warne swigs champagne on the dressing room balcony after yet another victory over England in 1997.

Gatt looked like somebody had nicked his lunch

SEE BACK PAGE

WARNEING

By PADDY DUPP

YOUNG Aussie cricketer Shane Warne bowled Mike Gatting yesterday with a ball that defied physics. His first delivery in Ashes Tests bounced 18 inches outside leg stump and spun back to hit off. Warne, 23, then got two other top batsmen out. A traumatised England insider said: "I've never seen anything like it."

Here it comes . . . ball drifts towards leg

Got it . . Gatt shapes to play as it pitches

Eh? Ball turns a mile to hit his off stump

This Aussie can SERIOUSLY damage your batting line-up

1994
SCHUMACHER, HILL, HUNT...
SUPERSTARS IN SUPERCARS

La Vie au Grand Air

Hungarian Francois Szisz (left), winner of the first ever Grand Prix, at Le Mans in 1906.

REGARDLESS of the many controversies of his career, Michael Schumacher is statistically the greatest driver in the history of Formula 1, the top competition in world motorsport. A century before him, another German, the engineer Karl Benz, made the whole thing possible.

Benz built the first petrol-powered motor car. His three-wheeled Motorwagen was completed in 1885 and had a top speed of 8mph.

Within ten years cars were being raced in earnest, the first event taking place between Paris and Bordeaux in 1895. More than 1,200km long, it was won by Emile Levassor in 48 hours. Levassor and his business partner Rene Panhard designed the modern car's forerunner, the Systeme Panhard, which had the engine at the front, a pedal-operated clutch and gearbox.

The first Grand Prix, organised by the Automobile Club de France, took place near Le Mans in 1906. Some 32 cars set off on 12 laps of the epic 64-mile circuit. Francois Szisz, driving a Renault AK 90CV, won at an average of 73.3mph.

The Monte Carlo rally and the Indianapolis 500 in America both started in 1911 and the Le Mans 24-hour race began in 1923.

A year after the end of World War Two motor racing initiated a new formula, originally called Formula A and soon as Formula 1. The first officially sanctioned race, at Silverstone in 1950, was won by Giuseppe Farina in an Alfa Romeo 158. The Italian went on to win the first Driver's Championship.

The following season saw the start of Juan Manuel Fangio's domination of Formula 1. The Argentine "grand master" won five titles – a record

which stood for 46 years – racing with four different teams: Alfa Romeo, Ferrari, Mercedes-Benz and Maserati.

The 1950s was also the era of Britain's Stirling Moss, regarded as the greatest driver never to win a Driver's Championship. He finished second four times and third three times, winning 16 Grand Prix during his ten-year career. The first Briton to win the Formula 1 title was Mike Hawthorn in 1958.

In 1959 the British-based Cooper team introduced a revolutionary rear-engine design which provided superior weight distribution and handling, helping Australian Jack Brabham to win back-to-back titles in 1959 and 1960. Aerofoils were attached to the cars' rear to create downforce, creating the now familiar shape of Formula 1 cars.

The 1960s was a golden era for British drivers. Graham Hill (1962 and 1968) and Jim Clark (1963 and 1965) both won the championship twice, with British teams (Lotus and British Racing Motors). John Surtees won in 1964 and Jackie Stewart won the first of his three

Graham Hill was the only man ever to have won the Triple Crown of motor racing: the World Championship, the Indianapolis 500 and the Le Mans 24 Hour race.

FRONT PAGE NEWS

Brazilian Ayrton Senna prepares for his final race – the San Marino Grand Prix at Imola in 1994. His car left the circuit at the infamous Tamburello corner and smashed into a wall at 135mph.

titles in 1969. James Hunt won the championship in 1976, driving for McLaren, who would dominate the 1980s and early 1990s.

The period was notable for the fierce rivalry between Frenchman Alain Prost and Brazilian Ayrton Senna, who between them won seven of the nine championships between 1985 and 1993. Prost's retirement in 1993 was followed a year later by Senna's death at the San Marino Grand Prix.

The vacuum he left was filled by Schumacher, who sealed his reputation for unsporting conduct by seemingly cutting across his only rival, Britain's Damon Hill, in the final race of the 1994 season in Australia and as a result securing his first championship.

Two years later Hill followed in his father Graham's footsteps by winning the title. But Schumacher dominated Formula 1 for a decade, winning seven championships before retiring in 2006.

Nigel Mansell is Britain's most successful Formula 1 driver ever in terms of race wins (31). He won the world title once, in 1992. Another Briton, Lewis Hamilton, made his debut in 2007, shattering records almost immediately, and looks set for a stellar future.

Lewis Hamilton celebrates winning the Canadian Grand Prix, the first victory in an amazing debut season for the rookie driver from Stevenage.

Argentine Juan Manuel Fangio started 54 Grand Prix races, winning a remarkable 24 times.

THE Sun

Monday, November 14, 1994   26p

OUR NIGEL NIPS IN TO NICK RACE

THERE was one crumb of comfort after Damon's disaster yesterday. The race was won by Britain's own Nigel Mansell in his Formula One comeback year. It is the 31st Grand Prix victory of his career. He was crowned world champion two years ago.

Bubbly . . . Mansell celebrates

Comeback . . George

Ali hails champ George age 45

By JERRY ATRICK

GEORGE Foreman was dubbed "The Greatest" by his old foe Muhammad Ali last night after regaining the world heavyweight championship at 45.

Ali, who gave himself that nickname after taking Foreman's title in the "Rumble in The Jungle" 20 years ago, was delighted by his pal's comeback.

He said: "It was a happy surprise. He's the greatest now."

Monster

Ali said he never wrote Foreman off against Michael Moorer in Las Vegas on November 5 even though he was losing hands-down. Ali said: "Power never dies."

Foreman, now a Texas preacher, felled the 26-year-old with one sudden, monster punch in round ten.

He said later: "We now know that the athlete of all athletes is between 45 and 55.

"All of you thinking, 'I don't know if I can do it any more', remember . . . if I can do it, you can do it."

PUNCH THAT'S WORTH $100M
BACK PAGE

SCHU RAT

Prang out of order . . Schumacher (right) drives across Damon

Smug . . . Schumacher raises a fist in victory after race

Uproar as German's F1 'accident' robs Damon

THIS was the controversial crash yesterday that ended Damon Hill's Formula 1 title dream — and handed it to Michael Schumacher.

Last night there were calls for action against Schumacher — although he and race officials insist it was an accident.

Britain's Damon, 34, was one point behind the 25-year-old German in the drivers' championship before the final race in Adelaide, Australia.

Schumacher was in the lead when on lap 36 he veered off the track and hit a wall. He drove back on to the circuit but was going so slowly that Damon saw a chance to overtake on the inside. Schumacher's car

From BERNIE RUBBA, Motor Racing Correspondent, in Adelaide, Australia

then drove into Damon's path, damaging both cars and forcing both men to retire from the race. Neither driver scored a point, so Schumacher won his first world title.

Damon remained dignified last night. He said: "I knew Michael had everything to gain should neither of us finish. I think he would have made it difficult for me to pass in any situation. That's understandable. After all, we were racing for the world championship."

Schumacher insisted: "We just ran over each other. That's racing."

Told that the British public were in uproar, he said: "They are allowed their opinion."

Schu The Jury — Pages 4 & 5

1996 THAT GOAL, AND THE RISE OF THE BECKHAM BRAND

DAVID Beckham rose from a gifted youth player at Manchester United to become the poster boy of English and world football, before becoming a global brand. One extraordinary goal set the lad from Leytonstone, East London, on the path to staggering fame and fortune.

On the opening day of the 1996-97 Premiership season, during a match against Wimbledon, 21-year-old Beckham spotted the goalkeeper a long way off his line. He shot sublimely from behind the half-way line, the ball floating over the goalie and into the net. The football world was stunned.

Barely a month later, the Man United midfielder was making his debut for manager Glenn Hoddle's England in a World Cup qualifier.

England duly reached the 1998 finals in France. A trademark Beckham free-kick against Columbia helped set up a second round tie against Argentina and the scene of his most notorious incident on a football pitch. After being tackled from behind by Diego Simeone, a prostrate Beckham petulantly kicked out at the Argentine and was sent off. England lost on penalties and Beckham was blamed for England's exit. The newspapers vilified him, fans taunted him and his effigy was hanged outside a London pub.

Beckham responded magnificently, dominating the midfield

Beckham celebrates scoring England's opening goal in the lacklustre 2006 World Cup campaign. He later surrendered the captaincy and was dropped by new England manager Steve McClaren but made a crucial impact on returning against Brazil in June 2007.

FRONT PAGE NEWS

1995	**Assassination of Israeli Prime Minister Yitzhak Rabin**
1995	**Rogue trader Nick Leeson bankrupts Barings bank**
1995	**American football legend OJ Simpson cleared of double murder in U.S.**
1996	**Prince Charles and Princess Diana divorce**
1996	**Oasis play biggest concert in UK history at Knebworth, Hertfordshire**

and turning in countless "man of the match" performances for Manchester United in the 1998-99 season, helping secure a unique treble – European Cup, Premiership champions and FA Cup winners.

He married "Posh Spice" Victoria Adams in Ireland in July 1999 after a very public two-year romance. They later had three sons, Brooklyn, Romeo and Cruz.

Beckham could do little wrong on the pitch, but off it he became derided for his lifestyle and dress sense.

Beckham finished the following season with another Premiership winner's medal and was voted second best player in Europe and the world. But his performances for England were still marred by persistent abuse from a large section of fans. After a prolonged series of taunts during England's 3-2 defeat to Portugal at Euro 2000, Beckham returned the jibes with a one-fingered salute.

The appointment of Sven Goran Eriksson as national coach ushered in happier times. He was made captain in 2001 and turned in some of his best performances, peaking with a heroic display in a crucial World Cup qualifier against Greece in 2002, which saw his injury-time free-kick draw the game 2-2 and secure England's passage to the finals. His redemption was complete.

He travelled to the finals despite recovering from a broken metatarsal in his left foot but his lack of match fitness hampered England's progress. They then lost to Brazil in the quarter-finals.

Beckham returned to domestic duty at Manchester United for one more season, marred by growing animosity between him and his manager Alex Ferguson, but he still collected a fifth league champions medal.

Beckham reluctantly sought out a new challenge at Real Madrid in 2003. His football continued to flourish, as did controversy in his private life.

Another World Cup ended in agony as England lost to Portugal in the quarter-finals in 2006. Beckham limped off in the second half, his World Cup dream over and so, it seemed, his England career.

In January 2007, having been dropped by new manager Steve McClaren and with his career in Spain seemingly on the slide, Beckham signed for LA Galaxy of the

Above: Danish referee Kim Milton Nielsen shows Beckham the red card for kicking Diego Simeone in England's second round match against Argentina in the 1998 World Cup.

U.S. Soccer League in a colossal deal worth $250million over five years, making him the world's highest-paid sportsman.

But McClaren bowed to a public clamour for Beckham's recall in the summer of 2007 – the midfielder repaying him with sparkling performances.

The Beckham phenomenon, as it enters a new phase in America, continues to fascinate.

Beckham strikes the free kick that saves England from a play-off against Ukraine in 2002. The stunning 93rd minute goal capped a heroic performance by England's captain.

SPORT SPOT

During a match against Austria in 2005, Beckham became the first England captain to be sent off, and the first player sent off twice for England.

THE Sun

Monday, August 19, 1996   26p

Grumpy Spice: Is it just a nice fella she really, really wants?

Glum . . 'Posh' Spice Victoria Adams   **Bizarre — Page 23**

GOAL-DEN BOY

Wonder strike by 'Becks', 21 . . superstar in making

Fame Beck-ons . . he celebrates

A MIRACLE goal by young Manchester United ace David Beckham was the talk of Britain yesterday.

Football pundits say the spectacular 55-yard strike makes "Becks" a certain choice for new England boss Glenn Hoddle.

Others tipped the young midfielder to become one of the game's greats. Beckham spotted Wimbledon

By WILL GOFAR

keeper Neil Sullivan off his line in the last minute of Saturday's game. His exquisite right-foot shot sailed through the air and dipped into the goal behind Sullivan's despairing leap.

Team-mate Jordi Cruyff said: "For most players it is a dream to do it. It was incredible." Eric Cantona

ran out from the bench wide-eyed with amazement and with his arms outstretched. Boss Alex Ferguson babbled excitedly.

Rueful Sullivan said: "I've not seen anything like it. My only consolation is that at least I'll be on telly every week."

Man of the Match Beckham had a hand in all the goals in United's 3-0 win.

Worth a punt . . . Beckham's long-range effort

He's done him . . . ball dips into Sullivan's net

HODDLE HAS TO PICK HIM NOW: SEE BACK PAGE

1999 PREMIER LEAGUE AND MAN UNITED'S TREBLE

MANCHESTER United's historic treble in 1999 confirmed Sir Alex Ferguson's team as the greatest of the Premier League era – and their return to European glory.

But it might all have been so different for United, and Ferguson, had it not been for Mark Robins, a 20-year-old striker who in 1990 scored the winning goal against Nottingham Forest in the third round of the FA Cup. Since Ferguson's arrival at Old Trafford in 1986, his teams had lacked consistency and a lowly league placing in January 1990 had prompted calls for him to be axed. Robins' goal saved his bacon, as United progressed to the FA Cup final and won it.

That victory heralded a remarkable upturn in their domestic fortunes during the 1990s, coinciding with the demise of the once-invincible Liv-

erpool, who won the last of 18 league championships in 1990. United had not won the league since 1967. In the same period Liverpool had done it 11 times, becoming the most successful club in British football history.

At the time, English football was at a low ebb. Hooliganism and a series of disasters – including the Bradford City fire in 1985 and the Hillsborough tragedy in 1989 – had tainted its reputation. But it was transformed by the introduction of the FA Premier League in 1992. The introduction of all-seater stadia and a huge influx of TV money from BSkyB turned the new league into the national ob-

Eric Cantona in action in the 1996 FA Cup final against Liverpool at Wembley. Manchester United won thanks to his late goal. Cantona was the first foreign superstar of the Premiership.

session the old one had once been – as well as a highly successful global product.

Manchester United won the inaugural title, their first in 25 years, and didn't look back. Former youth team talents such as Ryan Giggs, Paul Scholes, Gary Neville and David Beckham mixed with more experienced stars such as Bryan Robson, Mark Hughes and the mercurial Frenchman Eric Cantona, whom Ferguson had bought from Leeds for a bargain £1.2million in November 1992.

They dominated the Premiership for the rest of the 1990s, ending the decade with a dramatic last-gasp 2-1 victory over Bayern Munich in the 1999 Champions League final which secured an unprecedented treble (League, FA Cup and European Cup).

United continued to dominate domestic football, winning another two Premiership titles before their only real challengers, Arsenal – then emerging as an increasingly attractive and fluent side under Frenchman Arsene Wenger – won in 2002 and 2004. The Ferguson/Wenger duel dominated the Premiership for seven years.

The arrival of Russian billionaire Roman Abramovich, who bought Chelsea in 2003, heralded a new era. Already wealthy footballers began to receive even more money, with top players earning in excess of £100,000 per week. Hungry for an immediate return on his investment Abramovich

Above: Alex Ferguson has led Manchester United to nine Premiership titles since 1993 and has won more trophies than any other manager in the history of English football.

discarded manager Claudio Ranieri after one season for the highly-rated Portuguese coach Jose Mourinho. He, aided by seemingly unlimited funds, helped Chelsea win the Premiership in 2005 and 2006.

European success continues to elude Chelsea, but not Liverpool. Under Spanish manager Rafa Benitez, they knocked Chelsea out in two Champions League semi-finals, in 2005 and 2007, the first enabling them to go on to win their fifth European crown. Trailing a rampant AC Milan 3-0 at half-time, they engineered a famous comeback and then won a penalty shoot-out. Liverpool reached the final again in 2007, but this time AC Milan were too strong.

Right: Liverpool captain and midfielder Steven Gerrard lifts the European Cup in Istanbul, 2005, after his side pulled off the greatest comeback in any Champions League final, beating AC Milan on penalties.

Left: "Please don't call me arrogant, but I'm European champion and I think I'm a special one." Jose Mourinho has found Champions League success at Chelsea more difficult than with his former club FC Porto, whom he guided to victory in 2004.

FRONT PAGE NEWS

1997 Roslin Institute in Scotland announces birth of Dolly the Sheep, the first mammal cloned from an adult cell

1997 Labour sweeps to power in landslide, Tony Blair is Prime Minister

1997 Princess Diana killed in Paris car crash

1997 Britain hands over Hong Kong to China

1999 TV star Jill Dando shot dead on her London doorstep

Champs . . . Fergie and keeper Peter Schmeichel raise Cup

Two in two . . . Solskjaer's winner in dying seconds

Trebles all round

FERGIE BUBBLY FOR CUP HERO

WELL done, my son! Alex Ferguson congratulates match-winner Ole Gunnar Solskjær with bubbly last night after Man United clinched their incredible treble.

Substitutes Ole and Teddy Sheringham both scored in injury time to steal the Champi-

From LARS MINNIT in Barcelona

ons League trophy from Bayern Munich in two of the most amazing minutes of football ever known.

The Red Devils trailed the Germans 1-0 after 90 minutes in

Barcelona. Their two last-gasp goals left Bayern's players weeping on the pitch.

Fergie was almost speechless. He spluttered: "Football! Bloody hell!" After composing himself, he added: "This is the greatest moment of my life."

2003 HOW JONNY MADE RUGBY THE NEW FOOTIE (BRIEFLY)

NOT since 1966 had an English team won a major world sports trophy. For decades football had outshone its ancestral cousin, growing to be the game all the world played. But for a short period before and after the World Cup in 2003, rugby was the new football and Jonny Wilkinson was the new David Beckham.

For once, England's billing as pre-tournament favourites looked justified. In the past 12 months they had beaten South Africa, Australia and New Zealand. Led by a formidable captain, Martin Johnson, England were at long last a match for anyone.

They arrived in Australia to the usual heckling from a pommie-bashing media accusing them of being boring and calling the English pack (average age 29) "Dad's Army".

Apart from making heavy weather of a group game against Samoa, England made comfortable progress to the final, overpowering Wales (28-17) and France (24-7) in the knockout stages. Standing in their way was a rejuvenated Australian team who had comfortably beaten New Zealand's All-Blacks 22-10. In front of 83,000 spectators

Above: Coach Andy Robinson succeeded Sir Clive Woodward in October 2004 and won just nine of his 22 matches in charge of England.

at the Telstra Stadium in Sydney, Australia settled first and scored a try in the sixth minute. The jolt appeared to calm the English players, who went on to dominate the rest of the first half. Jonny Wilkinson, the fly-half, kicked three penalties before releasing Jason Robinson, who scored a try in the 38th minute to give England a 14-5 lead at half-time.

Australia clawed their way back in the second-half with two converted penalties, reducing the gap to three points. England were on the brink of victory when in the 79th minute referee Andre Watson awarded Australia a controversial penalty, which was converted by inside-centre Elton Flatley to tie the match 14-14.

Wilkinson kicked yet another penalty to put England in front, but in extra-time Aus-

> **SPORT SPOT**
>
> A mystery waitress known only as "Susie" allegedly poisoned the All Blacks on the eve of the World Cup final against South Africa in 1995. They lost 15-12.

tralia looked to have saved themselves again, Flatley converting another penalty to tie the score at 17-17 two minutes from time. With seconds remaining England drove deep into Australia's 22. Sensing his chance, Wilkinson dropped back and waited for scrum-half Matt Dawson to deliver the ball from a maul. Kicking with his weaker right-foot, Wilkinson hit the ball flush, and the ball sailed over the posts. There was no time for another Australian comeback. England had won 20-17 and Jonny was a superstar.

Australia's press ate their words, hailing the England team as "magnificent" and a heroes' welcome at Heathrow greeted the players on their return. Better was to follow as 750,000 fans flocked to Trafalgar Square after the team's victory parade around the streets of London.

In September 2004, Sir Clive Woodward stepped down as coach. His departure after seven years, and that of captain Johnson, ushered in a more unstable period for England who struggled to maintain their world champion status.

Under new coach Andy Robinson, England's game spluttered and eventually stalled. By the end of 2006, they had lost eight times in nine matches. Robinson was replaced by England's long-serving backs coach Brian Ashton, ready to defend the world title during 2007.

Another try conceded – the world champions' record since victory in 2003 has been woeful

Right: Clive Woodward wanted to carry on coaching England, but continuing disagreement with the RFU led to his resignation in September 2004. "You can't take short cuts if you're trying to be the best in the world," he said.

THE Sun

Monday, November 24, 2003   30p   www.thesun.co.uk

Hot shots . . . hero Wilkinson's drop goal, above, echoes Geoff Hurst's 1966 winning strike, top

RUGBY WORLD CUP 2003

SPECIAL EDITION WITH 12-PAGE PULLOUT

2005 BRITAIN IS HANDED THE 2012 OLYMPICS

Left: Dame Kelly Holmes and Steve Cram jump for joy in Trafalgar Square as they hear the news that London has won the right to stage the 2012 Olympics.

Above: IOC President Jacques Rogge (left) shakes hands with Sebastian Coe, chairman of the London 2012 bid, after the contract is signed and accepted.

THE surprise announcement that Britain was to host its biggest sporting event since 1966 came in a dramatic broadcast on live TV at 12.49pm on July 6th, 2005. Jacques Rogge, President of the International Olympic Committee (IOC), declared that the right to stage the 2012 Olympics had been won by . . . "London!"

The London 2012 bid team present at the Raffles City Convention Centre in Singapore jumped up and down in delight. So too did the huge crowd that had gathered in Trafalgar Square. Meanwhile a dejected throng of Parisians outside Paris Town Hall contemplated their third bid defeat in 20 years. Then it rained on them.

For the London team and its leader, track legend Lord Sebastian Coe, it was the culmination of two years' hard work. The planning and promotion, the last-minute lobbying of undecided IOC delegates by then Prime Minister Tony Blair and the defence of the bid against its many critics had all been worthwhile.

London has hosted the Games twice before, in 1908 and 1948. The latter was known as the "Austerity Games", with housing shortages and rationing still widespread three years after World War Two. By contrast, with the budget having already soared from the original estimate of £2billion to somewhere approaching £10billion, the IOC can expect the 2012 Games to involve nothing but state-

of-the-art facilities and modern comforts.

The centrepiece will be the 500-acre Olympic Park in the Lower Lea Valley in Stratford, East London. The area will be completely regenerated. The aim, according to Lord Coe, is "to stage inspirational Games that capture the imagination of young people around the world and leave a lasting legacy".

The site will include an 80,000-seat athletics arena, the athletes' village, an aquatics centre, a velodrome, a BMX track and a hockey centre. The rest of London's historic sporting infrastructure will also come into play, including tennis at Wimbledon, archery at Lords cricket ground and football finals at the new Wembley stadium.

The Games will reach as far north as Glasgow – with early matches in the football tournament at Hampden Park – and as far west as Weymouth, Dorset, which will host the sailing.

Organisers hope to provide a sporting legacy – an increase in numbers participating in sport – and a lasting legacy for the deprived East End too. The athletes' village will be converted into 3,600 apartments, mostly affordable housing, and the media centre will

become a base for the creative industries. As of 2007 the Olympic site has been cleared, 13km of overhead power cables hanging from 52 pylons are being rerouted underground and crucial infrastructure is being put in place so building work can begin in earnest in 2008.

For Lord Coe and his committee the path to 2012 has already proved controversial – as he found out when he unveiled the official London Olympics logo only to discover that the animated version could induce epileptic fits. But his mission to produce "the greatest show on earth" is on track to be realised.

SPORT SPOT

Sir Clive Woodward, director of elite performance at the British Olympic Association, believes Britain can climb to fourth in the medals table in 2012 and win 18 gold medals.

The controversial London 2012 logo was slated not only for its cost – £400,000 – but also for its garish angular design.

FRONT PAGE NEWS

2004 NASA's exploration rover, Spirit, successfully lands on Mars

2005 Four al-Qaeda suicide bombers kill 56 and injure 700 on London Tube and a bus

2005 Hurricane Katrina strikes U.S. coastal areas from Louisiana to Alabama, killing 1,800 people

2005 Prince Charles marries Camilla Parker Bowles

The Olympic Park development lies at the heart of plans for the long-term regeneration of East London. "It is very important that we're able to leave a legacy that lasts and facilities that are used by communities for generations to come," says Lord Coe.

THE Sun

30p

Thursday, July 7, 2005   30p   www.thesun.co.uk

HISTORIC EDITION
BRITAIN GETS THE GAMES

WE DON'T MEAN TO GLOAT BUT...

SEE PAGES 2, 3, 4, 5, 6, 7, 8, 9, 10, 11, 12, 13, 14, 15, 40, 41 & FIVE PAGES OF SUNSPORT

INDEX

ACKNOWLEDGEMENTS

Profuse thanks to the following:

Matt Marsh, for his creativity and great diligence; Mike and Tanya Tier for some terrific headline contributions; Lee Wells for his technical expertise and dedication; Phil Gregory, John Sear and the Sun Imaging team for processing the Sun pictures; Kath George and her graphics wizards; The Sun picture desk, notably Mark Hunte.

The following were most helpful too:

BBC Motion Gallery, Beccy Gillings at Getty Images, Diana Morris, Illustrated London News Picture Library, Jenny Page at Bridgeman Art Library, Liz Parsons at PA Photos, Mary Evans Picture Library and Popperfoto.com.

PICTURE INDEX

Getty Images
Page 8, 9 (top left), 10, 11, 14, 16 (top left), 17 (top right, middle right), 21 (top right), 22 (middle left), 23 (bottom right), 24 (top middle, right), 26, 27 (middle), 28, 29 (top right), 30, 31, 34, 35 (bottom right), 36, 37 (top right), 38 (top right), 39, 40, 42 (top middle, bottom left), 45, 46 (top right, bottom left, bottom right), 48 (top left, middle), 49 (top right), 52 (top, bottom middle, bottom right), 53, 54 (top right, bottom left, bottom middle), 55, 56, 57, 58 (top left, bottom left, bottom middle), 59 (top right), 60-61, 62, 63, 64 (top right, bottom right), 65 (middle left), 66, 67, 68, 69, 70, 71, 72, 74 (top right), 76-77, 78 (top left, bottom right), 79, 80, 81 (main, top right) 82 (top middle, bottom right), 84-85 (main), 88 (top middle, top right, bottom middle, bottom right), 90, 91, 92 (middle), 94, 95, 98, 99, 100 (top left), 101 (bottom right), 102 (top right, bottom left), 104, 108, 110 (top right, bottom right), 111, 112, 113 (top right), 114, 115, 116, 117, 118 (top right, bottom left), 119 (top right), 120 (top right, bottom middle, bottom left), 121 (main), 122, 123, 124 (top left, top right, middle), 125, 126, 128, 129 (main, bottom right), 130 (middle, bottom right), 132, 133 (main) 134 (bottom middle, bottom left), 135, 136, 138 (top left, top right).

PA Photos
Page 29 (main), 41 (top right), 48 (bottom right), 66 (bottom left), 73, 81 (middle left), 87, 88 (top left), 92 (top right, top middle), 96 (bottom left, bottom middle), 100 (bottom left), 102 (middle right), 103, 105, 106 (top right), 107 (main, bottom left), 109, 120 (top left), 124 (bottom left, bottom right), 127 (main), 130 (top right), 131 (bottom left).

Popperfoto
Page 38 (top right, middle, bottom), 42 (middle right), 43 (main), 44 (top left, bottom middle), 46 (top left), 47, 48 (top left, middle),

50 (top right, bottom right), 54 (top left), 64 (bottom left), 65 (main, top right), 74 (top left, bottom left), 75, 82 bottom right), 83, 84-85 (small pics), 86 (top middle, top right, bottom left), 92 (bottom), 96 (top right), 100 (top right, bottom right), 106 (bottom right), 107 (top right), 110 (bottom left), 113, 130 (top left, bottom left), 134 (middle left, top right).

Mary Evans Picture Library
Page 9 (main), 15, 16 (top right, bottom left), 17 (main), 18, 19, 20 (top left, middle right, bottom left), 21 (main), 22 (top right, bottom right), 24 (bottom left), 25, 32-3, 118 (top left).

Bridgeman Art Library
Page 6 (bottom left, bottom right), 12, 19 (top), 20 (top middle), 23 (middle and top), 50 (top left).

Ancient Art and Architecture Library
Page 7 (both pictures), 13 (main)

AllSport UK
Page 127 (inset)

iStockphoto.com
Page 6 (top right)

Graham Morris
Page 58 (top right)

News Group Newspapers
Page 52 (middle right), 58 (bottom right), 78 (bottom right), 86 (bottom right), 106 (bottom left), 119 (main), 121 (bottom right), 137, 138.

Illustrated London News
Page 49 (main), 59 (main)

London 2012.com
Page 138 (middle right, bottom right)

BBC Motion Gallery
Page 89, 97, 129 (sequence, left)

Offside / L'Equipe
Page 131 (main)

Photographersdirect.com
Page 101 (main)

Sporting Pictures (UK) Ltd
Page 91

Main picture, Page 51, **courtesy of Lion Television.**

Beckham goal images, Page 133, **courtesy of the Premier League Archive.**